THE MOTHERCARE GUIDE TO CHILD HEALTH

THE MOTHERCARE GUIDE TO CHILD HEALTH

PENNY STANWAY, M.D.

Consultant
Rosalind Y. Ting, M.D., M.P.H.

PRENTICE HALL PRESS
New York London Toronto Sydney Tokyo

CONTENTS

To Hilary Greaves

PRENTICE HALL PRESS
Gulf + Western Building
One Gulf + Western Plaza
New York, New York 10023

Library of Congress
Cataloging in Publication Data

Stanway, Penny
The mothercare guide
to child health:
keeping children healthy.
A-Z of illnesses,
coping with emergencies /
Penny Stanway,
Rosalind Y. Ting. – 1st ed.
p. cm.
"Originally published in
Great Britain in 1988 by
Conran Octopus Limited."
includes index.
ISBN 0-13-602921-3:$17.95
1. Pediatrics – Popular works.
2. Children – Health and
hygiene –
Popular works.
I. Ting, Rosalind Y. II. Title.
RJ61.S768 1989
649'.4–dc19 88-36572
CIP

Conceived, designed and produced by
Conran Octopus Limited
Manufactured in Hong Kong

10 9 8 7 6 5 4 3 2 1

First Prentice Hall Press Edition

INTRODUCTION

Health, and child health in particular, is something that concerns us all. As parents we carry the prime responsibility for our children's health. Health professionals are trained to share this responsibility, especially for a child's physical health, but when we look closely at all the different ways of caring for a child's health, it really is we parents who do the lion's share of the care.

In this book we look at how parents, and mothers in particular, care for the everyday needs of their children, because this care underpins a growing child's well-being. We consider the basic principles of keeping children healthy and how we can best achieve this. We see, too, how to help children learn to look after their own health and how necessary it is to look after ourselves.

If they are to grow up healthy, children need food, clothing, shelter, warmth, physical contact and protection from harm. This personal health care must be set against a backdrop of a reliable health care system and ready access to experienced health professionals.

But in addition to all this material care, a child needs love if he is to grow up with the best chance of being healthy in the widest sense of the word. Loving and being loved are a vital part of child health. It is no longer acceptable to talk about health without considering the area of emotional health. Mind and body affect one another at all levels, and when we look at why adults visit the doctor, we see that a large proportion do so because they are suffering from emotional "dis-ease." Both physical and emotional ill health can have their roots in childhood, so it is essential to discuss the mind as well as the body here. Too often, books on health fail to mention the emotions and concentrate solely on the medical "plumbing."

Any of us who have used the health care system have, at some time, been confused as to who does what and how they can help us. We look at who the caring professionals are and what they do. But before we get to a health professional, we need to know whether or not a child is ill and how we can best look after him. Medicines are considered from the practical aspect of how to use them as well as what they do, and some of the more common treatments and diagnostic procedures are explained.

In my work with parents, I find that they are often interested in knowing about the body and why it goes wrong. We've included a section on how the body works to help the reader understand the causes of the common childhood disorders and illnesses. A natural follow-up from this is to take a look at

Penny Stanway, M.D.
Since qualifying in 1969, Penny Stanway has worked both in general practice and as a senior medical officer for London's largest area health authority, looking after normal and handicapped children in the community. She pursued her special interest in child health by studying developmental pediatrics and child neurology at the Institute of Child Health, London University.

After the birth of her first child, she gave up full-time practice. She now concentrates on writing about child health and development and has written several bestselling books with her husband, Dr. Andrew Stanway, among them The Baby and Child Book *and* Breast is Best. *She also lectures, contributes to several magazines and is on the advisory panel of the National Childbirth Trust and the La Leche League. While her three children, now aged 12, 11 and 6, were young she set up and ran a mother and toddler group for five years.*

the symptoms of these disorders and illnesses and at what you and your doctor can do to help.

Accidents and emergencies account for a large amount of preventable suffering and death in children, which is why we look in detail at the area of safety and first aid. Much of this is true preventive medicine.

Self-help groups have grown in strength and influence in the last few decades, reflecting the fact that individuals are more willingly sharing the responsibility for health that for so long has been mainly entrusted to health professionals. We can do no more than include a list of addresses, but we join with the World Health Organization in acknowledging the increasingly valuable part they play in helping parents care for their children.

One of the roles of these groups is to support and encourage parents in their task of caring for sick or handicapped children. They, along with professional helpers, friends and relatives, "mother" parents, so enabling them to cope better. Supporting, encouraging, mothering, loving – it all comes down to the same thing and it's what parents do as they care for their children in sickness and in health.

Hopefully, we'll continue to fight against illness and to search for ways to make our children's lives more comfortable. But perhaps also, as we move towards the twenty-first century and as we become more aware of what health is all about, we and our children will learn to be more gentle with ourselves and to rejoice in the love and care that we can accept and share.

Penny Stanway

Reader's note
The pronouns "he" and "she" have been used in alternating sections throughout the book to reflect that the text applies equally to male and female children. Where this is not the case, the appropriate pronoun is used.

Dr. Rosalind Y. Ting, M.D., M.P.H.

Dr. Ting is Professor Emerita at the University of Pennsylvania School of Medicine, and Senior Physician at the Children's Hospital of Philadelphia. Dr. Ting joined the Children's Hospital of Philadelphia in 1961 and has been the attending physician in the Division of Child Development and Rehabilitation, as well as at Children's Seashore House. She is responsible for teaching Developmental Pediatrics and has been chief investigator in various research projects relating to child development. In 1976 she established an infant day care center in Philadelphia, and in 1980 she founded another model infant and child care center in affiliation with the Children's Hospital of Philadelphia for teaching and research projects.

During the last 15 years, Dr. Ting has also worked closely with pediatricians in China by giving lectures and presiding over workshops and research projects.

Part One

GENERAL HEALTH CARE

Looking after a child is perhaps the most important process in the world. In most instances our own experience, intuition, imagination and sensitivity equip us perfectly well to carry out this care and it helps if we have the confidence to listen to and learn from ourselves and our children. But we also need the wisdom to learn from others and to know how and when to ask for help. There are times for every parent when outside help in the form of encouragement, emotional support, advice or practical assistance is desirable or even downright necessary.

Modern means of communication enable information about child health to be shared easily between parents and professionals all over the country, so we have the potential to know more about children now than ever before. This first section aims to show the best ways of looking after children, both in health and sickness, up to the beginning of adolescence. As well as talking about the practical everyday care of young children and how to keep them healthy, we look at how *you* can best look after yourself in your busy life.

We explain how the health care system works so that if your child needs professional care you will understand who does what, and we hope the chapter on medicines, diagnostic procedures and treatments will help remove some of their mystery. Ignorance is certainly not always bliss when it comes to illness.

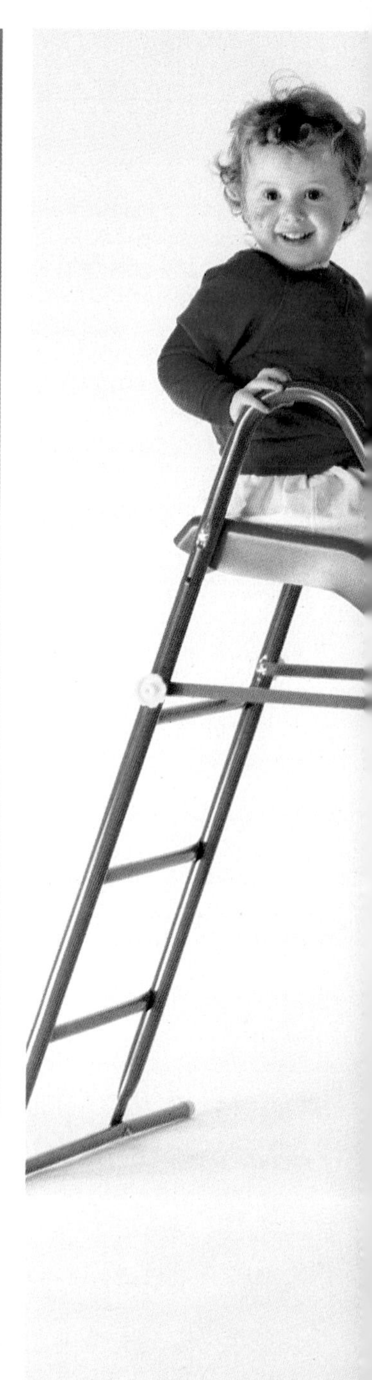

KEEPING HEALTHY

The opportunity to be with your child, to introduce her to the wonder and fascination of the world around, and to share in her interest and delight, is very precious.

Most of us realize that being healthy involves more than just being free from physical disease – it also includes emotional, social and spiritual well-being.

Today there is a growing acceptance of the idea that we are responsible for many of our ills and that individuals have at least some choice when it comes to looking after their health. We also know that if we are to bring up healthy children, it's up to us to set a good example by the way we live.

But however hard we try to set a good example, the fact remains that all of us go through physical and emotional suffering at some time. Although we share the responsibility for our children's health with others in the community – with health professionals, the pharmaceutical industry and the government – one of our important tasks as parents is to help our children learn and grow from their experiences in life, be they good or bad, so they can cope constructively with their own adult lives.

About five per cent of children have a long-term physical problem such as asthma, epilepsy, recurrent abdominal pain or headaches. Part of keeping them healthy includes encouraging them to avoid the label of being "sick." If we are to help our children be truly healthy, we must help them to accept life as it is and themselves as they are. Looked at in this way, the disabled child can be healthier than the Olympic athlete.

Improvements in health care

Over the past century, there have been enormous improvements in our general health and life expectancy. This is partly a result of the huge effort that has been put into basic public health measures – despite pollution scandals, we have generally clean drinking water, a good sewage system, adequate refuse disposal and cleaner air and rivers. There have also been great strides forward in medicines and treatments.

But beside all this, we have a greater awareness of how to prevent and treat illness in the home. Here we can bring our children up to a positive awareness of the importance of healthy living – we can eat sensible foods, exercise and avoid excessive smoking and alcohol.

Planning a healthy family

Becoming a parent for the first time alters the balance of your existing lifestyle dramatically. It makes good sense to look after yourselves especially well so that you can take the best possible care of your totally dependent baby.

You can start this caring process even before your baby is conceived. Like all parents, you want your baby to be born healthy. While there is still much to be learned about preconception care, making sure that you and your partner are as fit, physically and emotionally, as possible in the months leading up to conception can do nothing but good. Your doctor can advise you on general health matters, and some women's health centers, family planning clinics and hospitals now offer preconception advice, so find out what is available in your area. Diet is especially important – you may need extra vitamins and minerals – and you and your partner should consider the effects that drinking alcohol and smoking might have on your planned baby.

Genetic counseling

If there is any history of genetic disorder in either of your families, you should consult your physician before you become pregnant. He may refer you to a genetic counselor or to a physician who specializes in genetic diseases. The counselor may recommend tests to show whether or not you or your partner is carrying abnormal genetic material, which could affect the baby even though you yourselves may be quite healthy. The counselor can also help parents who have an affected child to decide whether or not to have another baby.

Some parents decide that the risk of having an affected baby is small enough for them to take a chance. They may opt for special tests during pregnancy to discover whether their baby is affected or not. This sort of test is only really worth having if you would be prepared to have your pregnancy terminated if the baby were found to be affected. If you wouldn't consider an abortion, the only benefit of having a prenatal test is the relief from worry that a negative result brings.

Prenatal care

Prenatal care is extremely important for every pregnant woman. It aims to detect any problems as soon as possible, so that the health of the mother and baby can be even more carefully monitored.

When you go to your obstetrician or clinic, you'll be asked to supply a sample of urine which is then tested for protein. Protein in the urine is one of the first signs of pre-eclamptic toxemia. Your blood pressure and weight will also be measured for the same reason.

Another part of each prenatal visit is the assessment of the size and shape of your growing womb. This gives a good idea of how well the baby is growing and, later in pregnancy, of the position in which the baby is lying. Ultrasound studies are widely used today. An ultrasound can detect certain abnormalities in the baby and repeated studies give an indication as to whether the baby is growing at a healthy rate.

Caring for your growing child

Once your baby is born, it's important to take advantage of the routine tests and developmental assessments (see pages 48–52) offered by your family doctor, health visitor or clinic doctor. These are a way of screening thousands of normal, healthy children in order to pick up problems in a few. The early detection of many problems can save both you and your child from unnecessary suffering or worry in the future. One such test is the Guthrie test, used soon after birth to detect the rare genetic disorder, phenylketonuria (see page 159). It involves making a tiny pinprick on your baby's heel and taking a few drops of blood for testing.

A hundred years ago, only six out of every ten babies reached adulthood and infectious diseases caused most of these deaths. Public health measures, improved nursing techniques and the availability of antiseptics, antibiotics and other drugs have cut down the incidence of infection. Perhaps most important of all has been the development of immunization (see page 53). No longer do vast numbers of children suffer or even die from polio and diphtheria, and smallpox has been officially declared eradicated worldwide.

Today, doctors and clinics offer immuninization against polio, diphtheria, tetanus, whooping cough, measles, mumps, German measles, Hemophilus influenza disease and tuberculosis if necessary. A close watch is kept on the number of children receiving immunization, the protection it achieves and its side-effects. When necessary, changes are made in immunization programs and from time to time it may be suggested that certain groups of children should or should not be immunized against particular diseases.

General health in the family

These happy, healthy-looking children are enjoying the benefits of fresh air and exercise, important factors in any child's general well-being.

Although we can count on professional health care to help us get through specific ailments, and on the federal and local agencies to provide a high standard of public health, it's up to us as individuals to keep ourselves and our children as healthy as possible. We can help ourselves do this by keeping up high standards of hygiene in our homes, by eating and drinking sensibly and by looking after ourselves both physically and mentally – and with any luck, our children will learn their standards from us.

Resistance to infection

In the early days, breast milk will give your child some protection against a variety of bacterial, viral and fungal infections – for instance, a breastfed baby has less gastroenteritis and tooth decay, fewer respiratory infections and isn't as likely to develop allergic disorders as a bottlefed baby. But whether you breastfeed or bottlefeed, your baby can fight infection better if he's well nourished.

AT HOME Resistance to infection is lowered by illness, emotional stress, poor living conditions and living in the same environment as a heavy smoker. Smoking may be limited in public places today, but there is no limit on smoking at home which is where children spend most of their time. Smoke coming directly from a cigarette is more irritating to the nose, throat and eyes than exhaled smoke, but both sorts can make a child more susceptible to chest infections, such as bronchitis and pneumonia, as well as to upper respiratory infections. Babies of under a year old whose parents smoke are twice as likely to develop a serious chest infection as babies of nonsmokers.

AT SCHOOL When you child starts preschool or school, he'll meet many infections he may not have encountered before. However healthy he is, he's bound to pick up some of them from other children. Researchers estimate that children get between six and nine upper respiratory infections a year in their first few years at school. One good thing is that a child gradually becomes more resistant to viral infections. In a sense, the infections seem to act as a form of immunization.

SMOKING IS BAD FOR YOU AND YOUR CHILDREN

If you really can't give up smoking, then at least follow these guidelines to minimize the harmful effect on your children:

- Keep a window open if you smoke when a child is in the room.
- Put out a lit cigarette if you're not actually smoking it.
- Never smoke if your child is in the car with you.
- Remember that children learn by example. If you smoke to relieve stress, it might be better to look at more constructive and healthier ways of dealing with your feelings.

Everyday hygiene

Teach your children to wash their hands thoroughly after using the bathroom and encourage the whole family to be particularly careful about hygiene. If anyone in the house has diarrhea, use a disinfectant to wash the toilet seat, flush handle and basin faucets. Soak soiled clothing and bedding in borax and water before washing.

Good personal hygiene and careful handling of food can help protect your family from gastroenteritis. Microorganisms called bacteria (see page 73) are normally present in many foods and do no harm. However, careless handling, storage, preparation and cooking can increase the number of these organisms to dangerous levels, or can cause contamination by certain organisms that can lead to food poisoning.

It's better to use a spoon rather than your finger to taste food as you're preparing it. Make sure all your kitchen counters and equipment are kept clean because bacteria can readily breed in food particles in warm conditions. Wipe up spills and wash dish cloths and hand towels regularly. Trash containers should be covered to keep flies away. Hot water and dish-washing detergent remove grease, but it's sensible also to rinse all dishes and all eating and cooking utensils to remove traces of detergent.

Cooked and uncooked meat should be kept separately and preferably covered in the refrigerator. Defrost frozen poultry completely before cooking and always cook meat thoroughly, especially pork and chicken. If you intend to reheat cooked meat, cool it quickly and keep it in the refrigerator, then reheat it really well. Food left out of the refrigerator should be covered to keep off flies. If you've let a carton of ice cream melt, it's better not to refreeze it. Anything containing egg is especially likely to go bad, so take no chances.

FAMILY PETS AND HYGIENE Children can catch worms and other infections from cats and dogs, so it is important to worm your pet regularly, both for its sake and yours, and take it to the vet if it has a skin infection or is scratching excessively. Train your dog to defecate in the gutter or in a part of the yard away from where the children play, and don't let your child kiss the animal or the animal lick the child's mouth. Keep your pet's food bowls separate from other pots and pans, and use a different scrub brush when cleaning them. Don't let your pet eat from the family's dishes.

Teach your child to respect animals – don't ever let him tease pets and don't let him approach strange dogs however friendly they may seem.

Your child's food

Obviously the sort of food your child eats plays a large part in determining how healthy he is now, but it's also known that some long-term diseases have their roots in the kind of diet eaten in childhood. For years, nutritionists and doctors argued about what foods were best for us. Now, for the first time, there seems to be a consensus on the kind of diet that combines being as nutritious as possible with protecting us against food-related diseases such as coronary artery disease, high blood pressure, obesity, strokes and dental decay (see pages 28–31 for feeding the family). A poor diet can not only lead to disease in later life but can also make a child feel less generally well than he should. In case you think we all eat well enough already, a 1980 study found that only fifteen percent of people were eating a diet that conformed even to minimum dietary recommendations!

A healthier diet

Base your family's meals and snacks on foods that are relatively low in fat, salt and added sugar. When shopping, buy fresh foods or foods that have been processed as little as possible. Increase the amount of fresh fruit and vegetables that you and your children eat and choose fish or white meat (such as chicken) rather than red, fatty meat. Buy or make whole-grain bread to provide dietary fiber and don't forget that cereal and flour can also be valuable sources of this.

FAMILIES AND FEELINGS

One of the most valuable gifts you can give your child is your time. Time, just for him, when he knows that you are there for him alone.

It's been known since ancient times that mind and body interact, one affecting the other profoundly. We all – adults and children alike – experience ups and downs in our daily lives and it's often obvious that these emotions can cause changes in our bodies.

From the time they are born, it can be seen that individual babies behave differently and are affected by different moods. Experienced mothers and nurses can often assess how easy a baby will be to look after just by watching him. How a baby behaves will affect his mother's actions and feelings, and this in turn will affect the baby. So if you have a difficult baby, or if you find looking after him very difficult, don't blame yourself. Try to discuss any worries or problems with your doctor or someone else who can help.

What does a child need most?

It's been said that if you love a child enough, you can do anything to him and he'll turn out all right. One advice columnist, commenting on years of answering problem letters from emotionally distressed people, said: "Not being loved enough and not loving enough – the problem is always the same." Research books back up what ordinary people know: a child needs to be loved and to feel loved if he is to thrive and grow up able to receive love and to give it to others.

As children grow up, they have to learn to cope with their own moods and feelings. Sometimes they build emotional and behavioral barriers to help them do this and to stop themselves from being hurt.

If a child doesn't feel loved enough when he is young, he'll grow up believing he's unlovable and may spend his life striving to make people love him, just as he worked so hard to make his parents love him by trying to get their attention by being "good" or even by being naughty. More tragically, he may give up in despair. This "love-hungry" behavior can be reflected in a variety of health problems in adult life.

The effects of emotions on health

Emotional distress such as depression in a parent can affect a child physically simply because his physical and emotional needs aren't being adequately met. If parents feel shocked or annoyed by their child's illness, this can alter how the child feels about being ill and may make him less able to get well.

An illness can be made worse if a child or parent finds it hard to communicate feelings about the illness, because unexpressed emotions can delay healing. A child who doesn't have a feeling of self-worth may also have difficulty in mobilizing his body's ability to heal itself.

Illness can be caused when a child's needs are misread. If, for example, a mother gives her child food every time he wants attention, the child learns that the way to comfort himself is by eating and hence he tends to overeat when upset.

And many childhood accidents, whether on the road or in the home, may also be influenced by the state of mind of the person looking after the child or by how the child himself feels.

Emotional distress affects the body in many ways including a well-recognized chain of hormonal changes starting in the brain and affecting every part of the body. Fear, anxiety or anger cause raised adrenaline levels which mobilize the body's resources to make it ready for action. If this energy isn't used, it has to be held in. With enough held-in or repressed energy, the body reacts by producing a physical disorder such as tummy ache, muscle tension or a headache.

Asthma, recurrent abdominal pain, juvenile diabetes mellitus, epilepsy and failure to thrive are just some of the illnesses which can be affected by a child's emotional state, although this isn't so for every child with these illnesses. Resistance to infection may also be affected by emotional distress.

Family life

At the core of a child's emotional world is the way in which his family behaves towards him and towards each other. He relates to other people according to this experience of his own family and those around it. Family life can be difficult and it can be wonderful. But one thing is certain – it's never perfect.

ENJOYING FAMILY LIFE

● Love your child unconditionally, even though you sometimes may not like what he does. This means accepting each child for what he is, a unique individual, not someone to be compared, favorably or unfavorably, with a brother, sister or friend's child. Competition is inevitable, but base your appreciation of your child's efforts on his own progress. Always remember to praise him when he has done well, rather than just criticize him if he hasn't.

● Look at your child when he's talking and really listen to him. Take an interest in him, his friends and his ideas and respect his feelings. Share your ideas, and even your worries sometimes, with him and let him help in family decisions if he can. This is all part of building his self-confidence and your mutual understanding.

● Have fun with your family and do things together. Give and enjoy lots of physical contact. Help your children be creative and appreciative of nature, music and art.

● Use your common sense and adopt consistent but flexible rules. Children feel safer if they know what is expected of them. Let him know that all members of the family have needs and try to help him understand whose needs are greatest at any one time. Share with and care for each other.

LOOKING AFTER YOURSELF

Making time for yourself can be difficult with a young child. It can help to find relaxing things to do together, such as swimming.

It may seem strange to talk about looking after yourself in a book on children's health, but it's important for anyone looking after a child to be healthy and well cared for themselves, especially when a child is ill. Remember that you are a person in your own right and you deserve and need to be looked after.

Becoming a mother

Many societies take special care of mothers, but in our society the idea of mothering the mother is rarely mentioned. When you have your first baby, your own need to be mothered resurfaces. Each of us has a childlike part inside us and we may need help at times of change and stress. You will be helping yourself a lot if you recognize this need and learn to accept help. Your partner may not necessarily be the best person to help you over this need to be mothered yourself.

It is important to understand that we can't love and look after our children as well as possible unless we value and look after ourselves. It's rather like the old injunction "love your neighbor as yourself" – in other words, you can only love your child as much as you love yourself.

Adapting to change

Pregnancy and childbirth are stressful periods both physically and emotionally, and caring for your baby brings exhaustion from sleepless nights and the continual routine of responding to your child. It's a time of enormous change and upheaval. It's even been called "the parental emergency"! It changes both parents' views of themselves and their relationship with one another and with anyone close to them.

Pregnancy and breastfeeding change the woman's body, at least temporarily, and may bring important social changes such as the woman giving up her job or reducing her hours, so increasing the father's share of the financial responsibility. And it firmly places the responsibility of attending to the long-term needs of another human being on your shoulders.

It's important to understand that we can only try to do our best at mothering – it isn't possible to do more – and that we don't have to be perfect for our children to develop healthily. All we need to do is to be "good enough" mothers. We need to respond to our children, to try to give them enough love, time, emotional availability and attention. We need to accept that it is perfectly normal to feel ambivalent about our children sometimes. Realizing that perfection is neither necessary nor expected can take a great weight off your shoulders and free you to be guided by your natural response and wisdom. Above all, try to put yourself in your child's shoes, see things from his point of view and understand his feelings. If he feels he's understood then he'll feel that you value him – and you will be the kind of mother that he really needs.

Accepting yourself as you are

Some of us ignore our feelings and pretend they don't exist, but out of sight does not also mean out of mind. If we suppress our feelings, we become prone to many emotional and physical ailments, including depression which is often based on suppressed anger or sadness. Or our feelings overflow explosively and inappropriately in times of trouble, leaving us feeling out of control. This in turn affects our children. If we can't accept our own feelings how can our children learn to accept theirs? Learn to recognize whether you're angry, sad, anxious, joyful or whatever, and accept your emotions as part of you and how you are now.

It's important to be positive about yourself – too many people, especially women, undervalue themselves and look to others for the love and approval they can't feel for themselves. Be aware of your skills and abilities and use them. Foster your self-confidence and learn to trust your own decisions.

Part of building up your confidence in yourself also means knowing your limits. Most of us were brought up to think we should never refuse anybody anything, and we run round like cats chasing our tails trying to help everybody with everything.

But this isn't healthy, for giving too much can mean taking too much from yourself and from your child. Learn to say "no" – it doesn't mean you're a bad person or that people won't like you. It means that they'll respect you for knowing yourself.

Enjoying motherhood

Remember to take pleasure in mothering. It's one of the most creative processes you will ever be involved in, and sometimes it will tax you to your limits. But most women say that in spite of the many difficult times, the high quality of the good times creates a positive and rewarding experience that most of them would want to repeat.

One advantage of being a mother is the opportunity for personal growth. Women notice that mothering makes them understanding, tolerant, confident, responsible and unselfish. They may also appreciate their own parents more!

Looking after your relationships

Having a child is often a real test of a relationship and if you and your partner are both to grow as individuals, and if your relationship is to be enriched by the irrevocable changes of parenthood, communication is a crucial area to work on.

The year after a baby is born is something of an emotional roller coaster. Many men and women experience greater highs and lows than ever before. Postpartum depression is only too common with one in six women becoming severely depressed, if only for a short time. And divorce and separation reach a peak, reflecting the stresses and strains a baby can bring to an existing relationship.

Try to get into the habit of being open and honest about yourself, your child and each other. Hidden and out-of-control emotions can damage a relationship if they're expressed as sarcasm, verbal abuse or physical violence. Being aware and open with each other can make you both feel very vulnerable because you risk being hurt through rejection or even ridicule, but if you support and encourage each other, your relationship will gain in understanding, honesty and intimacy.

It's all too easy to forget about being kind to one another in the turmoil of family life, but kindness, comfort and tenderness are the mainstay of a partnership. Try to maintain physical contact with cuddles and non sexual touching, to keep affection and warm feelings alive between you.

A deep level of emotional intimacy and good communication often leads to a rewarding physical relationship. If you can allow yourself to enjoy sex in an uninhibited, sensual way, you'll be in touch with the childlike part of you that is often forgotten. Both men and women need to receive as well as give and many couples encourage one another to be open about what gives them pleasure so that each can learn to become more sensitive to the other's needs.

You will find that making time for one another, perhaps just being quietly alone together, recharges your emotional batteries and enables you to cope with the demands of parenthood.

And don't forget your friends – spending all your time with a young child won't bring out the best in you. Most people enjoy life more if they have some adult company. So nurture your friendships and don't be afraid to reveal your feelings and needs. Your friends can't give you what you need, or even respond appropriately, unless you allow them to know you well.

Your children and your marriage

Children learn to relate to other people by what they experience in their own family. Your relationship with your partner will affect how your child will relate to his or her partner in the future. Children seem to know instinctively how important it is for them that their parents have a good relationship with each other. If it's in danger of breaking down, children naturally struggle hard to keep their parents together. Help is available, where there is a marriage problem, from a number of sources including your local marriage and family therapist association and other professionals. The usefulness of marriage counseling is widely recognized. It is very important to keep children out of the battlefield, if at all possible. Try always to avoid running your partner down in front of your children. If you and your partner are separated, one of the most loving things you can do is to help your children keep in touch with the other parent.

Awareness of your body and mind

We've talked a lot about feelings and how, if you suppress them, they'll surface in the way your body functions, in the way you move and hold yourself, and perhaps in actual physical disease, such as frequent infections, indigestion and headaches. Muscle tension, for instance, can be related to how you hold yourself, which may in turn be affected by your state of mind – some people talk of muscle tension as an armor that stops us from experiencing our feelings.

Learn to listen to what your body is telling you and to attend to its needs. Illness is the body's way of making us slow down. If you are sensitive to it, you'll notice its early warning signs when you're not looking after yourself properly and be able to take remedial action. Awareness of the state of your body can make you feel more alive, with better co-ordination and a heightened responsiveness to the pleasure of living in a well-tuned, healthy body.

Regular exercise makes you feel brighter as well as look better. If you join an exercise group, you will also find yourself enjoying the contact with other people.

Taking care of your body

Lots of parents lead very busy lives and find it difficult to switch off and be still. Raising children means we are constantly on the go and don't often finish the task at hand. But "busy-ness" can be a way of avoiding tuning in to ourselves and discovering our needs. You owe it to yourself to make time at least once a day to be completely calm. Some people relax in a hot bath, others by taking short naps, meditating, or lying down and tightening then relaxing one group of muscles at a time.

Even if you feel your energy is low, exercise will make you feel better. It's best if it's really enjoyable rather than just done because it's good for you. Try to exercise for at least twenty minutes three times a week. This will speed up your metabolic rate, help burn up excess fat and give you a feeling of well-being because of the natural hormones (endorphins) your body produces during exercise. If you've just had a baby, go to a postnatal exercise class and gently step up the exercise you take. Walking, swimming and dancing are good all-round types of exercise.

You are what you eat and your body will function better if you put good food into it. If you are breastfeeding, you'll need to eat particularly sensibly. If you don't look after yourself, your body will suffer because it will give up its nutrients to the baby. To get an idea of what constitutes a healthy diet, see page 15. If you are feeling anxious and jumpy, try reducing your intake of coffee, tea, chocolate and cola.

Many busy men and women don't think about what they're eating. Take time to concentrate on the nourishment you're absorbing and savor each piece of food.

Everyone needs a certain amount of sleep to function well and if your sleep is broken once or several times a night, try to catch up on it somehow.

Taking pleasure in your day

Parents often say they have too little time for themselves, but if you can make time to do something especially enjoyable for you each day, you'll feel more cared for. It doesn't have to be anything particularly amazing or difficult to arrange – it could be seeing a friend, reading a favorite book or preparing a special meal. Anticipation is half the pleasure and enjoying the memory is important too.

If you do paid or volunteer work, take a tip from the many people who actively enjoy life and try to ensure that you like what you are doing. Of course, some of us have jobs we dislike, but a change of attitude can sometimes work wonders.

The mental and social stimulation you obtain from working can balance your life and make you better able to enjoy both being a parent and a partner. Organize childcare so you don't have to worry about it. Spending time on arrangements that work is a way of caring for yourself as well as for your child.

EVERYDAY CARE

This child is obviously enjoying – and benefiting from – the loving attention of her parents who care for her and make her feel special.

Children rely on their parents to look after them for many years and at first they are totally dependent. A baby needs to be fed, protected from the cold and heat, cleaned, handled, moved from place to place and loved. As he grows older he gradually learns to look after himself, though from time to time he may take a backwards step and want to be "babied." As we spend time with our babies and young children, we not only attend to their physical needs but also enable them to experience what it is like to be looked after. One day they'll care for their own children and we'll see our love, care and concern echo from one generation to another.

Close contact

The first thing most new mothers do is pick up and hold their baby. Babies are able to wriggle and kick, but they can't get up and move around – we have to do that for them. At first, a baby can't even roll over or lift up his head – he has to spend many hours practicing and strengthening his muscles before he can manage the most basic of movements. We hold our babies to feed them, to cuddle them and to take them from one place to another almost without thinking about it. Some mothers like to carry their babies around with them in a baby sling or carrier because they believe it makes them more contented. Certainly some recent research bears this out. Babies who were carried around for at least three hours a day were found, at six weeks

Carrying your baby firmly against your body is very comforting for him. Babies obviously enjoy the warmth, security and movement.

old to cry in the evenings only half as much as other babies. There's nothing like crying to distress parents, especially at this time of day when many babies are difficult to comfort. So from both the baby's and the parents' point of view, it appears that being carried a lot is a good idea. Other research has found that babies who receive only minimal handling are much less likely to thrive.

Don't feel that you will spoil your baby if you pick him up, hold, cuddle and carry him as much as you like. He has been used to motion in your womb and this, together with your familiar reassuring voice, body sounds, smell and touch, is why he's comforted by being carried around. Children of all ages, boys and girls, benefit from hugs and cuddles when they want reassurance, comfort or just to know you're there.

You might like to try massaging your baby with oil. Use gentle, stroking movements over his arms and legs, feet, hands, trunk and head. Babies love it and it's a good way for you to get used to your baby. Older children enjoy it too – it's an age-old form of comfort and pleasure.

Feeding your child

Whether you choose to breastfeed or bottlefeed your baby in the early months, try to make each feeding an enjoyable and relaxed time for you both. The health advantages of breastfeeding are discussed on page 14 under Resistance to infection.

Breastfeeding

Mothers who breastfeed have a special and unique relationship with their babies, and many say how much pleasure being able to nourish and comfort their offspring brings. Breast milk is the natural food for babies. Breastfeeding is also convenient and cheap and protects a baby against some illnesses. It isn't without problems, but virtually all of these can be prevented or overcome. The problem most often experienced with breastfeeding is insufficient milk, which is a shame because it is a preventable problem.

Breastfeeding works on a demand and supply basis – the more time the baby spends at the breast, the more milk is made. One exception to this is if the baby isn't sucking efficiently. If you don't think your baby is sucking well or have any other feeding problem, ask your pediatrician, pediatric nurse or a breastfeeding counselor for advice. Good sources of mother-to-mother help for breastfeeding problems are La Leche League leaders (see page 217 for addresses).

If your breasts feel tender, lumpy or swollen, take some milk off as soon as you can by putting your baby to the breast or by hand-expressing. Hold your baby at the breast in different positions to drain the breast more evenly. The longer you leave overfull breasts, the more likely you are to get a blocked milk

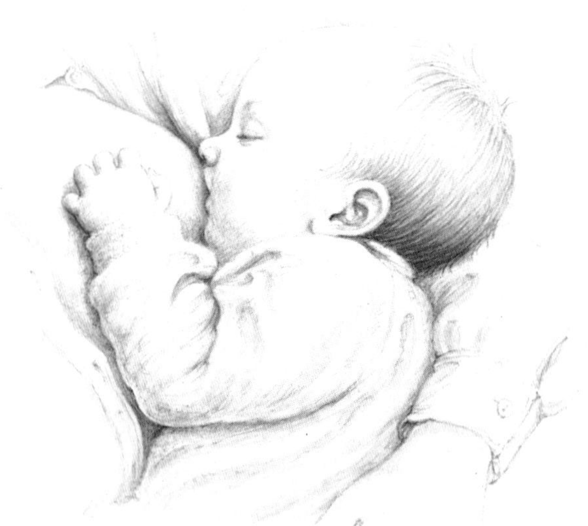

Breastfeeding your baby whenever he needs it will make him feel satisfied, content and secure and will help you make plenty of milk.

duct. This can make you feel flu like and irritable and can lead to a breast infection if you don't know what to do about it or don't ask for help.

Sore nipples are common at first, but they get better in time, especially if you change your breastfeeding technique.

Put your baby to the breast as often as he wants (or as often as you do, if your breasts are full), day and night, and don't be afraid to wake a sleepy baby if he isn't feeding enough to stimulate your breasts to make milk. Some babies quickly fall into a routine of their own while others don't for a long time, but the commonest mistake breastfeeding mothers make is to think they're giving their babies too many feedings. Once the average woman begins to ration her baby's time at the breast, she's in danger of her milk running out. Women would probably get much more satisfaction from breastfeeding – and their babies would benefit more – if they didn't start weaning their babies from the breast when they started introducing them to solids. There is no need to do this – after all, bottlefed babies go on getting their bottles. The point is that at the very time when breastfeeding is becoming second nature and when mother and baby are working really well as a team, society encourages the mother to think she has to stop!

LOOKING AFTER YOURSELF

If you are breastfeeding, make sure you eat and drink enough. It's better to eat small, frequent, nourishing meals than to have a couple of snacks during the day and one large meal in the evening. If there is a history of allergy in the family, try not to eat too much of any one food in case it affects your baby via your milk.

Bottlefeeding

If you decide to bottlefeed, your pediatrician or pediatric nurse will show you how to make up a bottle of formula. It's very easy, but has to be done carefully. An important point is to use exactly the recommended amount of formula powder or concentrate in order to make the feeding the correct strength. Ready-to-feed formula is also available, but is more expensive. Make sure that you know how to sterilize the bottle, nipple and cover properly. Dirty bottles and nipples or half-empty bottles left lying around are a good breeding ground for germs which can cause diarrhea in a baby.

If your baby is restless after finishing a bottle, try to calm him by sitting him up, leaning him forward slightly across your arm and rubbing his back. He might be happier if you give him something to suck. The crook of your bent (and clean) little finger will do or a sterilized pacifier. Bottlefed babies often like to suck for longer than a bottle feeding allows them.

If you're going out, don't forget to take bottles and formula with you. You never know when you are going to be delayed. It's not a good idea to make up a feed before you go unless you can keep the bottle in a cooler. Either take a thermos of water or ask for some water at a restaurant or someone's house, then warm the freshly-made formula to the right temperature by shaking the bottle gently under warm running water.

Your doctor or pediatric nurse will help you with any bottlefeeding problems.

Your baby will enjoy having his own spoon and will have fun trying to feed himself. Formula or breast milk remains an important part of his diet and most babies go on wanting their bottle or to be breast fed for quite some time.

Weaning

It's better to wait until your baby is at least six months old before you start trying him on foods other than formula or breast milk. If you're breastfeeding, there's no need to give other drinks unless you're ready to begin cutting down your milk supply. Some mothers continue breastfeeding until their babies are well over nine months old and perhaps into their second or third year, or longer. Older babies find it very comforting to be put to the breast if they're upset or unwell. If you're bottlefeeding, carry on until your baby is used to eating solids and is getting quite a large proportion of his nourishment from them.

Give your baby one new food at a time and wait at least three days before introducing another. This way if something doesn't agree with him you'll know what it is and you'll be able to avoid it until he is older, when you could try it again. Good first foods are tastes of rice, banana or applesauce. You can feed your baby the same food as the rest of the family as long as you make it the right consistency for him, adding extra liquid if necessary, and as long as it doesn't contain added salt. Avoid sweetened foods too because this can produce a "sweet tooth" and isn't good for your baby's teeth.

Family food

Children need a diet made up of a balance of carbohydrates, proteins, fats, vitamins, minerals and fiber, just as adults do, in order to stay healthy and allow them to grow. They learn most about eating from the food they eat with their family. If everyone eats a sensible and healthy diet most of the time, this is the best lesson in healthy eating there is. On pages 30-31 you'll find some ideas for healthy eating and information on the make-up of food.

Children inevitably have likes and dislikes, and there may be times when you are really worried that your child isn't eating well enough. Most children tend naturally to balance their own diet over a period of a week or so if they're offered a selection of foods and if they have very little added sugar. But it's difficult to be comforted by this if your child goes through a phase of wanting nothing but cereal, for example, or if he refuses to eat vegetables or fruit. It is possible for children to be poorly nourished, however much or however little they eat, if their diet is lacking in essential nutrients or if it contains too much fat or refined carbohydrate. If you think this may be true of your child, discuss it with your doctor.

Many of us find high-fat and sugary foods appealing and there's nothing wrong with eating them occasionally, provided it doesn't make us lose our appetite for the other foods we need. If your child has eaten sweet or fatty foods, try to counter-balance this later in the same day, or the next, by offering plenty of high-fiber food that is low in fat, with no added sugar. Consider buying foods such as unusual fruits as treats, rather than candy or cookies. And if you like home baking, learn to make cakes and cookies with plenty of fruit, nuts (finely chopped, not whole) and seeds in them, as well as wholewheat flour (or a combination of wholewheat and white if you don't like wholewheat alone), and less sugar. Many recipes can be adapted to make them "healthier."

Family mealtimes are important both in setting up healthy eating habits and in providing time for children and parents to relax together.

UNDERSTANDING WHAT YOU EAT

Food is made up of six basic groups of nutrients: fats, carbohydrates, proteins, fiber, minerals and vitamins. Some foods consist mostly of one of these groups, while others contain all or several of them. Certain nutrients can be stored in the body, but others, such as protein and vitamin C, should be eaten on a regular, preferably daily, basis.

Fats: necessary for the building and working of the body's cells and used to make fat stores that insulate the body against cold and provide energy if a child isn't eating enough – found in all dairy products, margarine, meat, nuts and seeds, oily fish (such as herring), vegetable and nut oils, cakes, cookies, pastry and lard.

Carbohydrates: essential for the body's metabolic processes – found in cereal grain or flour (such as in bread and breakfast cereals), other grains (such as rice), food containing natural or added sugar (such as fruits, milk, onions, peas, beans, cookies, cakes, puddings, jams, honey and candy) and vegetables and fruits containing starch (such as potatoes, other root vegetables and bananas).

Proteins: used to build and maintain every living part of the body – found in fish, meat, eggs, cheese, milk, nuts, cereal grains, rice, seeds and beans.

Fiber: prevents constipation and guards against overweight – found in whole cereal grains (such as wholewheat breakfast cereals, oatmeal and wholewheat flour), wholegrain (brown) rice, all fruits and vegetables, beans and seeds.

Minerals: used in a wide variety of ways – some, such as calcium and magnesium, are used in relatively large amounts, while only small quantities of trace elements such as iron and zinc are needed. **Calcium** keeps bones and teeth healthy and aids some of the body's chemical processes – found in milk, cheese, beans, green leafy vegetables, broccoli, nuts and seeds. **Magnesium** is essential for many metabolic processes and is concentrated in the teeth and bones – present in whole grains, green leafy vegetables, nuts and soy beans. **Iron** is used to make hemoglobin – found in liver, kidney, heart, egg yolk, beans and cocoa. **Zinc** is necessary for many metabolic processes – present in meat, nuts, peas, and wholewheat bread.

Vitamins: needed for a wide variety of functions. **Vitamin A** keeps eyes healthy and cell membranes stable and uses up excess oxygen in the body – found in liver, kidney, eggs, milk, butter, margarine and any green, yellow or orange vegetables. **Vitamin B1** enables the body to use carbohydrates – found in whole grains, meat, beans and brown rice. **Vitamins B2** and **B3** are necessary for the production of many enzymes. B2 – found in milk, cheese, cereal, meat and green leafy vegetables. B3 (niacin) – found in meat, milk, fish and whole grains. **Vitamin B5** (pantothenic acid) is necessary for the use of carbohydrates, fats and amino acids – found in eggs, wholegrain cereals and meat. **Vitamin B6** is important for protein metabolism – found in meat, fish, egg yolk, wholegrain cereal, bananas, avocados, nuts, seeds and some green leafy vegetables. **Vitamin B12** and **folic acid** are vital for the working of the central nervous system. B12 – found in liver, kidney, heart, meat, fish, milk, cheese and eggs. **Folic acid** – found in liver, kidney, green leafy vegetables, eggs and wholegrain cereals. **Vitamin C** keeps bones and connective tissues healthy, helps healing, is necessary for blood clotting and several metabolic processes and uses up excess oxygen in the body – found in most fruits, green vegetables, liver, kidney and potatoes. **Vitamin D** is essential for healthy bone growth – found in fatty fish, eggs, dairy products and margarine. **Vitamin E** uses up excess oxygen in the body – found in most vegetable oils, eggs, nuts, seeds, soy beans and lettuce.

TEN TIPS FOR HEALTHY EATING

1. Start when your baby is young by giving him suitably prepared food with no added sugar or salt.
2. Buy only what you are happy for your children to eat.
3. Watch what your children drink. If they want sweet drinks, give them diluted fresh fruit juices that are naturally sweet and have no artificial sweeteners and colorings.
4. Practice what you preach.
5. Learn from cookbooks how to make your children's food look appetizing.
6. Take pleasure in foods as you grow or buy and prepare them. Your children will sense your interest and delight.

Healthy eating doesn't have to be boring. Ingredients such as fish sticks, baked beans and tomatoes can be made into an appealing meal for children.

7. Try to make mealtimes happy, relaxed, sociable occasions.
8. Enjoy your own food. Eating healthily should be a positive pleasure, not a chore.
9. Encourage regular teeth brushing after meals.
10. If you and your children really like high-fat, high-sugar food, give yourselves a treat occasionally. A little of what you like does you good.

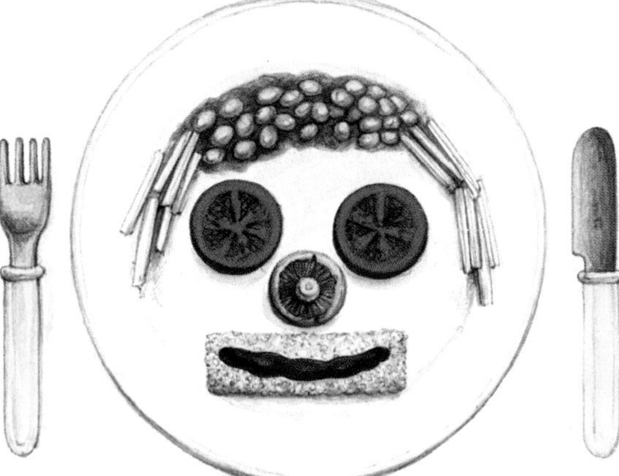

TEN DON'TS

1. Don't think that all is lost if your children haven't been eating well up to now. You can change your family's eating habits slowly and with common sense.
2. Don't make the mistake of thinking that you're depriving your children of love if you don't give them junk food.
3. Don't let your children believe that the only treats are fatty, sugary ones. Healthy foods can be treats.
4. Don't give your children sweets, chocolates or cookies when they're bored, tired, hungry between meals or for ease when you're traveling. You'll all be happier if they eat well.
5. Don't automatically sprinkle sugar over cereals, puddings or fruit and don't add it to hot drinks.
6. Don't be misled into thinking your child needs more food than he wants. Let his appetite be the judge.
7. Don't forget to plan and buy ahead. Food bought in haste may not be the best choice.
8. Don't leave too little time to prepare meals with the result that you fill your child up with convenience foods.
9. Don't forget that children's need for food fluctuates with age, state of health, level of activity, season and how they are feeling.
10. Don't ignore the food that your child eats at school. If you think school meals could be improved, say so and join up with other parents to form an action group to offer constructive advice.

Diaper changing

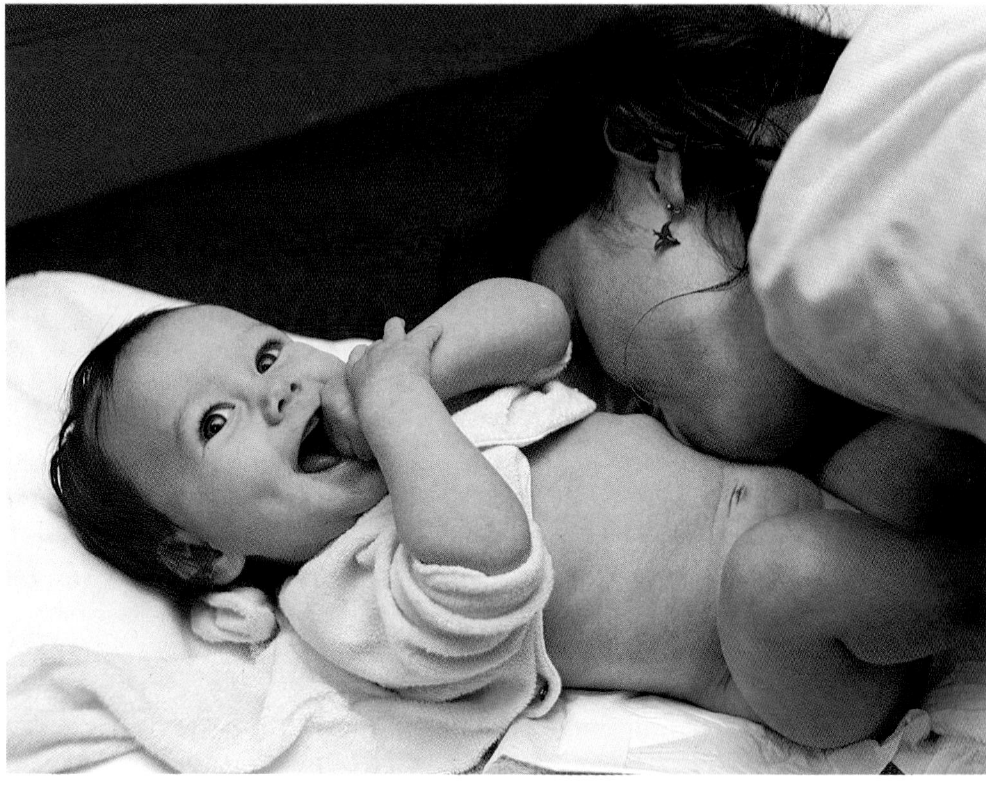

Even a task as routine as changing a diaper can give you the opportunity to play with your baby who will respond gleefully to your attention.

Whether you choose cloth diapers or disposables, don't leave them on your baby too long once they're wet and especially when they're dirty. If the skin is the slightest bit sore, diaper rash begins all too easily. Some mothers like to use a waterproofing cream, such as zinc oxide or a silicone-based cream, on their baby's bottom before they put on a clean diaper. This protects the skin to some extent. If the skin looks reddened, let your baby spend as much time as possible without a diaper on to let light and air get to the skin. Lay a young baby on a double cloth diaper, but make sure that the room is warm enough. Change the diaper more often than usual and consider using a one-way diaper liner to keep the skin drier.

Washing your baby's bottom

When you've taken off the old diaper, the best thing to do is to wash your baby's bottom with plenty of warm water, then pat it dry with a soft towel. If his bottom is soiled, use soap as well, as long as the skin isn't too sore or dry. If soap would sting or dry the skin too much, clean his bottom with a cream or lotion.

BOWEL MOVEMENTS A young breastfed baby may pass bright yellow liquid feces at first. The feces tend to become much less frequent and more formed as he grows older, and they have a distinctive, sweetish smell. Early on, you may see a daffodil-yellow stain on every diaper. A bottlefed baby passes much bulkier and more smelly bowel movements.

Once you start your baby on foods other than formula or breast milk, you'll notice that the bowel movements change. They become bulkier and contain particles of undigested or partially digested food, especially vegetables. This is quite normal. As your baby grows older, he'll become more able to digest many of the foods that at first seem to pass right through him.

Toilet training

Perhaps the only real problem for children when it comes to toilet training is if *you* are too eager to do it and attach too much importance to what is after all just a natural stage in development. At one time, mothers used to try hard to "train" even young babies to use the potty by holding them on it after a meal. This may have saved some washing, but couldn't be said to produce true self-control. It's better – and just as easy – to wait until your child is ready to let you know when he wants to move his bowels or empty his bladder before you encourage him to do so on the potty.

A child who is clean and dry at an early age isn't in any sense "better" than a child who achieves this later – he's just different. Children vary in the age at which they are able to learn, but most are ready to start practicing before their second birthday. Being clean usually comes before being dry.

CLEAN AND DRY

When you begin toilet training, take your child's potty with you when you go out. He's more likely to use a familiar one.

- Remember that your older child may wet or soil his pants if he is upset or unwell. It's far better to accept that these accidents will happen from time to time and not make a fuss about it.
- Teach your child how to wipe his bottom well after he has gone to the bathroom to avoid soreness and itching.
- Your daughter should also learn how to wipe her bottom from front to back.

Cleaning a baby girl

When you change your daughter's dirty diaper, clean the folds of her vulva well, so that she doesn't get sore. Always be sure to wipe from front to back to avoid wiping any potentially harmful bacteria from the bowel movement to the vulva.

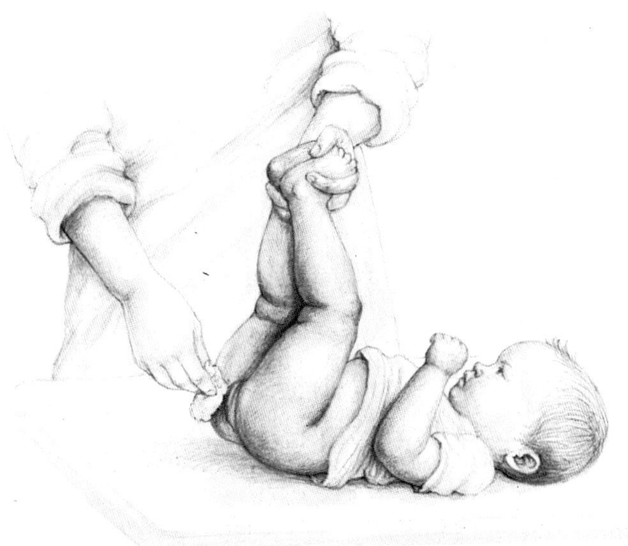

Bath time

You probably will be shown how to bathe your baby by a nurse in the hospital. Pay special attention to washing under his arms, in the folds at the tops of his thighs, behind his knees, round his chin and behind his ears. In other words, wash and dry the skin folds and creases well because a build-up of dirt and sweat can lead to soreness fairly quickly. Your doctor will show you how to look after your baby's bellybutton (umbilicus). If it starts weeping or looks at all sore, remember to tell your doctor. Dry the bellybutton well after washing your baby. Your family soap will probably suit your baby, but some mothers prefer an unperfumed soap and others find that soap dries the skin and so choose a soapless washing liquid. If you use soap, try to avoid getting it in your baby's eyes and keep his soapy hands away from his eyes too.

It's a good idea to bathe your baby when he's content. If you bathe him when he's hungry, he'll probably cry and no one will enjoy it, and if you bathe him soon after a meal, he may be sick.

There's no need to bathe your baby every day, but it is a good idea to "top and tail" him – to wash his face and bottom. Dry him carefully, particularly in the folds, using his own towel. Use cornstarch powder after drying him if you like, but take care not to shake it around too much or your baby may breathe it into his lungs.

THREE GOLDEN RULES WHEN BATHING A BABY

1. Check the temperature of the water before you put the baby in it. Try dipping your elbow in – it's a more sensitive guide to temperature than your hand.

2. Make sure that the room where you bathe your baby is warm. If your bathroom is rather cold and you have a baby bath, move to a warmer place, such as the living room.

3. Never leave your baby unattended in a bath. Even a baby old enough to sit up steadily can very easily fall over and could drown if you were out of the room for only a minute or two.

Washing and drying a baby

Your baby will enjoy being bathed if he feels secure, so hold him firmly with one hand around the top of his arm, supporting his shoulders on your forearm.

Make sure your baby stays warm as you are drying him after his bath and dry him thoroughly in all his creases, especially at the tops of his thighs and around his neck.

There's nothing wrong with cuddling and washing your baby as you take your own bath, provided that the bath water isn't too hot for the baby and that there's another adult with you to pass him to you once you're safely sitting down in the bath and to take him from you afterwards. Bathing with a baby can be lovely for both parent and child.

Bathing your older child

Older children need just as much supervision in the bathroom as do babies when it comes to checking the water temperature and not leaving them alone. They will gradually learn to wash themselves, but need help for a long time if most of the dirt isn't to end up on the towel! Wash your daughter's bottom gently between the folds of her vulva. Your son's foreskin may or may not pull back easily. If it does, then gently wash underneath it. If it doesn't, never try to force it back but simply try again in a few months time. It will loosen eventually and no amount of fussing will hurry it up. Teach your child to wash and dry well between his toes. This will help avoid athlete's foot (see page 116).

Looking after the skin

If your baby has a dribble rash on his cheeks, chin or neck, protect the skin with petroleum jelly or a silicone barrier cream. This can also help to prevent soreness under the nose when your child has a cold. Encourage children to dry their hands thoroughly to help prevent chapping in cold weather.

Most children enjoy playing in the bath and it can be a good way of winding down at the end of a busy day!

Hair care

A baby's hair needs to be washed only once or twice a week. Use a tearless baby shampoo or a plain, mild soap. Don't be afraid of soaping the soft spot on top of the baby's head – it is covered by a tough membrane. When you shampoo your baby's hair, try not to get shampoo into his eyes. A plastic halo shampoo shield is really helpful for this.

Cradle cap is very common at first and will disappear on its own in time, though you can speed its departure if you wish (see page 128). There's no special merit in washing hair frequently, but some children run their hands through their hair a lot and this, combined with dirt from playing and from the environment, can make hair smell unpleasant after a while. As your child gets older, you'll probably notice that his hair becomes greasy more quickly. When you wash your child's hair, rinse the shampoo out thoroughly and use a conditioner if his hair tangles readily, to make it easier to brush.

Nail care

You may find it easier to cut a young baby's nails while he's asleep. Use blunt-ended scissors for all children's nails in case they wriggle and you stick the points into them.

Toenails are easiest to cut after a bath when they are soft. The only reason why people suggest cutting toenails straight across is that if shoes fit badly, a child is less likely to get an ingrown toenail. If shoes fit well, you can follow the line of the quick, but make sure you don't leave a spike of nail at the edge. Fingernails are best kept short and smooth.

Don't try to clean under fingernails or toenails with any kind of manicure implement. If the nails are dirty, cut them, then let the child have a long soak in the bath followed by scrubbing the nails with a nailbrush. White flecks in the nails can be caused by knocks or possibly by a shortage of zinc in the diet (see page 30 for foods containing zinc).

HOW TO SHAPE FINGERNAILS AND TOENAILS

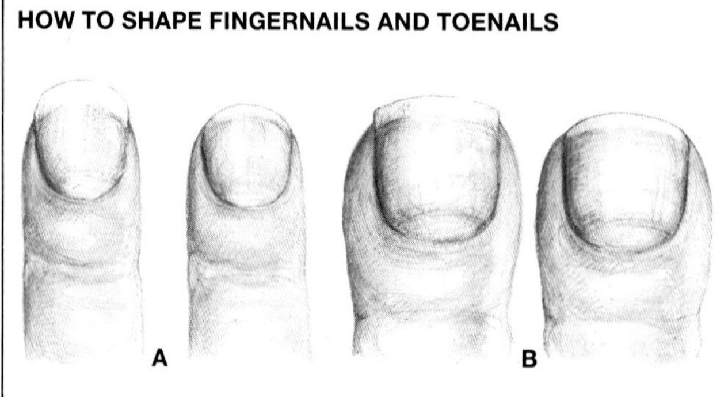

Make a habit of checking your children's nails regularly at bathtime. You can stop their fingernails from breaking or tearing – and discourage nail biting – if you cut them short and smooth (A). Toenails are more comfortable if cut straight across (B) and this also makes them less likely to become ingrown.

Caring for teeth

Dental decay, or caries, is still a problem in children today. Undoubtedly some children have teeth which are inherently stronger and more resistant than others. However, dental decay is to a great extent preventable. The following four points are particularly important.

Try only to give your child food containing added sugar *with* meals and not between them.

Look after baby teeth just as carefully as the second set. Decay in a baby tooth can affect the permanent tooth which lies underneath waiting to come through.

Clean your baby's teeth regularly with a toothbrush and toothpaste in order to get rid of as much of the sticky layer of plaque as possible. Teach your growing child the importance of looking after his teeth if he wants to avoid losing them prematurely.

An adequate amount of fluoride in the diet protects teeth against decay. Ask your dentist or pediatrician whether your child needs additional fluoride in either tablet or drop form – this will depend on the amount of fluoride in your drinking water. Be very careful not to exceed the recommended dose because too much can discolor the teeth.

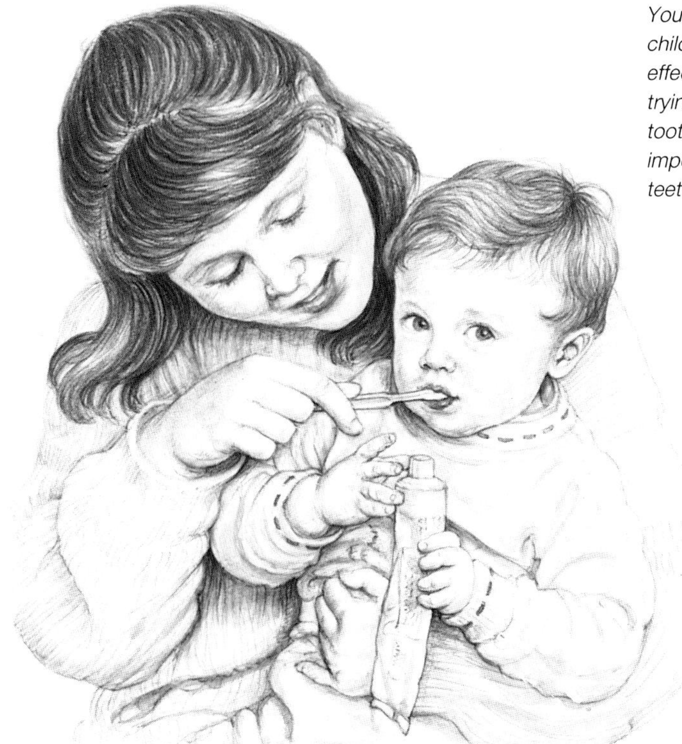

You will need to help your child to brush his teeth effectively, though he'll enjoy trying it on his own with his toothbrush. It is very important to look after his first teeth.

Clothing and footwear

When you are choosing clothes and footwear for your baby and child, bear in mind the practical considerations of his development and comfort.

Practical points on clothing

In cold weather several light layers of clothes are warmer than one or two thicker ones. Don't forget the old saying that if the head, wrists and neck are warm, the whole body is warm. Although gloves and scarves are a nuisance to put on and easily get lost, they are worth using. Mittens are easier and if you attach them to your child's coat or jacket, they're much less likely to get lost when you're out. Try joining them with some ribbon or yarn long enough to pass one mitten up one sleeve, across the back and down the other sleeve before you put your child's coat on. This way you can swap the mittens from one garment to another and take them out to wash them. Some children get pain in their ears in cold or windy weather. Choose a hat that covers the ears but isn't annoyingly tight.

Warm nightclothes insulate a child from cold at night better than extra layers of bedding. When you are buying or making nightwear, make sure the fabrics used are not flammable.

In hot or cold weather, your child will be much more comfortable in cotton, wool or other natural fibers than in synthetics. Natural fibers "breathe," while synthetics trap moisture and can be hot and sweaty in warm temperatures, and cold and clammy in cold weather.

Caring for growing feet

The twenty-six bones in a growing foot are soft and pliable, and can readily be distorted by pressure from badly fitting shoes, socks, stretch suits and even tightly tucked-in bed covers. Cut the feet off a stretch suit if they become too tight before your baby has grown out of the suit. Check the fit of socks and tights regularly and remember that they can shrink and become too tight. Stretch socks can easily compress small feet. If you want to put shoes on your baby when he starts standing or walking, choose very soft ones that can't interfere with the developing feet.

Once a foot begins to grow out of shape, it can be difficult to find well-fitting shoes and so a vicious circle develops which is hard to break and can lead to painful bunions, corns and calluses. Many children unfortunately end up with a foot abnormality that could have been prevented with a little care. Children's feet tend to grow in spurts, so even if your child's feet seem to have stayed the same size for a long time, have them measured regularly. Never buy shoes without trying them on your child. Let children go barefoot when it's warm and safe.

CHOOSING SHOES FOR A GOOD FIT

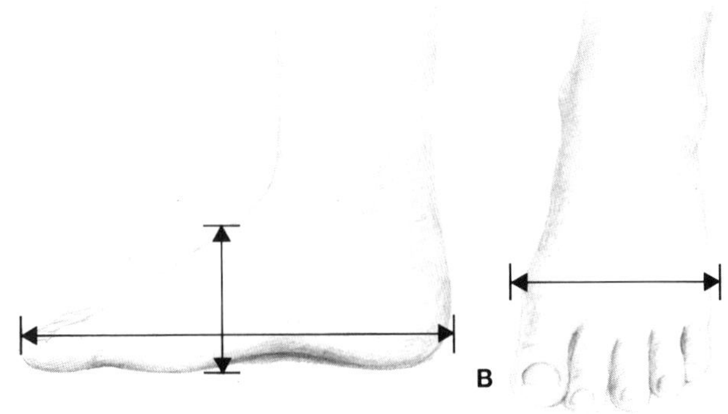

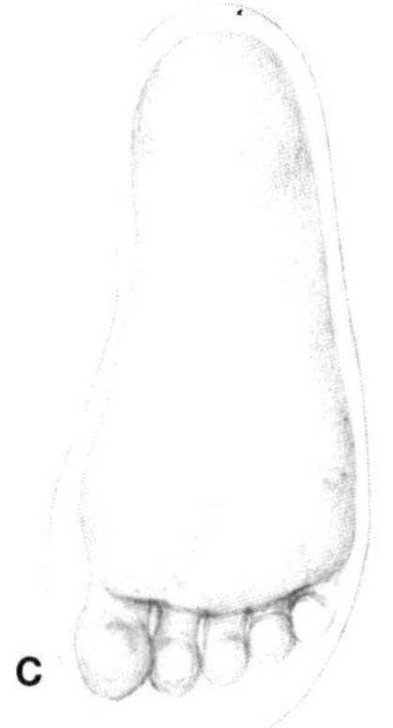

Make sure your child's shoes fit every dimension of his feet, checking the length and height of his instep (A), the width (B) and that the shoes allow ample room around the shape of his foot (C).

- If your child's toes seem to curl over, take special care that his shoes fit well and don't rub at the toes.
- Check that new shoes are big enough in length, width and height and that the inner edge of the shoe is straight, following the line of the foot. In other words, choose foot-shaped shoes.
- Don't choose shoes that are too stiff or heavy. Shoes which are supple and have natural "give" in them where the toe joints bend are much more comfortable.
- Shoes that are uncomfortable when first tried on should be left in the store. Feet shouldn't have to "break in" shoes.
- If the top of the back of the shoe hurts your child's heel, don't buy them. A bony callus can easily develop on the heel to protect the foot from the shoe and once there it makes the future buying of shoes much more difficult. This is often a problem in shoes that aren't high enough at the back: the top of the back of the shoes should reach above the most prominent part of the child's heel for greatest comfort.
- Choose shoes with leather soles or uppers, or sneakers with natural fabric uppers. All-synthetic shoes don't allow sweat to evaporate and so tend to create the moist, warm conditions between the toes that the athlete's foot fungus thrives on.
- Buckle shoes or sandals are better than slips-ons for children's feet because they hold the foot in place in the shoe and stop it from sliding forward and compressing the toes. Slip-on shoes slip off very easily and mean that the foot muscles have to work hard to keep them on. Shoes that come off readily are dangerous as children run around.
- Make sure that there's plenty of growing room between the ends of your child's toes and the front of the shoe when you buy new shoes.

Sneakers or soft play shoes with canvas uppers are a useful extra.

Leather buckle shoes hold the foot in place and allow it to "breathe." Choose shoes with a flat or very low heel and non-slip sole.

Sleep

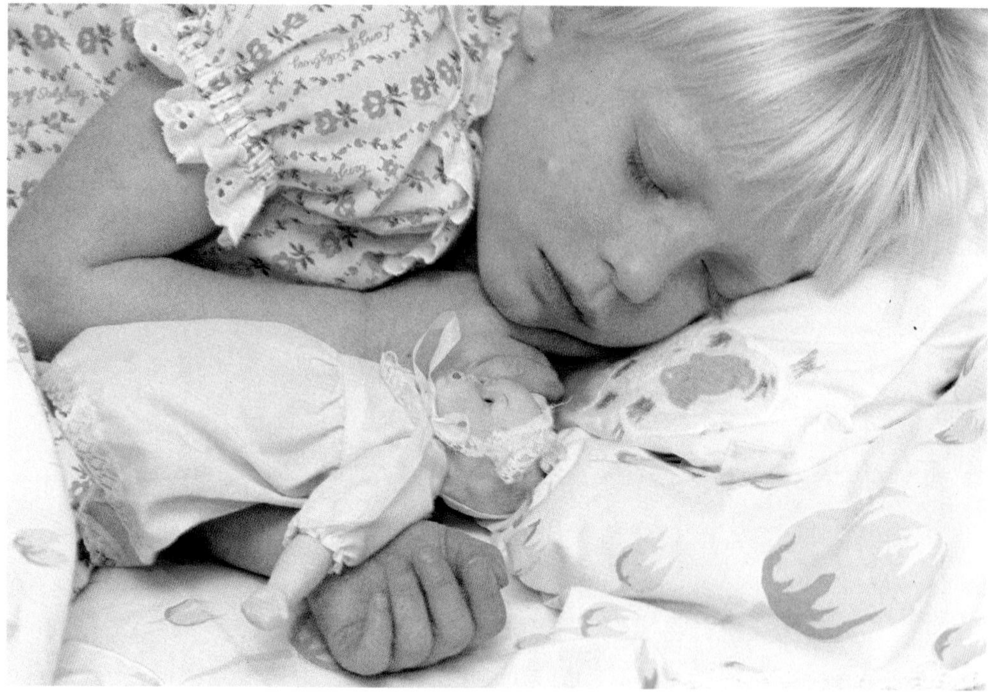

A favorite doll, toy or cuddly blanket can help a child fall contentedly asleep and can also be a comfort if she wakes in the night.

When parents talk about their children's sleep problems, they usually mean that *they* are the ones with the problems. Children tend to get as much sleep as they need simply by falling asleep whenever they are tired. The problem for parents is if the child falls into a pattern of sleeping more by day than by night and then disturbs their sleep by waking often or by not wanting to sleep at all. Some children need little or no more sleep than their parents – and sometimes even less!

It's important to work out how to handle a sleep problem because it's all too easy to become tired and run-down by broken sleep. Your pediatrician will be happy to discuss it with you. You should aim to be consistent and firm, so that your child knows what is expected of him, yet at the same time loving and flexible enough to take into account his desire to be near you and his natural fear of the dark.

Sleep patterns change over the months, especially in babies, but even a few nights with badly disturbed sleep can be difficult to cope with. Some mothers use the time that their baby sleeps during the day to rest themselves, rather than to dash round doing all the chores. It's tempting to get things done, but much more sensible to look after yourself. If you mother yourself enough, you'll be able to enjoy mothering your baby more.

Sleep and the young baby

Young babies can't last through the night without being fed several times. Be prepared to accept this and try to catch up on your sleep when you can during the day. If your breastfed baby starts sleeping through the night early on, try to hand express some milk during the night. You make more milk at night than during the day and if your baby is not nursing, your milk supply may begin to fail.

Some parents enjoy having their baby in bed with them. This makes breastfeeding easy because the mother can simply nurse her baby as they lie next to each other. And because the baby may nurse relatively frequently, she makes plenty of milk. However, the baby will grow up believing that the parent's bed is his bed too, and may find it difficult to adjust to moving into his own bed later. Don't have the baby in bed with you if you or your partner have taken any drugs (including sleeping pills or tranquilizers), have drunk too much or are very overweight.

Babies are much less likely to inhale regurgitated milk if they are not laid down flat immediately after a feeding. If you want to put your baby down, either strap him in an infant seat or prop up the legs of the crib about six inches at the head end. The safest position for a young baby to sleep in is on his side. You may find that it helps to keep him there if you put a rolled towel at his back.

It's important that you're near enough to hear your baby at night. If not, buy a baby monitor you can plug in wherever you are in the house.

Sleep problems in an older child

Children feel secure and comfortable if they have a regular bedtime routine which might include a last snack or small drink, undressing, washing or bathing, putting on nightclothes, getting into bed and having a little time for a story or to talk about the events of the day and what will happen tomorrow. Many parents share a short prayer time with their child too. But however reliable a pattern you have set, there will be times when your child doesn't want to stay in bed, can't get to sleep, wakes up and comes downstairs or into your bed, or cries and doesn't want you to leave him.

Try to work out why your child is behaving like this. He may be feeling sick, uncomfortable, cold, hungry or afraid of the dark or being left alone. He may have had a disturbing dream or want to go to the bathroom. More likely, though, is that he simply would prefer to be with you, especially if he thinks you're having a good time and he's left out of it. Attend to his physical needs and let him stay with you if he's sick or afraid or if you are happy to have him up. If you feel he won't get the sleep he needs unless he's in bed, or you need some time to yourself, take him back to bed and stay with him until he's happy to be left or falls asleep.

General well-being

Encourage your child to play outside in the fresh air. He will enjoy it and feel much better for the exercise.

Fresh air and exercise

The ultraviolet light in sunlight enables your body to make and store vitamin D which is important for the development of bones. Unfortunately this light is filtered out by glass, so a child has to be outside in the fresh air in order to benefit from it. Enough sunlight comes through the clouds to make it valuable so it's worth taking a baby out every day and encouraging a young child to play outdoors for some of the time, whatever the weather. In that way, sufficient vitamin D can be made and stored to last a child through the grayer months.

Our bodies are made to move and a child's muscles, joints and bones need regular activity to be healthy. Plenty of exercise not only makes a child feel well, helps his muscles grow strong, keeps him slim and helps him sleep, but also helps his body to burn up excess energy and keep him warm. The beneficial effects of exercise last for a few days, but it's still sensible for a child to get some exercise every day.

Getting regular exercise isn't always easy if your family relies on a car for transportation. But even young children benefit from walking, so try to set aside part of every day for walking, swimming, playing outside or some other form of activity that you and your child enjoy. Even if it's raining you'll both feel better for the exercise, though it might be more tempting to stay inside. If your child is at school, check how much exercise he has there and supplement school gym and games with out-of-school activies if necessary.

Learning about life

The stimulation that comes from being involved in what's going on around him is essential for a child to develop normally. Children love to be with people and can become very board if left alone. They need to be played with, talked to, smiled at, laughed with, shown things, and included in family meals, outings and other activities. They need to feel part of the family and – as they grow – of the wider community, rather than just left to be passive observers. Perhaps what's most important is having enough time with one person concentrating on them alone and taking a real interest in them.

Choose a time to give your full and undivided attention to your child when *he* is ready for it. It's no good expecting a tired or hungry child to enjoy even your best efforts to play with and talk to him just because it's a good time for you. The more you talk with your child and listen to him, the more capable he'll be of understanding and talking himself.

You may find that there are some situations when it isn't appropriate or convenient to have a baby or young child with you. Then it's better to leave him with someone else he knows rather than to be frustrated and annoyed because his presence isn't welcome. He'll probably enjoy himself more too.

Spiritual care

If the spiritual side of life is important to you, tell your children about it. It's easy for a child to grow up never knowing what his parents think and feel because they are embarrassed, can't find the words or don't want to brainwash him. Yet many people, old and young, draw comfort and sense of meaning in life from their faith in a source of goodness, or "God," beyond themselves and potentially present in each of us.

If you're not sure what you believe or have no spiritual beliefs, it's still worth encouraging your child to consider other people's ideas.

You could also try and find a way of developing a broader perspective on life, something that goes beyond you. You might, for instance, be aware of a sense of wonder at the beauty, majesty and power of nature, or you could entrust yourself to a creative and loving power even though you don't understand what you're doing.

THE HEALTH CARE SYSTEM

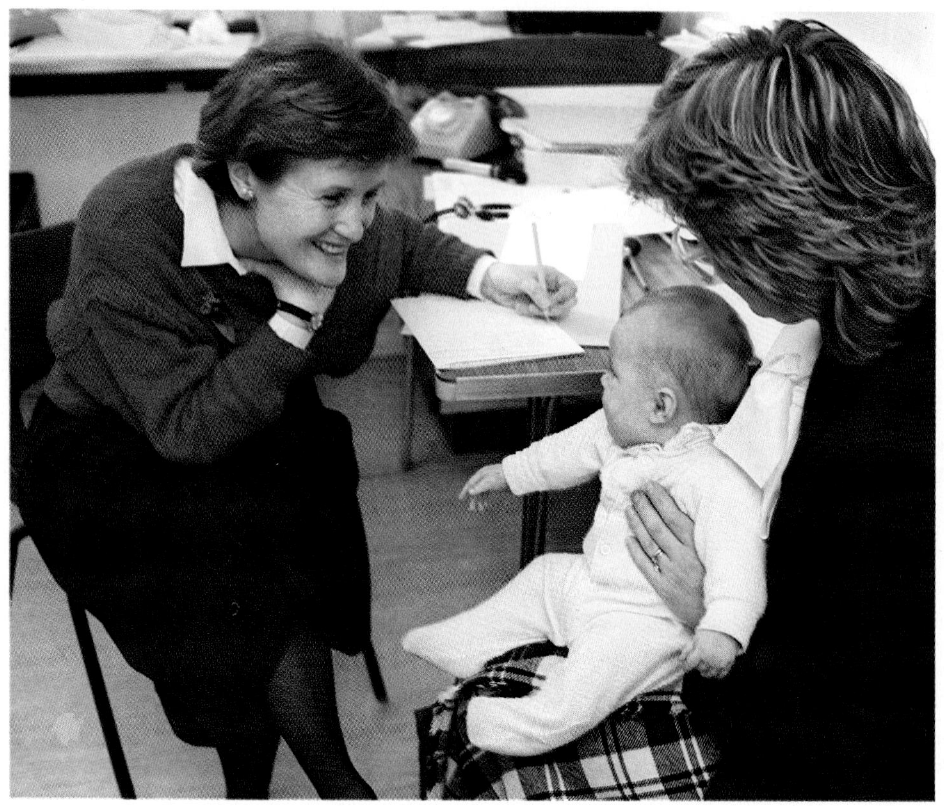

Most family doctors are very good with small children and very understanding about a mother's concern for her child's well-being.

The aim of our health care system is not only to diagnose and treat disease or disability but also to prevent it. In other words health professionals want to keep children healthy and this is why there is such emphasis on the word "health" such as in the terms "health professional" and "health care service." We now know that much disease can be prevented, saving untold misery to children and their families.

However, prevention isn't necessarily easy, quick or cheap. Health education takes time, effort and expertise, and cooperation from patents, children and the local community (including schools) is essential. There are also hundreds of volunteer organizations and self-help groups working on the promotion of good health (see pages 216-18 for addresses).

When we talk of "health," we're not just talking about physical health but also about emotional health. Children need healthy minds in healthy bodies. Health professionals today are well aware of this and no longer think about and treat physical and emotional problems separately.

The health care professionals

How a parent chooses a doctor and other health care professionals for a child depends upon a variety of factors. In small towns and rural areas, where there are few doctors and clinics, the decision is a relatively easy one because there may be only one practitioner within a reasonable distance. In cities and suburbs, parents can choose from among many kinds of physicians and specialists, medical practices and payment schedules.

Choosing a doctor

There are two types of doctors that provide primary medical care for children: pediatricians and family physicians (or family practitioners). A pediatrician is a physician who has had three years of extensive training after completing medical school in the care of infants, children and adolescents. A family practitioner (which is not the same as a general practitioner) is a doctor who has had at least three years of residency training in the care of families – adults as well as children. About half of all children in the U.S. are cared for by family practitioners.

In many small towns, there may not be a pediatrician. But whether you select a family practitioner or a pediatrician to care for your child, you should, ideally, meet with the doctor – or at least talk to the doctor on the phone – before the baby is born or, if you have moved to a new area, before bringing in your children. The best way to find a doctor is through friends and neighbors and other knowledgeable professionals in the community. You can also call the nearest accredited hospital (preferably a teaching one) and request a list of pediatricians or family practitioners on the staff as attending physicians. "The Directory of Medical Specialists," available in the local library, and the county medical society, listed in the phone book, will also provide the names of qualified family practitioners and pediatricians in your area.

Just as important as determining a doctor's medical credentials and competence is knowing whether the doctor is someone with whom you can communicate and feel comfortable. This is why a preliminary visit is so important. You should ask about the doctor's training and hospital affiliations. In addition to being licensed and board-certified, you want your doctor to have admitting privileges at a hospital near you which has emergency care facilities. You will also want to ask whether the physician is in solo practice (without partners) or part of a group. With a solo physician you often have more assurance of continuity of care and find that you develop a closer relationship, but a group practice may offer a wider range of "in-house" specialities, as well as expanded and more flexible office hours. You will also want to ask about fees and the cost of the immunization program. Other questions to ask are:

What are the doctor's office hours? Does the doctor have telephone hours for answering routine questions?

What is the role of your doctor's nurse or receptionist? Some physicians' practices include a pediatric nurse practitioner, who is a registered nurse with additional training in pediatric nursing. Often the nurse or the receptionist will act as an intermediary between you and the doctor, answering routine questions and making suggestions. You should decide beforehand if you would feel comfortable with this type of arrangement.

How can the doctor be reached in an emergency? Who takes the doctor's calls and how are messages relayed to him? Does the doctor call back promptly? Does he make house calls?

How long do you have to wait for an appointment?

Does the doctor's office have a separate waiting room for children with infections?

Will the office staff handle insurance forms?

Who is the "back up" physician when the doctor is away? How far will you have to travel to this doctor's office?

The medical care of a child involves a three-way partnership between physician, parent and child. Sometimes, for one reason or another, this partnership breaks down. You may feel that you cannot communicate effectively with your doctor or that you are not receiving satisfactory medical care. Remember that most doctors want you to be satisfied with the care you receive. So be sure to talk over the concerns and questions you have with your doctor first, if possible. If you are still not satisfied, you should select another physician. Remember it is your responsibility as a parent to your children to provide good medical care, even if it means changing doctors several times.

If your family belongs to a Health Maintenance Organization (HMO) where you receive prepaid medical care and are usually assigned to a doctor, you can ask to be transferred to another doctor. This can usually be accomplished without much difficulty.

Specialists and pediatric subspecialists

Part of the job of your pediatrician or family physician is to make certain that your child gets appropriate care from the right specialist or pediatric subspecialist, if a referral is necessary. For example, if your child suffers from chronic ear infections, your physician may request that the child be seen by an otolaryngologist (an ear, nose and throat, or ENT, surgeon). In some cases, it may be necessary for your child to be seen by a pediatric subspecialist, such as a pediatric allergist, cardiologist or endocrinologist. Generally it is your doctor who makes these referrals, but parents are free to go to such physicians without being referred. This is called seeking a "second opinion," and it is a common practice.

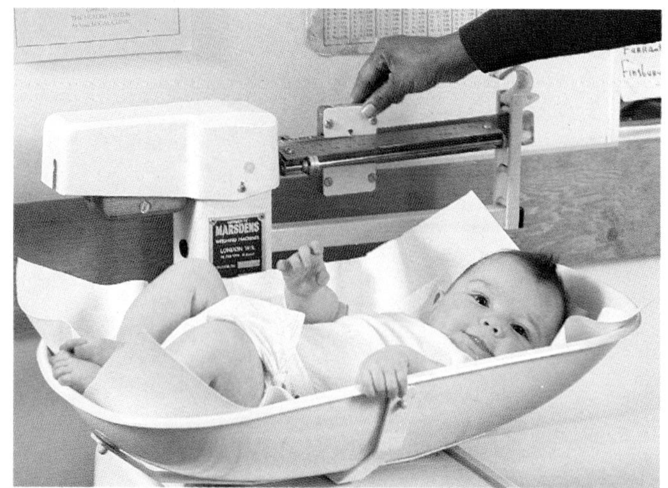

Your baby's weight gain in any one week is much less important than the average weight gain over a few weeks. If your breastfed baby is gaining very slowly, remember that you can always increase your milk supply by feeding more often and longer each time.

Clinics

There are "well-baby clinics" at many hospitals or child-health stations throughout the country. These clinics provide good medical care at less cost than a private doctor. They are staffed by doctors and nurses who work as a team. At many of these clinics your baby can have routine checkups and immunizations. However, some assign you to a different doctor each time you come, see only well babies, and require that you have an appointment in advance. Others will see your baby if he's sick and have walk-in services where no appointment is necessary.

To find out the whereabouts of these clinics in your area and other specifics, such as eligibility, fees and services offered, contact your local hospital or the state and county department of health or social services.

The school physician and nurse

School physicians may also work as family doctors and pediatricians and they work in close collaboration with the school nurse. When routine physicals are done varies from district to district, but usually they are performed when a child enters first grade and high school and before participating in any interscholastic sport. Vision and hearing tests are usually done every year by the school nurse. The school nurse is often involved with health education and counseling in the school and she carries out routine activities such as weighing and measuring the children and taking their blood pressure.

The dentist

If you live in a large community, you may be able to find a pedodontist or pediatric dentist, who specializes in the dental care of children. Other dentists care for both adults and children. It is recommended that you begin taking your child to the dentist every six months, beginning at age two. Try to find a dentist who makes that important first visit fun for children. Your child's doctor will usually refer you to a dentist.

Other health care services

Sometimes children may require medical or other related services not ordinarily provided by a pediatrician or family doctor. It's best to get a specific referral from your doctor, your child's school, or another knowledgeable professional.

DIETARY ADVICE Many disorders are caused or worsened by the food a child eats. While others require a temporary or permanent change in the diet as part of the treatment. Dietary manipulation is becoming increasingly sophisticated and your doctor may recommend that you consult a nutritionist for detailed advice and supervision.

COUNSELING AND PSYCHOTHERAPY Emotional problems in children can show up as depression or anxiety, behavioral problems, learning difficulties or physical illness, and are often associated with tensions and problems within the family. The family doctor or pediatrician may refer the child, or even the whole family, for skilled help from an individual or a team trained to cope with such issues. Sometimes this help has to be given over a long period and requires considerable patience and perseverance.

EDUCATIONAL PSYCHOLOGY A child with learning or behavioral difficulties at school may be referred to a licensed school psychologist for help and guidance. The psychologist will look at the many aspects of the child's intellectual ability and potential and will also take emotional and other considerations into account. He will serve as a liaison between parents and teachers and may ask the school physician to become involved if there's any chance that medical problems, such as deafness or poor vision, are contributing to the child's difficulties.

SPEECH PATHOLOGY Speech pathologists are health professionals specially trained to work with children who are particularly slow at beginning to talk, with children who have conditions such as cerebral palsy or a cleft palate that interfere with speech, and with children with very indistinct speech. The pathologist serves as a liaison with the child's doctor to work out the basic cause of the child's problems and then plans a course of treatment which will probably take place both with her in her office and with the parents at home.

Developmental screening

Your pediatrician or family physician may do routine screenings of your child's development. The doctor usually does them in conjunction with routine physical examinations. However, there are no systematic requirements for doing developmental screening in the U.S., so it is up to the parents to see that they are done. In some states, developmental screenings are available free of charge for preschool age children through the school district. Some areas also have early intervention programs which offer screenings for children from birth up to the age of three.

Children are individuals and as such develop at their own unique rate and in their own way. However, there are certain well-recognized developmental "milestones" – mental and physical skills which children acquire in much the same order. For example, your baby will probably be able to smile at six weeks, learn to sit before he stands, and talk in simple sentences at three years.

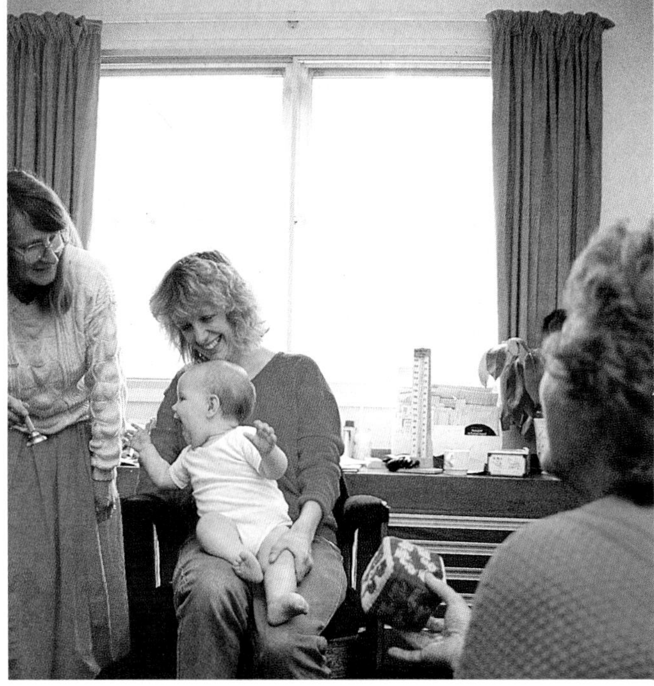

A 7- or 8-month-old baby may respond very clearly to a hearing test, but if she doesn't, the test can be repeated another time.

If your child seems to be developing slowly you should mention this at your next routine visit to your physician or clinic. Your doctor will closely monitor your child's progress to see if he catches up, or he may recommend that special help be sought. Problems and potential problems can be spotted sooner if regular screenings are done.

If your child needs a more thorough evaluation, he may be referred to a developmental assessment team where he'll be seen by a team of experts which is headed by a developmental pediatrician and includes a psychologist, a learning disabilities teacher, a speech pathologist, an occupational and/or physical therapist, a social worker and a nurse.

AVERAGE DEVELOPMENT AT DIFFERENT AGES

Age	Vision	Hearing	Speech
Six weeks 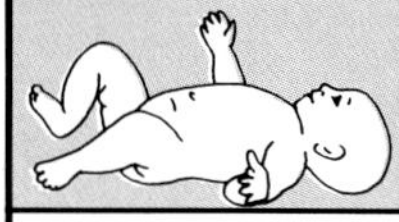	Follows a moving object from side to side within a limited range and up and down.	May startle at a loud sound.	Coos and gurgles.
Six months 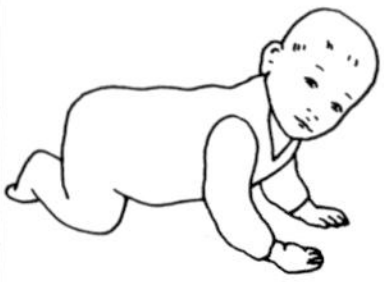	May grasp 1 inch (2.5 cm) red wooden cube at a distance of 12-15 inches (30-38 cm) in sitting position. May make contact with whole hand on a red "M&M" candy at a distance of 12-15 inches (30-38 cm).	May turn to sounds, but this is unreliable. Listens attentively when talked to.	May babble with sounds such as "ba-ba" and "a-da."
One year 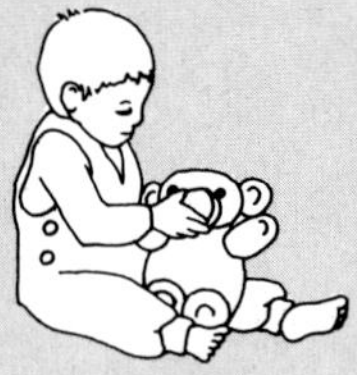	Can see as well as an adult.		May be able to say the names of a few objects, but understands many more. May have his own jargon or verbal "scribble" language.
Two years 	When small toys of varying sizes are held up one at a time, he may match the toy from an identical set in front of him.		Can put several words together and chatters a lot. Uses the pronouns "I," "me" and "you." Sometimes echoes what he hears.
Three years 	May cooperate with a vision test in which he has to look at letters of varying sizes a certain distance away and match them against letters in front of him.		Becoming much more fluent now, can talk in sentences and uses prepositions, such as "with," "from" and "into," and plurals. May learn rhymes or stories by heart.

Social	Movement
Smiles. Fascinated by faces.	Beginning to have some head control and can bring the hands together. Kicks vigorously.
Probably objects strongly when you go out of his sight.	Sits alone for a few moments only, but sits well when supported, holding his head firmly and his back straight. Lifts his head up when lying on his back and may roll over. Pushes himself up on outstretched arms when lying on his tummy. Reaches for objects, passes them from one hand to another and uses his fingers to feed himself.
Understands that if you leave him you will come back. Enjoys games such as stacking cups, sorting shapes and pat-a-cake, and likes to look for hidden objects and imitate you.	Crawls on hands and knees or on hands and feet, or may be a bottom-shuffler. May be able to pull himself up to stand and walk around furniture, or even walk alone. Picks up tiny things with thumb and finger and may be able to balance two or three blocks on top of each other. Uses a pencil to do circular scribes.
Plays alone even if with other children. Likes to say "no" and do the opposite of what you want. Enjoys exploring from a safe base.	Can easily start and stop running, and jumps with both feet. May be able to kick and throw a ball and walk on tiptoe. Draws straight lines and likes playing with building blocks. Can unscrew a lid and use a spoon well. Slowly learns to cope with buttons, undressing and washing hands.
Beginning to share toys. May have a make-believe friend. Enjoys helping adults and is beginning to be able to wait for things more calmly.	Runs around corners and climbs. Goes upstairs like an adult, but comes down one step at a time. Can pedal a tricycle and use a paintbrush and blunt-ended scissors. Tries to draw people and thread beads. Uses a knife and fork and may dress himself.

Vision tests

The American Academy of Pediatrics recommends that all newborns be examined for eye problems and checked again at six months of age. Your pediatrician or family doctor will probably perform these tests during routine checkups. If necessary, your child will be referred to a specialist for more sophisticated testing. Most states require that children have their eyes tested before entering the first grade.

This baby is fascinated by the doctor's ophthalmoscope as his eyes are checked for any sign of a squint.

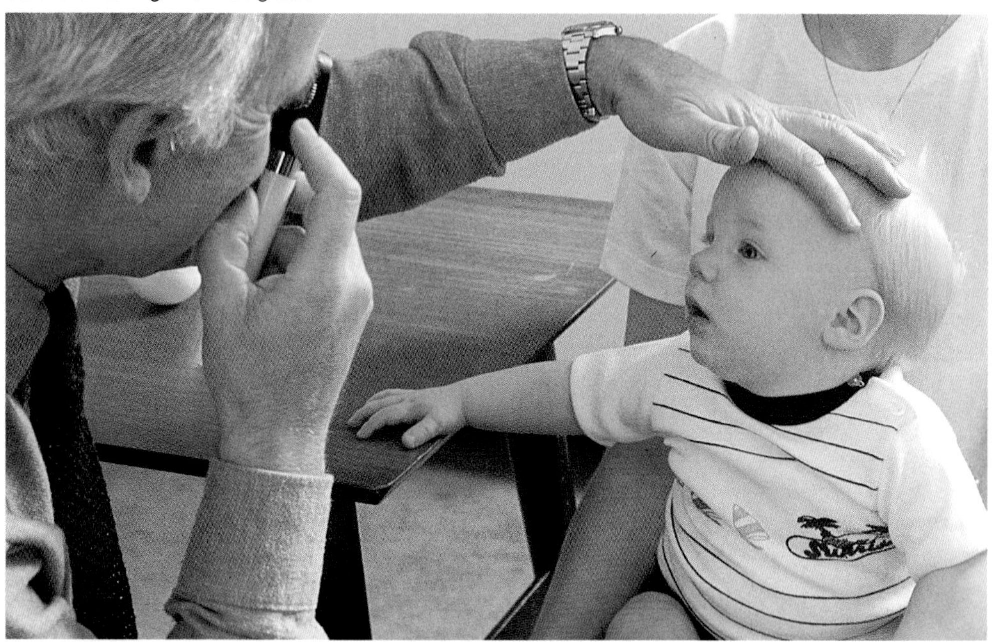

Hearing tests

The doctor should test your baby's hearing at birth, and then again when your baby is between four and six weeks old.

Hearing is then usually checked informally during developmental screenings at well-baby visits. If your child develops language problems or delay, and frequent ear infections, formal hearing tests by an audiologist may be recommended by your doctor.

Immunization

You may choose to have your child immunized by your family doctor at his office or by the clinic doctor at the well-baby clinic. Either way, the same immunization schedule is followed and your family doctor or his nurse will advise you about this and discuss with you any worries you may have. Occasionally there may be indications against certain immunizations, such as when a baby has had a convulsion or suffered any brain damage at birth. Immunization against diphtheria, tetanus, whooping cough, polio, measles, mumps, rubella, Hemophilus influenza disease and – if necessary – tuberculosis is offered to all children.

It is better to postpone immunization if your child is ill and especially if he has a fever or, when he's due to be given the polio vaccine, diarrhea.

After the DTP vaccine (which provides immunization against diphtheria, tetanus and pertussis, or "whooping cough") your baby may become irritable and feel very hot about twelve to twenty-four hours later. The skin where the needle entered may react by becoming slightly raised, hot and red, and sometimes the lump stays for several weeks. If your child has a severe reaction, such as persistent screaming, strange behavior or a convulsion, contact your family doctor at once. A further dose of whooping cough vaccine is probably best avoided, but the baby should continue with the full course of diphtheria, tetanus and polio immunization. After the measles vaccination, your child may have a slight measleslike rash and a raised temperature about a week later. He is not infectious and the symptoms are usually mild.

Recommended immunization/vaccination schedule

Age	Immunization
2 months	First dose of the DTP vaccine, containing diphtheria, tetanus and pertussis (whooping cough) vaccines, given by injection. First dose of polio vaccine given as drops by mouth.
4 months	Second dose of the DTP and polio vaccine.
6 months	Third dose of DTP vaccine.
1 year	TB test.
15 months	Measles, mumps and rubella vaccines given by injection.
18 months	Fourth dose of DTP vaccine.Third dose of polio vaccine. Hemophilus b conjugate vaccine (Prohibit) given by injection.
4-6 years	Booster dose of DTP and polio vaccines.
14-16 years	Tetanus-diphtheria vaccine given by injection.

WHEN YOUR CHILD IS ILL

An ill child will always need lots of comfort and cuddles, so be prepared to give him as much time as you can.

Knowing when your child is ill

Most parents are so closely tuned in to their children and so used to their normal behavior and appearance that they can usually tell the moment that their child starts to become ill. If you believe that your child is coming down with something, follow your instincts – you're almost certainly right. Indeed, many parents find they know if their child is going to become ill even before symptoms are apparent.

This "tuning in" to your baby is a natural part of learning about being a parent and explains why so many new parents feel jumpy or anxious about their babies. It's quite normal and it's far better to be over-concerned than over-confident when it comes to babies, because a slightly ill baby can become rapidly worse. It's much safer to seek medical help sooner rather than later if you're in any doubt. In fact, if you have a young baby, it is probably sensible to consult your doctor in person or by phone any time that you are worried. You owe it to yourselves and your baby to hand over the burden of medical decision making to the doctor, rathor than to try to shoulder it alone and wait until illness is all too obvious and perhaps more difficult to treat.

Your pediatrician and possibily the pediatric nurse should be a very important source of help and advice about babies and young children and they will help you to learn to distinguish what is normal and to be expected from what is not. Regular office visits and discussions with them will soon give you more confidence in your judgment.

Where to take an ill child

If your child is acutely and seriously ill, or has an accident and needs emergency care, he may have to go to the hospital. The quickest way to get him there is by car if he is well enough to travel and if you are not too anxious and can drive safely. If not, phone for an ambulance. If you take your child yourself, always phone to check that the emergency room is open, unless you know that it offers a twenty-four-hour service.

If your child is too ill to be taken to your doctor's office, but doesn't need to go to the hospital as far as you can tell, phone your doctor's office and explain the situation. Make sure the nurse/receptionist understands the urgency of your child's condition. If necessary, the doctor will send your child to the hospital to see a specialist either at once or later by appointment.

If you are very concerned about an ill child, but you can't contact your doctor and don't think it's safe to wait, take your child to the local hospital emergency room. It might be sensible to phone the emergency room and speak to a doctor or nurse first to explain the situation.

If your child is well enough to be taken to the doctor's office, but you think that he may have an infectious illness, phone and tell the nurse/receptionist. You may be asked to come when few people will be there or to wait somewhere apart from the main waiting area, to avoid spreading infection. Alternatively, the doctor may visit your child at home.

If you are not sure whether your child needs to see the doctor, phone him or ask his nurse for advice.

What to do at night

Sometimes a child who has been well or only slightly under the weather all day becomes worse at night. The doctor should always be contacted as soon as possible if a baby is ill, but you may find it difficult to know what to do about an older child. A child who feels ill at night often feels frightened – perhaps of the dark, or of waking you up, or of whatever it is that's keeping him awake. This is the time to stay with him and give him as much cuddling and physical comfort as he wants, and this reassurance may make him feel a lot better. However if you are

When to call the doctor

Most symptoms and signs of illness are obvious to parents, but watch in particular for the following:

Symptoms	Indications that the doctor should be consulted
	ANY illness or change of behavior in a young baby
Headache	If continuous If combined with repeated vomiting, a fever, a stiff neck or severe pain elsewhere If recurrent
Rash	Unless you are quite sure it's nothing to worry about
Thirst	If your child is drinking much more than you would expect him to, especially if he is also losing weight
Fever	if above 103°F (39.4°C) If combined with any other signs of illness If you are worried
Appetite loss	If combined with other signs of illness
Breathing	If shallow or unusual If fighting for breath If painful or noisy
Vomiting	If frequent or violent If it lasts for more than one hour in a baby, or four to five hours in an older child If combined with a headache, fever or neck stiffness
Diarrhea	If it continues for more than a day
Urine	If little or none being passed
Emergencies and injuries needing immediate first aid are covered on pages 194–215	

still worried and your child's symptoms seem to be getting worse, don't hesitate to contact the doctor. He may be able to reassure you over the phone, but if he's in any doubt he'll certainly visit. If for some reason you cannot get hold of the doctor and you're alarmed about your child, take him to the local hospital emergency room.

When you're with the doctor

Sometimes when you take your child to see the doctor, you forget to ask all the things you wanted to know, either because you're nervous or because they simply go out of your head. You may find it helpful to write down your questions so that you can check you have all the information you need.

It's equally easy to forget what your doctor has told you. You might like to go over what he has said again, or even jot down a summary of his advice. If you haven't understood something, say so and ask him to explain it again. Good communication is essential when you're responsible for a sick child. If you disagree with the doctor's ideas or advice, have the courage to air your point of view. A good doctor will accept your concern and your child's interests will be best served by a joint discussion of any problem.

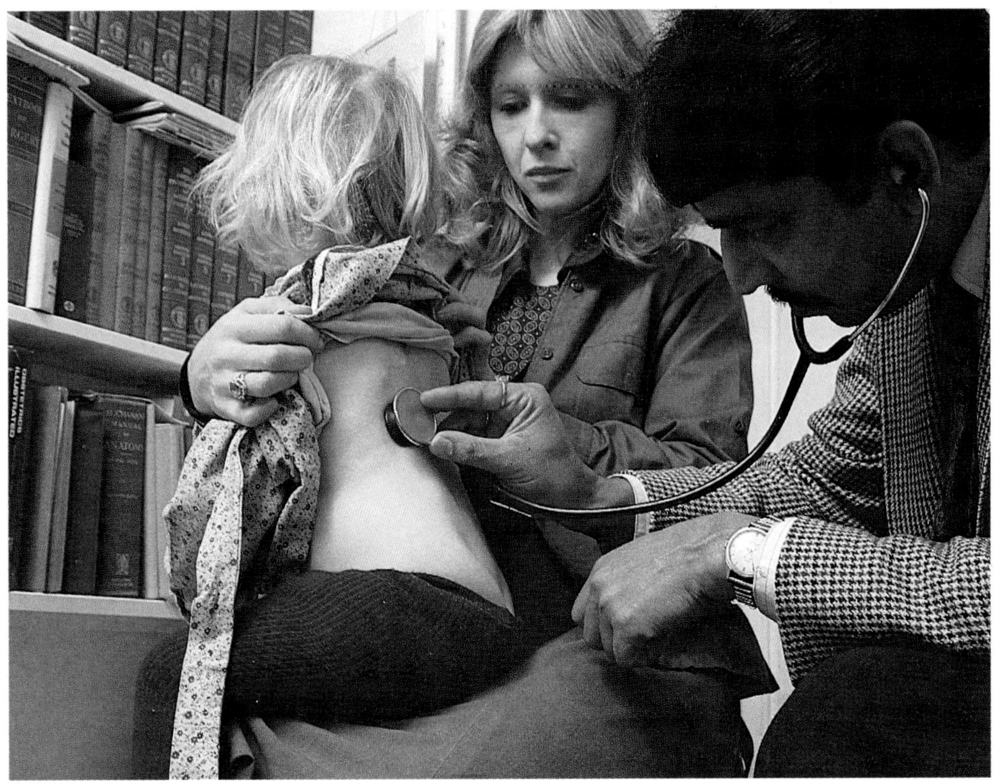

The doctor may use a stethoscope to listen to your child's chest from the front and from the back. It will help your child to feel more at ease if you hold her firmly and confidently.

Preparing your child

The doctor's examination instruments and other equipment can frighten a young child, especially if he doesn't feel well. You could help to familiarize him with some of these instruments by giving him a doctor's or nurse's toy kit to play with. This usually includes commonly used equipment such as a stethoscope.

Sick children often need to have their chests or tummies examined by the doctor, so it makes sense to dress your child in clothes that are easy to remove or pull up or down if necessary. The last thing you want is to have to struggle with tight clothes or difficult fastenings which might upset him.

Your doctor will tell you if he wants your help while he examines your child. Usually this simply means holding the child confidently and calmly to reassure him by your closeness and also to keep him still. It's particularly important that the child stays still if the doctor wants to look at his eardrum with an otoscope. Any wriggling can jog the instrument and make it hurt your child's ear. Sit your child sideways on your lap with the ear that is to be examined facing the doctor. If your child is facing to your left, hold his head above his ear with your left hand and put your right arm around his chest and right arm to hold his left hand with your right hand.

CARING FOR AN ILL CHILD

There's a lot that you can do to help your child when he's ill. He'll find it comforting to be close to you, for example, when he's having his temperature taken.

Sickness in children can develop quickly and unexpectedly, especially with an infectious illness. Once you have made your child as comfortable as possible, you will need to make arrangements for any practical necessities such as picking up other children from day care or school, doing the shopping or contacting the person who will look after your child if you have to go to work. Some childcare providers are happy to look after an ill child in their home if the child is not too sick to be taken there. Sick children usually prefer to have their parents with them rather than anyone else, even if they know them well. However, it is often difficult for a working parent to take time off work.

When your child becomes sick, your plans may have to be abruptly altered if he needs to stay at home and you have to look after him. It may sound selfish even to mention the possibility of you feeling frustrated and disappointed at the disruption to your routine, but it's a natural human response and is better acknowledged from the start.

Making your child comfortable

A really ill child tends to become lethargic, so there's no difficulty in deciding that he would be better off lying down. But it isn't necessary to keep a child in a proper bed unless he really would be more comfortable there. A young child will probably be much happier near you and you won't be able to spend all your day in the bedroom with him, so think about improvising a bed in the room where you're likely to be spending most of your time. An older child may be happier in his bedroom where it's quiet. You can always move a child from one room to another if necessary.

Babies and small children tend to need lots of comfort and closeness when they're ill, so be prepared to interrupt whatever you're doing and have a cuddle. If your child goes to sleep on your lap, you can gently transfer him to his bed.

A table placed beside the bed is useful for drinks and toys and an older child could have a tray (preferably one with a stand or legs). It may be helpful to have a potty close to the bed and a basin if he's feeling sick.

Bedding

A child who is ill in bed will be more comfortable with a light quilt or comforter rather than heavy blankets. Cotton or polycotton sheets are better than synthetic ones. Straighten the sheets and other bedding every so often, especially if the child is restless. If he has been sick, change the pillowcase fairly soon because it'll probably be rather smelly even if he wasn't actually sick on it. An older child who is sweating from a fever will appreciate clean sheets and pillowcase.

Room temperature and humidity

For a child who is ill at home but without a fever, a room temperature of 68–70°F (20–21°C) is comfortable if he is wearing ordinary clothes or pajamas and is sitting or lying in bed. But if a child has a fever, it makes sense to lower the room temperature by opening a window and turning the heating down or off. On a hot summer's day, open doors and windows to produce a draft or use an electric fan or air conditioner. Remember to watch the child in case he becomes chilled.

If your child has a respiratory complaint, such as croup, he'll be more comfortable if the air in the room is relatively humid. Most heating systems tend to dry out the air. To counteract this, many people have humidifiers connected to their heating systems or use individual humidifiers (or even bowls of water placed near the radiator in the baby's room).

Giving fluids

Children who are feverish, sweating or vomiting, or who have diarrhea, lose a lot of fluid and need plenty of drinks to replace it in order to avoid becoming dehydrated. Anything the child likes will do, but remember that milk contains relatively less water than plain water or diluted fruit juice. A tasty drink can be made from meat or vegetable bouillon cubes as long as it doesn't contain too much salt, because salt can make dehydration worse.

Meals

A child who is not well may want little or nothing to eat, and it's best not to force him. When he starts to improve, his appetite will return slowly. Encourage it by giving him small portions of his favorite foods, temptingly presented and easy to eat. If you're worried about him not eating, consult your doctor. Constipation can be a problem after a period of not eating so remember to include high-fiber foods (see page 30) in your child's diet as soon as he will take them.

Hygiene

If your child has gastroenteritis, wash your hands thoroughly every time you touch him or his soiled diapers, clothing or eating utensils. Remind your older child to wash his hands after going to the bathroom and make sure that you keep the toilet and sink especially clean.

If he has an infectious disease, warn visitors – particularly the elderly or anyone who is pregnant or with very young children – in case they would prefer not to be in contact with the infection. Teach your child not to cough or sneeze without putting his hand, or preferably his handkerchief, in front of his mouth.

Entertainment

Early in the day, when you're feeling fresh, think about the games, toys and books your child might like. A sick child may only be able to cope with simple toys and books that would normally be too young for him. The TV or video cassette recorder can be very useful for keeping an ill child amused. Most children want plenty of attention when they're sick, though they do tend to sleep for part of the day, which can give the people looking after them some welcome respite.

One of the best medicines is your time, but it is often the hardest for a busy person to give. Try to make caring for your sick child your priority, but remember that you won't be able to keep this up for long unless you have some practical support and unless you take care of yourself too.

Giving medicines and treatments

The different types of medicines that are commonly prescribed for children are described in the next chapter (see pages 68–72). When a medicine or other treatment is prescribed for your child, make sure that you fully understand the instructions. If you have any questions, you can always telephone your doctor or ask the pharmacist who is making up the prescription. See also opposite page for dos and don'ts for medicines.

Most medicines are flavored to make them palatable for young children. If your child doesn't like the taste, give him a drink afterwards. If it's going to taste nasty, tell him – he can always brush his teeth to take away the taste.

Applying eye drops or ointment

It isn't pleasant having anything put in the eye and your child will probably wriggle when you apply eye drops. Reassure an older child that it won't hurt, but that it may feel strange and he may not see clearly for a little while afterwards. Lay the child on his back and pour the correct number of drops into the hollow between his eye and nose. Don't worry if he closes his eye, as the drops will run into the eye when he opens it. Try to stop him rubbing his eye.

If you are applying an ointment, ask the child to keep still or find someone to hold him. Separate his eyelids with your finger and thumb, squeeze some ointment on to the eye and then close the eyelids. The ointment will be spread over the eyeball when he blinks.

Giving nose drops

Nose drops are best given with your child lying down so the drops don't run straight out again. This is particularly important if you are giving them to prevent or treat middle ear infection (see page 157 for otitis media), as you'll need them to run back to the openings of the Eustachian tubes in the throat. Do this one side at a time: lay the child down with his head to one side and slightly tilted back, and put the correct number of drops in the lower nostril. Wait a minute or so, then repeat the procedure with his head to the other side.

Giving ear drops

To give ear drops, lay your child down with the ear to be treated uppermost and put in the correct number of drops. Wait a minute or two. Putting a piece of absorbent cotton in the ear will prevent any excess fluid running out, but don't wedge it in too tightly. Repeat on the other side if necessary.

DOS AND DON'TS FOR MEDICINES

- When your doctor makes out the prescription, tell him if your child has ever had an allergic or other unpleasant side effect from any medicine before.
- Only give medicine prescribed by the doctor when it's been prescribed for your child and for that illness.
- Make sure the medicine is within any expiration date on the bottle.
- Follow the instructions on the bottle exactly. See page 68 for more information about giving medicines.
- Use the correct measuring spoon – you can get a 5 ml spoon from the pharmacist (see page 70).
- Never give medicine to a sleeping, unconscious or sleepy child because he might choke.
- If your child vomits within an hour, give another dose of the medicine.

Giving drops

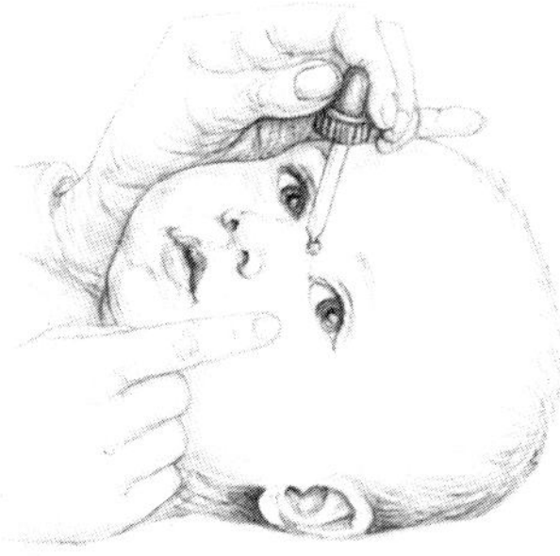

Your child will probably close his eyes automatically as he sees the dropper coming.

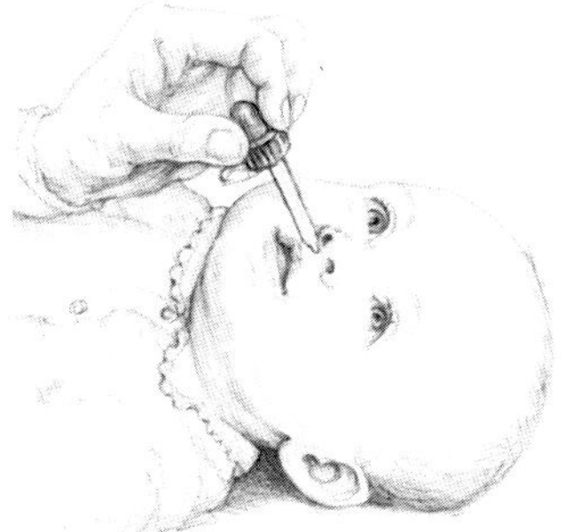

When you are giving nose drops, try not to touch the applicator against the nose.

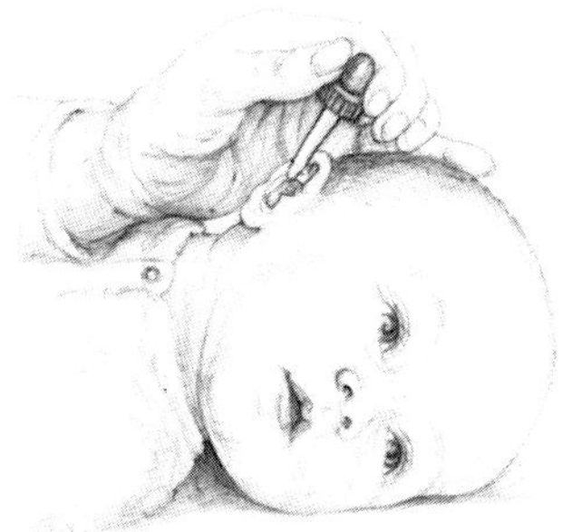

The ear drops may be a little cold and may tickle your child's ear as they go in.

Coping with fever

A fever is common with an infectious illness and it's important to know how to make a child comfortable. Not only is it unpleasant to be hot and sweaty, but it can also make a baby or young child dangerously dehydrated and overheated and make a febrile convulsion (see page 128) more likely.

Knowing if your child has a fever

Most parents know by their child's flushed face and ears and dulled eyes if he has a fever. You can also get a very good idea by feeling how hot his forehead is, though this isn't always reliable. A feverish child usually stops eating, sleeps fitfully, perhaps has nightmares, is irritable, tends to cry, may have a headache or pain behind the eyes and feels generally achy.

If you have a thermometer you will know definitely whether your child has a high temperature and may decide to call your doctor to see about setting up an appointment immediately. If the child has a rising temperature, or if he is very hot already, it's a good idea to cool him down (see opposite page) before seeing the doctor, to make him more comfortable and to reduce the risk of him having a convulsion. Occasionally, however, using a thermometer can be misleading, for with some illnesses the child can be very sick, but may nonetheless have a low or normal temperature.

Taking your child's temperature

There are three types of thermometer for home use: the standard glass clinical thermometer, the liquid crystal thermometer (fever strip) and the newer, digital thermometer. However, fever strips are not very accurate and are not usually recommended.

If you decide to buy a glass thermometer, choose a stubby-ended one that can be used in the mouth or under the arm for children older than two years; for children less than two years of age, it should be used rectally. Don't take his temperature if your child has had a hot bath within the last hour and remember that if he's had a hot-water bottle with him, it might alter the temperature reading if it was near his cheek or armpit. Obviously a hot drink within the last half hour will affect the reading if you take his temperature by mouth. Whichever method you use, make him sit or lie down quietly for five minutes before you take his temperature.

Reading a glass thermometer

Hold the thermometer at eye-level with the degree markings facing you. You will see an arrow that indicates where "normal" is. Roll the thermometer slightly backwards and forwards between your thumb and finger until the light catches the thick grey line of mercury. The number where the mercury stops indicates the temperature.

Using a glass thermometer

Hold the thermometer at the opposite end to the silver mercury bulb. Shake the mercury level down with sharp flicks of the wrist to well below the average normal temperature 97–99.5°F (36–37.5°C) measured in the mouth; approximately 1°F (0.5°C) lower if measured under the arm).

Depending on the age of your child, decide where you're going to take his temperature. Don't take it in the mouth of a baby or very young child because he might bite the thermometer, break the glass and swallow the poisonous mercury. The safest and most accurate place to take it is rectally.

To take a rectal temperature, have your baby lie comfortably on his back. Lift his legs and hold them with one hand while inserting a lubricated rectal thermometer into his rectum. (You can use petroleum jelly as lubrication.) Keep one hand on the thermometer at all times. Remove the thermometer after three minutes and read the temperature.

To take an axillary temperature, sit your child on your lap and place the thermometer in his armpit, folding his arm to keep it in place. Hold your child still to get an accurate reading.

Leave it there for three minutes at least and add approximately 1°F (0.5°C) to the reading to give an estimate of the child's inner body temperature.

An older child can have his temperature taken by mouth. Put the thermometer, bulb end first, under his tongue and tell him to close his mouth gently without biting. He should breathe through his nose. If he has to breathe through his mouth because of a heavy cold, the reading will not be accurate, so it's better to take the temperature under his arm.

When you've finished, wash the thermometer with rubbing alcohol and put it away in its container.

THERMOMETERS

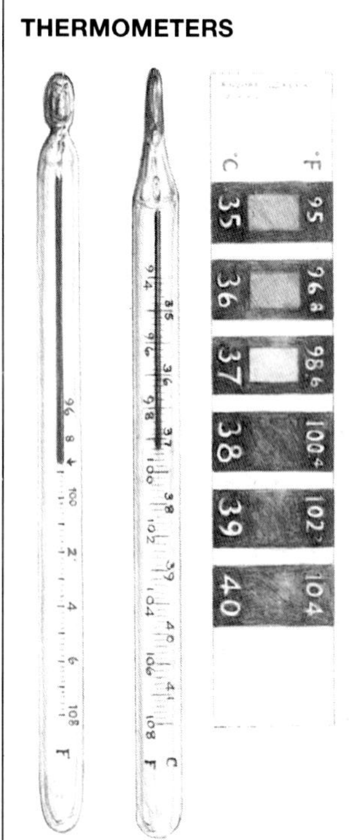

A stubby-ended glass thermometer (left) is more practical for young children than a narrow-ended one (centre). A fever strip (right) gives a rough estimate but isn't as accurate as a glass or digital thermometer.

Using a fever strip

Place the strip across his forehead, which must be dry. Take the reading after fifteen seconds.

Cooling a child

You can make a feverish child comfortably cooler by removing his clothing and bedcovers, controlling the room temperature, giving cool drinks, giving children's acetaminophen in the recommended dose, and by giving him a cool, not cold, bath.

If he's too unwell to have a bath, cool him by tepid sponging. This is a useful technique to know if your child has a temperature of more than 103°F (39.4°C). Undress him, lay him on his bed (preferably on a plastic or rubber sheet), get a bowl of warm water and sponge him all over with it. Don't dry him because the evaporation of the moisture has a cooling effect. Leave a warm wet washcloth on his neck and another two on his groin, and check his temperature every ten minutes until it comes down to 100°F (37.8°C).

Going into the hospital

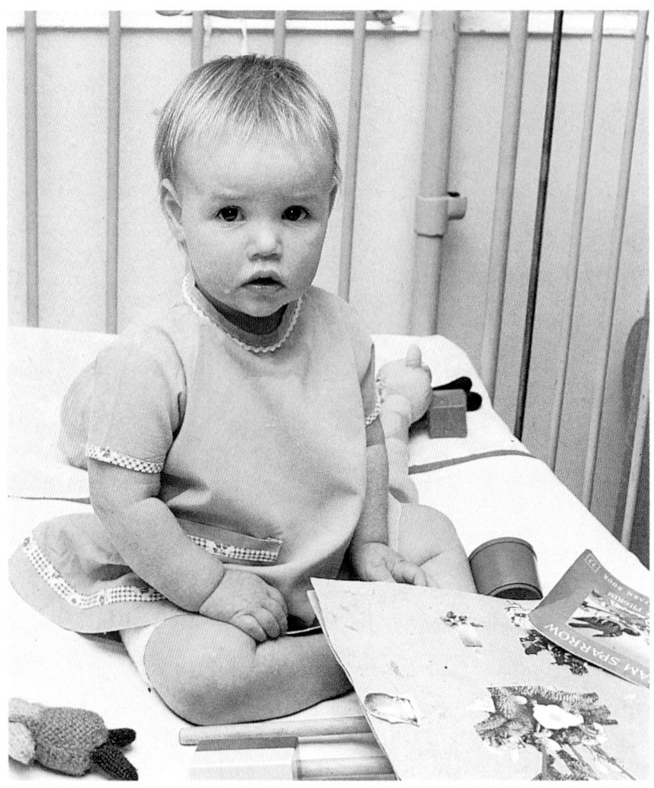

Most hospitals are very sympathetic to the emotional needs of young children. Familiar toys are a great help, but best of all is your presence if you can stay with the child.

Hospitals can be very frightening to a young sick or injured child so it makes sense to introduce him at an early stage to the idea of hospitals and what they do. Point out the hospital as you pass it and explain who works there. If you have friends or relatives who are health professionals or who work at the hospital, this will help your child associate it with familiar people and thereby make it seem more normal.

If you have to go to the hospital, your child will pick up a lot about what goes on simply by coming with you to the outpatient clinic or by visiting you in the hospital. Many things that you take for granted must seem strange to a child, such as the smell, the uniforms and the beds being wheeled around, so talk to him about everything and try to let him see hospitals as helpful rather than frightening places.

Many young children have to stay in the hospital at some time, so it's a good thing that hospitals today are likely to be welcoming and child-centered. Both parents and staff are aware of the adverse effects that being alone in the hospital can have on a young child's emotional well-being and parents are usually encouraged to stay with their children as much as they can. However loving and caring a nurse may be, a child will always prefer his mother or father to be with him. Some hospitals offer parents a bed in their child's room while others have special rooms nearby where a parent can sleep. An older child may be quite happy to stay in the hospital without you as long as he knows when you'll be visiting.

If you stay with your child, you may want to ask your partner, another member of the family or a friend to spend some time with him each day to give you a break – it'll do you good to get some fresh air and exercise. Eating well is also important and it's a good idea to pack snacks and drinks for yourself as it may be difficult to get anything during the evening or at night in the hospital. However, don't give your child anything to eat or drink until you've checked with the staff that it's quite safe for you to do so.

WHAT TO TAKE TO HOSPITAL

For your child:

- nightie or pajamas
- slippers
- robe
- washing things
- favorite toys, books or games

For yourself:

- change of clothes
- sleepwear
- toiletries
- a book

Organizing things at home

It'll help enormously if you are happy with the arrangements for the care of other children. Friends and family are usually only too happy to help out in times of crisis, so don't be too proud to ask. You may also want to spend some time with your other children. If your sick child doesn't want to be left, you could either ask your partner or a friend or neighbor to bring them into the hospital, or you could run home for an hour or so when someone else is with your sick child.

If you are unable to stay with your child in the hospital, don't forget to tell the staff any special names he might use for the bathroom, and don't forget to take his favorite cuddly toys or blanket with him.

New games, activities and friends make the long hours in the hospital pass more quickly for an older child who is beginning to feel better.

Caring for the chronically ill child

It's human nature to believe that chronic illness or mental or physical handicap is something that only afflicts other people's children. That is, until it happens to your own child. Many pregnant women worry about whether their unborn baby will be born normal and healthy; some even dream about giving birth to a handicapped or deformed child. This fear is almost universal, though it's understandably worse for mothers who have had problems in a previous pregnancy or pregnancies, or who have a chronically sick or handicapped child already.

If a newborn baby is obviously handicapped or becomes ill very early in life, parents may react with shock, followed by numbness and denial, sadness and depression. Later, there's a period of reawakening of their energy, which is often combined with much anger. These stages are well-recognized parts of the normal process of grieving. They are mourning for the normal, healthy baby that might have been. The realization that a baby is mentally handicapped often dawns more slowly, which in a way is a blessing.

Talking about your feelings

Whenever an illness or a handicap begins, it helps to be aware of your feelings about the situation and the inevitable changes in your family life that will follow. Marital difficulties can be a problem right from the beginning. One major factor behind this is a lack of open and honest communication of feelings between the parents which leads, in turn, to insufficient and inappropriate support and care for each other. If you are to give the best to your child, it's essential to look after your relationship with your partner.

If you have other children, you must be sensitive to their need for a fair share of your time, interest and energy. Feelings of jealousy and even hatred are natural as their lives are inevitably changed. Older children may well worry about what will happen to their brother or sister once you are no longer there. Don't forget that not only do the well brothers and sisters have ambivalent feelings, but the affected child does too. These all need to be talked over to make them easier to cope with. Whatever the problems – the physical exhaustion and the emotional strain – there are positive sides to caring for a chronically sick or handicapped child. Many parents say that for the first time they understand what life is all about and that the child's presence has enriched them in a way that they could never have foreseen.

Living with chronic illness

With long-term conditions, such as diabetes, epilepsy and cystic fibrosis, both you and your child will need to become used to the medicines or treatments that have to be given, day in and day out. And with certain conditions, such as food intolerance and diabetes, there is the additional burden of always having to remember to be scrupulously careful about what the child eats. Severe chronic eczema can be a truly distressing problem, bringing sleepless nights for both parents and child from itching that is at times intolerable. Some children with chronic illness or with a physical handicap have to go into the hospital from time to time if their condition becomes acute or needs special treatment.

Short-term hospital care can give parents of a chronically sick child a necessary break from the demands of day-to-day care. There is a patchwork of public and private day care and educational facilities available for physically and mentally handicapped children. But these vary from state to state and county to county and are usually inadequate to meet the long-term needs of working parents. The Association for Retarded Citizens of the United States offers day care provisions for all ages in some areas, but spots are usually limited. Special education classes are mandatory in most states and are part of the public school system. To find out what is available in your area, contact your local school district and the state and county department of social services.

Overprotection

It's quite easy while caring for a chronically ill or handicapped child to be overprotective, smothering or overconcerned about the condition in front of the child. Children, quite naturally, lap up fuss and attention and can become unreasonably demanding. Your protectiveness may be caused by your inability to accept that it is normal to feel angry and resentful at times towards your child while still loving and caring for him. Give him your love and time, and try not to feel guilty and so over-compensate for any angry feelings you may have.

One of the best gifts you can give your child is the ability to care for himself, and you won't be able to do this if you do for him what he should be learning to do for himself. And unless you demonstrate that you can look after yourself and accept help from others, your child will be left with a huge burden of guilt because he'll feel responsible for making you run-down and unhappy. You may be a very capable person with lots of love and willingness to care for your child, but you don't have to be perfect. If you try to be, you won't be doing yourself, your partner, the rest of the family or your sick child any favors. Ask your family, friends and neighbors to help out so that occasionally you can have the luxury of some time to yourself. This will help restore your emotional and physical energy and gives them the chance to show their love and support. Most important of all, it allows you to feel loved and to replenish the well of love which you are constantly drawing upon to give away.

SELF-HELP GROUPS

Local and national self-help groups exist for almost all the problems causing chronic illness or handicap, and can be of enormous benefit. They offer support, provide information and arrange meetings for the exchange of ideas. Many groups have regular meetings, a newsletter, fund-raising events and counselors who are usually parents of a child with the same condition. These groups are especially valuable during the initial period of shock or grief, offering support and encouragement and later providing inspiration and hope once energy has returned. They are also excellent at arranging for the vast experience accumulated by parents to be shared by others in a similar situation. Your family doctor or pediatrician will be only too pleased if you become involved and may refer other parents to you for information later. See pages 216-18 useful addresses.

ALL ABOUT MEDICINES

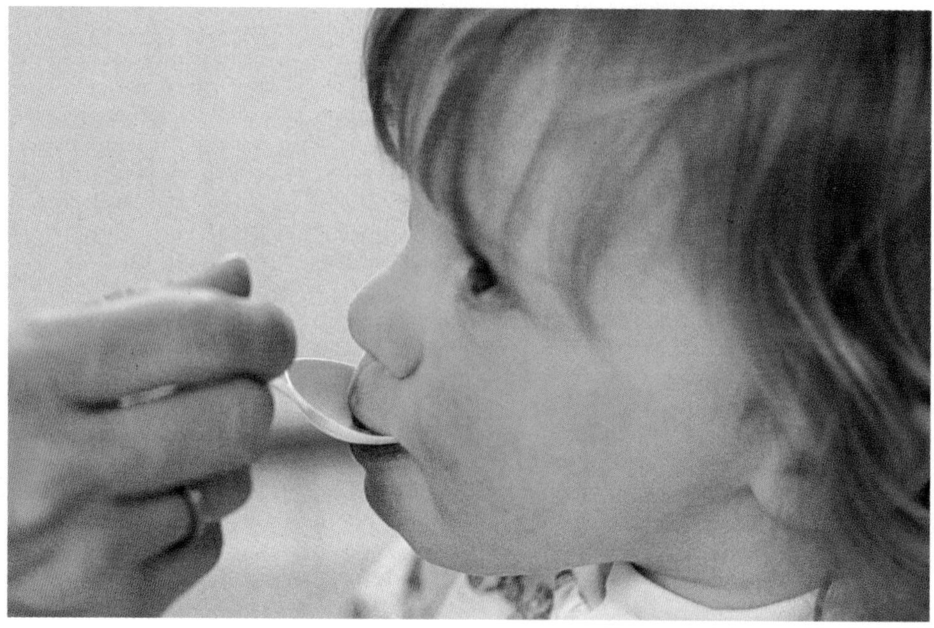

Always give your child her medicine from a proper measuring spoon as the exact dosage is very important.

Medicines have always been used to prevent disease, relieve or suppress symptoms and cure underlying conditions. Today for the first time many old and new remedies have come under the scientific microscope and some have been found ineffective or have been proved to have unacceptable side effects. Medical and pharmaceutical research means that we have access to powerful groups of drugs, such as the corticosteroids, antibiotics and anticancer drugs, and it is now possible to treat many disorders, both serious and minor, with medicines that have been proved to work.

With the vast majority of childhood ailments, the body heals itself given enough time and often medicine is actually unnecessary. But to many parents, giving medicine is a symbol of loving and caring. There's nothing wrong with this, providing that medicine isn't used as a substitute for attention, that it does no harm and that we also look beyond the illness to what might have caused the child to become ill in the first place.

Instructions and side effects

Some medicines are available only by a doctor's prescription, but this doesn't mean that the ones you can buy over the counter are not effective or even sometimes potentially dangerous. Any medicine can have unpleasant and perhaps even dangerous side effects if used wrongly, if given in the incorrect dose or if given too often or not often enough, so it's always extremely important to follow the doctor's or the manufacturer's instructions, especially when it comes to treating young children. The dose of any medicine for a baby or young child is very carefully worked out according to the child's weight or age. Liquid medicine is prescribed either by the teaspoonful or by dropper. For a baby, a calibrated dropper or plastic graduated syringe is easier to use. Older children can take medicine from a calibrated plastic spoon or measuring cup. Do not use domestic teaspoons as they are not accurate.

When your doctor prescribes medicine, he weighs the benefits of using the particular drug or drugs it contains against their potential side effects. If the side effects are likely to be serious, he will only use the drug if it is essential. If there are specific instructions about how to take a medicine, there will be a good reason. For example, when taking medicines by mouth, the absorption of the drug is affected by the fullness of the stomach and sometimes by particular foods and drinks in the stomach.

When it comes to antibiotics, don't stop giving them just because your child seems better. If you do, it's likely that the infecting organisms will not have been completely destroyed or incapacitated as they would be if the prescribed course of treatment had been completed. The microorganisms may then multiply again, with the added disadvantage that by this time they will probably be resistant to the antibiotic your child has been having, so another will have to be prescribed and you'll have to start all over again.

Medicines prescribed for one child should *never* be used for another. Leftover medicines are best discarded once the child is better, unless they have been prescribed for a chronic condition that is likely to recur. Some medicines don't have a long shelflife and should be disposed of by flushing them down the toilet.

How a medicine is made up

A medicine usually contains one or more active ingredients. It may be made up in one of several forms: liquid, tablets, chewable tablets or capsules for taking by mouth; lotions, cream, paste, powder, ointment or spray for putting on the skin; liquid, skin rubs or capsules for inhaling; drops for the eyes, nose or ears; liquid for injecting; and liquid or suppositories for administering rectally.

Medicines to be given by mouth to children are often made up as syrups or "elixirs." These have the advantage that some children find them more pleasant to take, but the disadvantage that others may dislike the sweet taste and that the sugar in the syrup can cause dental caries, particularly if taken frequently or given last thing before going to sleep without cleaning the teeth afterwards.

SAFETY AND MEDICINES

- If you buy any preparations for your children over the counter, make sure you ask for a junior or children's medicine.
- Never give your child any medicine that has been prescribed for anyone else or that you have bought for yourself.
- Always follow the exact instructions given for a medicine or other treatment. See also pages 60-61 for giving medicines.
- Make sure all medicines are kept out of the reach of children.

Drugs commonly have three names each, which can be confusing. They each have a full chemical name, a general name which is used by doctors and pharmacists and one or more proprietary, trade or brand names given by the manufacturers. Variations and different formulations of the same drug may have certain advantages and disadvantages, but unless these are particularly important the cheapest form of a drug is usually prescribed.

Medicines available without a prescription often contain additives to improve the smell, taste or ease of application, and you may end up paying a lot more money than necessary.

GIVING MEDICINE

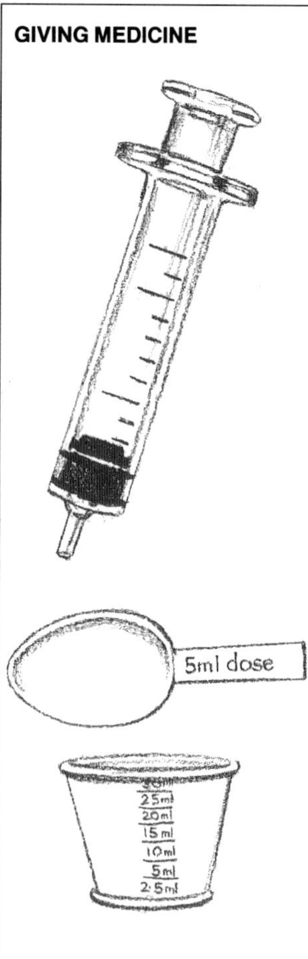

The right equipment makes giving medicine both easier and safer. You can use a plastic graduated syringe (top), a calibrated dropper or a 1 tsp (5 ml) measuring spoon (center). For larger doses, use a graduated 1 oz (30 ml) measuring cup (bottom).

Some medicines used for children

These are some of the types of medicine that are most commonly used in treating children's ailments.

Pain relievers

Acetaminophen by mouth is the recommended drug for relieving pain at home. It is reasonably effective and it will also lower a fever. Possible side effects include skin rashes, blood disorders and, if taken for long enough in a large enough dose, kidney damage. Never leave an adult's acetaminophen tablets within reach of a child because poisoning can seriously damage the liver.

Aspirin is no longer considered suitable for children because of the possibility of a potentially serious condition known as Reye's syndrome (see page 163). More potent pain relievers are available from the doctor if necessary.

Decongestants

Nasal congestion is difficult to treat in infants. However, attempts should be made to relieve the condition if it seems to interfere with feeding or sleeping. Sterile salt water nose drops may help to loosen excessive mucus, which can then be suctioned out with a soft bulb syringe.

For older children, phenylephrine decongestant nose drops are widely used. However, after four or five days of regular use there is often renewed congestion. The drops may also irritate the lining of your child's nose. A highly humified environment is helpful in alleviating symptoms and oral decongestants are sometimes useful.

Antihistamines

Drugs such as chlorpheniramine, trimeprazine, triprolidine, diphenhydramine and carbinoxamine are used for some allergic skin conditions such as reactions to insect bites and stings, for hives, for hay fever and for travel sickness. They have little effect on allergic asthma. Possible side effects include drowsiness and an inability to sleep restfully, and a few children become hyperactive. Antihistamines are sometimes included in cold and cough remedies because they tend to dry up the secretions in the nose and respiratory tract and so provide some relief. However, this very action may lower natural resistance to the infection. When applied on the skin, antihistamines can sometimes cause an allergic skin reaction.

Cough medicines

Cough suppressants subdue a cough and expectorants are supposed to liquefy secretions so that they can be coughed up more efficiently. Coughing should only be treated with suppressant drugs, such as dextromethorphan or codeine, if it is preventing your child from getting enough sleep to aid recovery, or if it is very painful. Expectorants aren't recommended because they seem to be of little use.

Cough drops don't contain sufficient concentrations of drugs to be of any use, but they increase the production of saliva, which can soothe a sore throat.

Asthma medicines

Bronchodilators are drugs such as metaproterenol, albuterol and theophylline which widen the airways and are usually given orally, but may also be given in aerosol form. Adrenaline by injection may be necessary for a severe asthma attack, and corticosteroids such as beclomethasone in aerosol form are also useful. Cromolyn sodium from a special inhaler is effective if used right at the beginning of an allergic asthma attack. It can cause a slightly sore throat, especially if the child has a respiratory infection. This drug is also used to prevent hay fever.

Antibiotics

Many different classes of antibiotics are used to treat infections with bacteria and fungi. Some of the better known ones are the penicillins (such as ampicillin, dicloxacillin and amoxicillin), erythromycin, trimethoprim sulfa and cefactor. Antibacterial drugs such as nitrofurantoin and nalidixic acid are alternatives used for urinary tract infections. Antibiotics are usually given by mouth and can also be used in preparations for the skin, eye and ear. Antifungal antibiotics include nystatin and griseofulvin. Antibiotics aren't effective against infection with viruses or protozoa. Your doctor chooses the antibiotics according to the type of bacteria he believes is responsible for a particular infection. Sometimes it helps him to decide if a specimen from the infected area is tested by the pathology laboratory.

A problem with antibiotics is that bacteria tend to become resistant to them and this is one reason why their use is restricted to prescription only. Possible side effects include allergy and the risk of infection with other microorganisms such as monilia (see page 73 under Fungi).

Skin preparations

Drugs contained in the base of a skin preparation include antiseptics, antibiotics, antiviral agents, steroids, zinc, calamine, antiparasitic drugs, antisunburn substances, antiitching agents, local anesthetics and astringents. The base is chosen according to the job it has to do. A watery or alcoholic lotion is used for cooling acute conditions with unbroken skin. Calamine lotion is used to cool the skin in scabbed and dry skin disorders. Powders are used between folds, pastes are used for scaly skin, and creams and ointments are used for various conditions. Sensitivity to antibiotics, local anesthetics and antihistamines can be a problem in some children.

Many skin conditions are more itchy at night when your child is hot, so it's a good idea to apply cream or ointment before bedtime.

What causes infection?

Contact with potentially infectious microorganisms such as bacteria, viruses and fungi is common. A child's normal resistance is usually enough to prevent the organisms from taking a hold in the body, but if the organisms are very virulent or if a child's resistance is low, then an infectious illness results. Infections spread from person to person, sometimes directly and sometimes via food or another medium.

Bacteria

Bacteria come in three basic shapes: spherical (such as the streptococci and staphylococci), rod-shaped (such as E. coli and whooping cough bacilli) and spiral (such as cholera bacteria). Bacteria can live in a wide variety of environments such as in soil, food and in the body. Certain types are normally present in parts of the body such as the bowel and on the skin, and many perform useful functions, helping the body to run smoothly. Illness can be caused by an overgrowth of these "normal" bacterial colonies or by invasion of the body by disease-provoking or "pathogenic" bacteria. Bacterial infections can be treated with antibiotics.

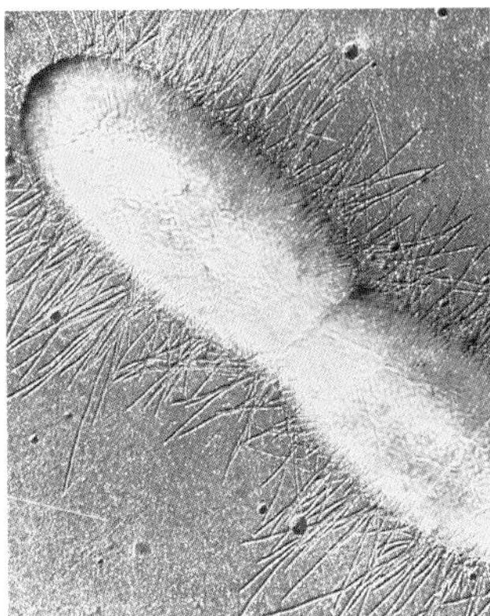

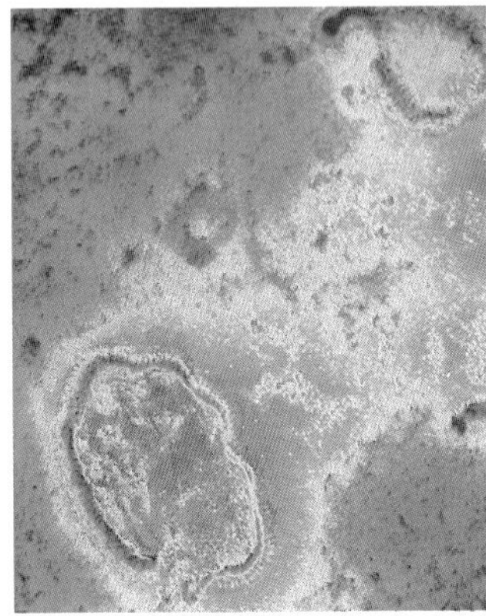

Far left This E. Coli bacillus has been magnified many thousands of times and clearly shows the distinctive rod shape of this type of bacteria.
Left The microscopically small virus particles enlarged here are from the respiratory syncitial virus which is one of the major causes of bronchiolitis in babies.

Viruses

Viruses are minute living particles and the largest of them are just bigger than the smallest bacteria. Viruses can only multiply inside a host cell in the body. As new viruses are formed, they either stay in the host cell until it bursts (such as in polio), or they are continually released from the cell (in flu and herpes). Some viruses can survive outside the body for weeks or even months. Progress is being made with antiviral drugs such as acyclovir (sometimes used for herpes simplex and chickenpox).

Fungi

Some fungi, such as monilia, live on or in the body without doing any harm. However, if your child's immunity is lowered or if other microorganisms living alongside the fungi are killed, so destroying the natural balance locally, the fungi may multiply and cause illness. Some premature babies and chronically ill infants who have received antibiotics for other infections may develop serious fungal infections which are very difficult to treat. In normal children, common fungal infections can affect many areas including the skin (such as in monilial diaper rash), the mouth (in thrush), the scalp (in ringworm), the feet (in athlete's foot) and the lungs.

Diagnostic procedures

If your child has to have a diagnostic procedure of some sort, it helps if you know what will actually happen. If you are nervous and apprehensive, your child will sense your anxiety and may begin to be afraid, but if you are relaxed and confident, he's much more likely to cope with the situaiton well.

Out-patient clinic

Although some tests can be done at the doctor's office, many are carried out in the out-patient department at a hospital. Many treatments are also done in clinics. Most hospitals are much more thoughtful than they used to be about making the pediatric unit a pleasant place for children. There are usually toys and books and there may even be small furniture and rugs to play on.

Should a special procedure such as an X-ray be needed, talk to your child about it beforehand if he's old enough, so that he knows what to expect. Try to stay with him if you can to reassure him – hospital equipment can look very frightening.

Blood samples

Blood tests are an important feature of modern medicine and are done to help discover the cause of an illness, check the progress of treatment, identify a child's blood type and estimate blood loss after bleeding. The samples of blood taken are usually small and for some tests a few drops of blood taken by pricking the heel or finger are sufficient. Usually, though, blood is taken from a vein using a syringe and needle. In babies, a vein in the scalp or neck may be used and in older children a vein at the inside of the elbow. It would be untrue to say that having a blood sample taken isn't painful, but the worst moments are when the needle is pushed into the skin and taken out. While the needle is actually in, it really doesn't hurt. If you make sure that your child is warm before the sample is taken, the superficial veins will be dilated and it'll be easier for the doctor to find a suitable one. With an older child, the doctor will further encourage the vein to stand out by putting a tight cuff around the child's upper arm and perhaps by patting the vein and asking him to clench and unclench his fist several times. The skin is quickly cleaned with a swab of alcohol or antiseptic and then the needle is inserted almost parallel to the skin. Once the sample has been taken, the cuff is loosened, the needle withdrawn and the puncture site is pressed until any bleeding stops. Sometimes there is a bit of bruising afterwards.

Urine tests

Parents are often asked to collect a urine sample from their child as this can prove very helpful in the diagnosis of certain conditions. If the urine is to be tested for infection, it is especially important to wash and dry your child's genitals and area around the rectum well, before taking the sample. Ask an older child to urinate into the toilet or potty and as he does so, hold the sterile container your doctor has given you under the stream and fill it. To collect urine from a baby or an untrained toddler, ask your doctor about special bags that fit over the penis or vulva to catch some urine. In some babies, it may be necessary to perform urinary tract catheterization.

Stool tests

Your child's bowel movements (stools) may need to be tested for infection with microorganisms, worms or other parasites, blood or various chemicals. Ask your child to defecate into a clean potty and put some of the stool into a marked sterile container. If your child isn't potty trained, scrape some of the stool off his diaper.

Throat swab

If your child has a bad sore throat, the doctor may want to take a sample of the mucus from the back of his throat and have it tested by the laboratory to find out what organisms are present and which antibiotics would be most suitable. He'll take a stick with an absorbent cotton swab attached to the end and gently pass the swab across the back of your child's throat. It shouldn't hurt at all, but may cause your child to gag.

X-rays

X-rays are frequently used to help in diagnosis. The most common X-rays done on children include X-rays of bones, the chest, the abdomen and the urinary system. A good X-ray

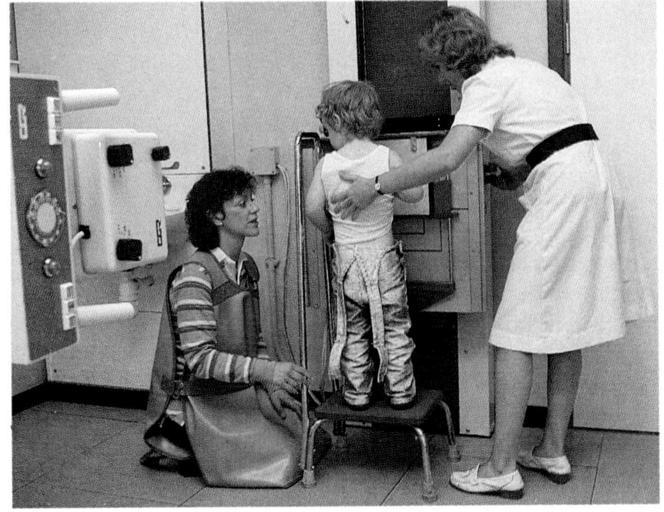

The machinery and equipment used for an X-ray can seem frightening to a child, so stay close to reassure him.

picture of the urinary system is obtained by first injecting a vein with a special substance that will register on the X-ray. This is concentrated by the kidneys and passed down the ureters into the bladder and thus into the urine. A barium swallow is a special X-ray of the stomach taken after the child has drunk some flavored barium-containing liquid. The barium shows up clearly on the X-ray, giving a good picture of the stomach.

You will probably be given a protective apron to wear if you hold your child while he has an X-ray. This is particularly important if you are pregnant or in the second half of your menstrual cycle (when you could be pregnant). Your child won't feel anything as he is X-rayed, but may need reassurance if he is frightened by the appearance of the X-ray equipment.

CAT scan

A CAT (computerized axial tomography) scan is a special set of X-rays of soft parts of the body, such as the brain, which is integrated by a computer. It produces very precise pictures that enable a more accurate diagnosis to be made.

Biopsy

A biopsy is a procedure in which a tiny piece of tissue is taken from the body to be examined in the laboratory for signs of illness. For a skin biopsy, the skin is cleaned and sterilized with antiseptic, then some local anesthetic is injected so that the insertion of the biopsy needle doesn't hurt. A tiny piece of skin is cut out and the area closed with a stitch. For a kidney biopsy, the skin over the kidney is sterilized, local anesthetic is injected, then a special "punch" biopsy needle is used to penetrate the kidney and remove a small section of tissue. The bone marrow, lung and liver are biopsied in a similar way. If the small bowel needs to be biopsied, your child has to swallow a fine plastic tube with a special instrument attached to the swallowed end. The position of the instrument is checked by X-ray and then a biopsy is taken.

Skin tests

These are sometimes done to find out which substance may be responsible for a skin allergy. Small drops of a solution of each substance in question are put on the child's forearm and a little prick is made with a needle through each drop into the skin. A welt developing within fifteen minutes may indicate that the child has an allergy.

Audiometry

This is the measurement of hearing by an audiologist using an electronic instrument called an audiometer. It doesn't hurt at all, but takes a long time and requires concentration, so is best done when your child is not too tired. The child wears headphones through which the audiometer sends a pure tone sound of a chosen frequency (pitch) into one ear. A young child indicates whether he can hear anything by putting a toy or bead into a box when he hears a sound. An older child might tap the table or raise a hand. Sounds of the same frequency but of gradually decreasing volume are sent to the child's ear until he can't hear any more, and the last audible sound is plotted as a mark on a graph called an audiogram. The test is continued using notes of differing frequencies, each also marked on the audiogram, and then the other ear is tested. A complete audiogram measures sound conduction through the bone of the skull as well as through earphones. An audiogram is very helpful because it shows whether a child has a hearing loss, whether one or both ears are affected and what sorts of sound are difficult for the child to hear. This information, combined with a history of the ear problem and a medical examination, allows the family doctor, pediatrician or ENT surgeon to work out the best treatment for the child.

Lung function tests

These include using a little gadget called a peak flow meter to measure the force of exhalation and give some idea of the efficiency of the lungs. The child is asked to puff into the meter as hard as he can several times. Most children enjoy trying to make the needle in the meter swing as far as possible.

Lumbar puncture

Meningitis and several other diseases of the nervous system produce specific changes in the fluid surrounding the brain and spinal cord. A sample of this cerebrospinal fluid can be taken by lumbar puncture. Your child lies on his left side with his knees drawn up to his chest; the skin over the lower spine is cleaned and local anesthetic injected to numb the area: then a needle is inserted between two bones in the spine to suck out some of the fluid. Your child will be asked to stay lying flat for a while afterwards in order to avoid getting a headache.

Electrocardiogram (EKG)

An EKG is a paper trace or TV picture representing the electrical currents created by the heart muscle as it beats. It can give useful information about the state of the heart and is quite painless and safe. The child lies still and electrodes are attached to his wrists, ankles and chest, which have been treated with a watery gel to improve conduction.

Electroencephalogram (EEG)

An EEG is a paper trace representing the electrical acitivity of the brain and is taken by attaching several electrodes to the scalp with glue. It takes about an hour to do and is quite painless and safe. It is particularly useful when diagnosing epilepsy (see page 135).

Treatments

Intravenous drip

Sometimes an ill child needs fluid, chemicals or food, yet can't take anything by mouth. These are then given as drip fluid via a vein into the blood system. A suitable vein is chosen and the skin over it is cleaned. A needle is put into the vein and the tube from the plastic bag or bottle containing the drip fluid is connected. The needle is then strapped and bandaged into position and the child's arm may be restrained so that he can't pull over the drip pack with its hanger. It isn't very pleasant having a drip put in, but in skilled hands it is very soon over. The fluid dripped into a child's vein is very carefully measured, as is his urine output, so that he doesn't get too much or too little fluid. The nurses make frequent checks on an intravenous drip, but if you are with your child and you notice the drip bag or bottle running out, or if the skin around the end of the needle swells or becomes painful, tell the nurse at once.

Nasogastric tube

A low-birth-weight baby who doesn't suck, or a child whose bowel isn't yet working properly after an abdominal operation, may need to have a fine plastic tube inserted down his nose into the stomach. Milk or other food can be passed down this tube or gastric secretions sucked up through it. The free end of the tube is taped in place on the baby's face and closed off when not in use with a plastic plug. A baby can easily practice sucking at the breast or bottle with a nasocastric tube in place and as he gets better at sucking he takes part of his milk down the tube and part direct from the breast or bottle. A wider bore

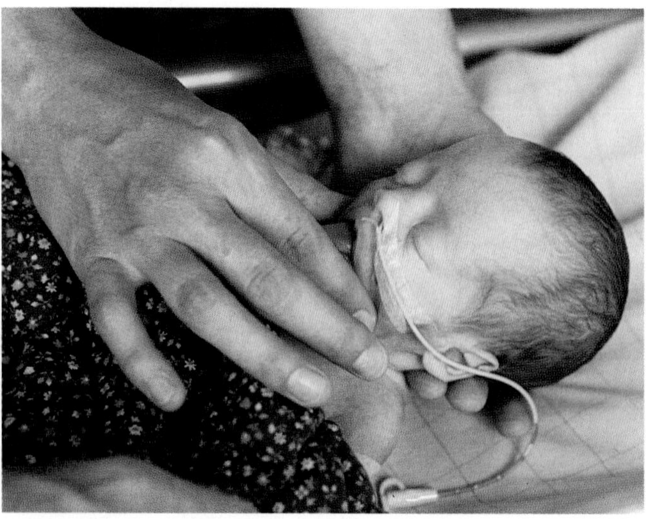

However sick or immature a baby is, he'll do far better with lots of cuddling and closeness, so hold him and talk to him as much as you can.

tube is used to pump out the contents of the stomach if a child has swallowed a poisonous substance.

Traction

Sometimes after a fracture a child's muscles pull unevenly on the broken bones and tend to distort them as they heal. Traction is the use of weights to counteract this effect and allow the bones to set correctly. The traction apparatus is set up differently according to the site of the fracture. The treatment may be painful at first.

Dialysis

Dialysis aims to take over the job of the kidneys in a child with kidney failure and is a process in which waste products are removed and the balance of water, salts and other chemicals in the body is maintained artifically. This can be done in two ways. In hemodialysis, the child's blood is passed from an artery in his arm through a tube into a kidney machine where it is filtered and then returned into a vein. When a special fluid is put through a tube into the space around the abdominal organs and gradually sucked out and replaced, it is called peritoneal dialysis. Hemodialysis can be done at home, but both sorts need to be done several times a week.

Physiotherapy

Physiotherapy covers the many forms of physical treatment that may aid healing or prevent worsening of a condition. It is particularly concerned with problems to do with muscles, joints and nerves and aims to make the most of their action. Treatments range from methods used to increase the drainage of fluid from the lungs in cystic fibrosis (see page 130), to exercise for the strengthening of a weak muscle after a muscle injury or after prolonged immobilization following a fracture, and to the use of interferential short wave treatment to aid healing of an inflamed muscle. Many of these treatments need to be repeated frequently and regularly and physiotherapists usually encourage parents to undertake some of the therapy at home.

Alternative therapies

Increasing numbers of people are becoming interested in alternative therapies to use alongside or instead of conventional medical treatment. Some medical doctors practice alternative therapies in conjunction with conventional medicine, but it is more usual to have to consult a private practitioner. Most alternative practitioners are not medically licensed. The box to the right offers a few examples of alternative therapies that are available in the U.S. today, but the list and descriptions are intended solely as a source of information, not as an endorsement.

SOME ALTERNATIVE THERAPIES

Herbal medicine
Until this century, most medicines came from plants. Now, many are synthetic imitations and those few which still come from plants are highly purified. Increasingly, people use herbal remedies because they believe that they have natural healing properties and fewer side effects than conventional medicines.

Chiropractic therapy
Chiropractic therapy involves the manipulation of the spinal column in an effort to restore normal function of the body.

Homeopathy
Homeopathy is based on the idea that illness can be cured by giving minute doses of a substance which, in larger doses, would cause the same symptoms as the illness. Diluting the substance increases its power to heal. The homeopath treats each person as an individual with a particular complex of symptoms, rather than treating a disease as such.

Acupuncture
Treatment with fine needles is part of an ancient system of medicine which aims to correct the unbalanced flow of energy along the fourteen main energy flow lines, or meridians, in the body. It has been found useful in a wide variety of conditions including asthma, headaches and digestive problems.

Part Two

HOW THE BODY WORKS

The more you know about the human body and how it works, the more wonderful and amazing it seems in its complexity. The inborn mechanisms for fighting disease and injury are also fascinating in their ingenuity.

Most parents find that an understanding of how the body works is enormously helpful. This is especially true during the times of rapid growth and development in early childhood and during illness when it is very useful to have a good idea of what is happening to your child.

Not only does an awareness of the anatomy and working of the body give you more confidence in understanding what is happening to your child, but it can guide you as you care for your child from day to day. It may also give you some insight into why your doctor suggests a certain treatment or plan of action. Learning about the body's immune system, for example, will help you understand the benefits of immunization and knowing about the shape and structure of the middle ear and the Eustachian tube will make the doctor's instructions for treating middle ear infection (otitis media) much more comprehensible.

We have separated the body into systems for the purposes of clarity, but in practice they all interact with each other to make up the fascinating creature that is the human being.

The eye

The eyes lie in bony sockets in the skull. The eyebrows keep sweat from running into the eyes and the **eyelids**, when closed, protect the eyes; the **eyelashes** help keep out foreign bodies such as dust or insects. Blinking keeps the eyes moistened with tear fluid produced by glands above the eyes. This salty fluid washes away dust and contains a natural antiseptic, lysozyme. Extra tear fluid is made when crying or when something irritates the eye. The tear ducts drain excess fluid into the nose.

Each eyeball consists of several layers: the outer one is the **conjunctiva**, a membrane which covers the eye and lines the eyelids. Underneath is a tough fibrous layer which forms the white of the eye (**sclera**) and the clear central part (**cornea**). The next layer is the colored muscular **iris**, with a hole in the center called the **pupil**, which lets light into the eye. When it's bright, the iris alters its shape so that the pupil becomes smaller and lets less light in; when it's dark, the pupil enlarges to let in more light. Behind the iris is the **lens**, held in place by ligaments attached to the **ciliary muscles**. These muscles can make the lens thinner or fatter in order to focus light on the innermost layer of the eyeball, the **retina**. This is made of nervous tissue and contains light-sensitive cells called rods and cones. The image that forms on the retina is relayed – via the **optic nerve** –

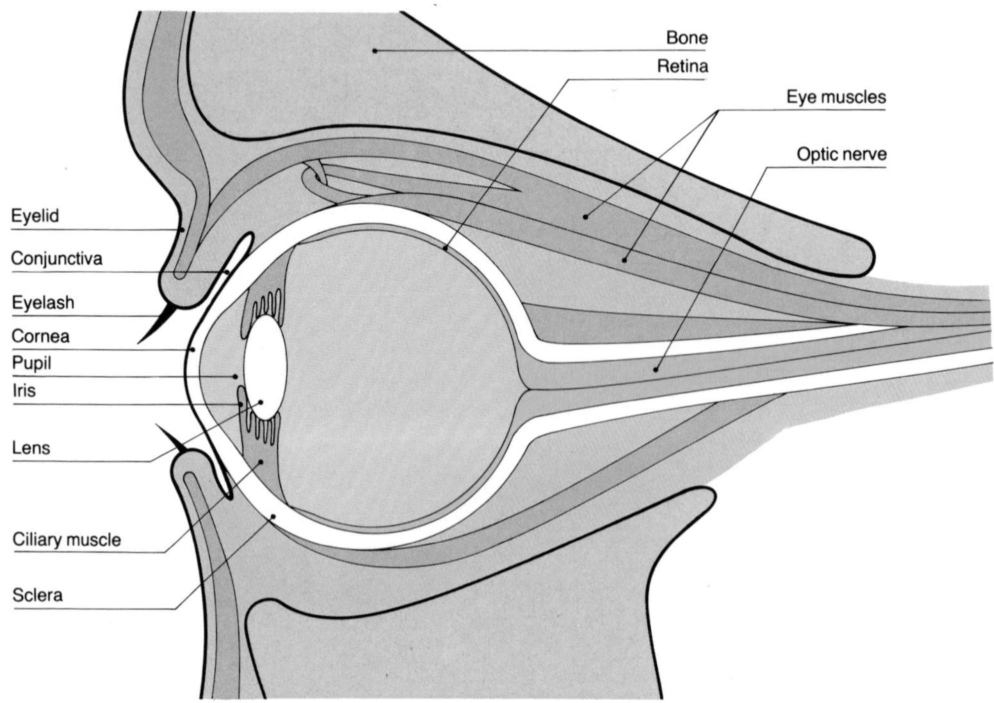

to the brain to be interpreted as what we see.

The **eyeball** is filled with watery fluid in front of the lens and jelly-like fluid behind it. Each eyeball is moved by six small **eye muscles** attached to the bones of the eye socket. Coordination of their action allows very fine, precise eye movements. The two sets of six muscles enable the eyes to be moved together so that the brain receives two very slightly different pictures of the same object, giving 3D or binocular vision. The nearer the object, the more difference there is between the two views. A newborn baby can focus only on things about 8 inches (20 cm) away, but as she grows older she becomes able to see things clearly at varying distances.

Color vision is only possible if there is enough light, because the cones (which register color) in the retina need light of fairly high intensity to function. The rods work in low light, but only give black and white vision.

ASSOCIATED SYMPTOMS

- Blurring
- Discharge
- Double visiuon
- Itching
- Redness
- Tears

WHEN THINGS GO WRONG

A strabismus, or squint, is a common example of something going wrong with the eye's function. It is usually caused by an imbalance of the small strap-like muscles that move the eye. If one of the sets isn't perfectly balanced, the pictures received by the brain are too different for it to put together, so one picture is ignored. If the condition goes untreated, the brain eventually learns to do this permanently and the child becomes blind in one eye.

Nearsightedness (myopia), farsightedness (hyperopia) or astigmatism can also lead to a squint. Some children develop a temporary squint brought on by tiredness, illness or worry.

An eye specialist will find out why the child is squinting and check that nothing serious is responsible. If there is any visual defect, it will be corrected. Sometimes, one or more operations may be needed to correct the squint.

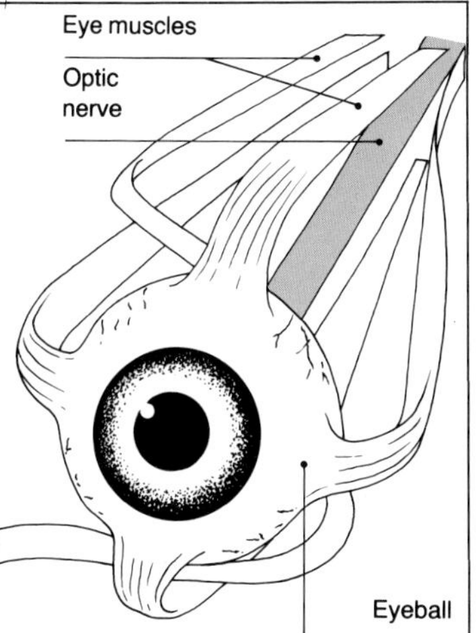

ASSOCIATED CONDITIONS

- Astigmatism
- Blepharitis
- Blocked tear duct
- Blindness
- Cataract
- Color blindness
- Conjunctivitis
- Farsightedness
- Nearsightedness
- Nystagmus
- Squint
- Stye

The ear

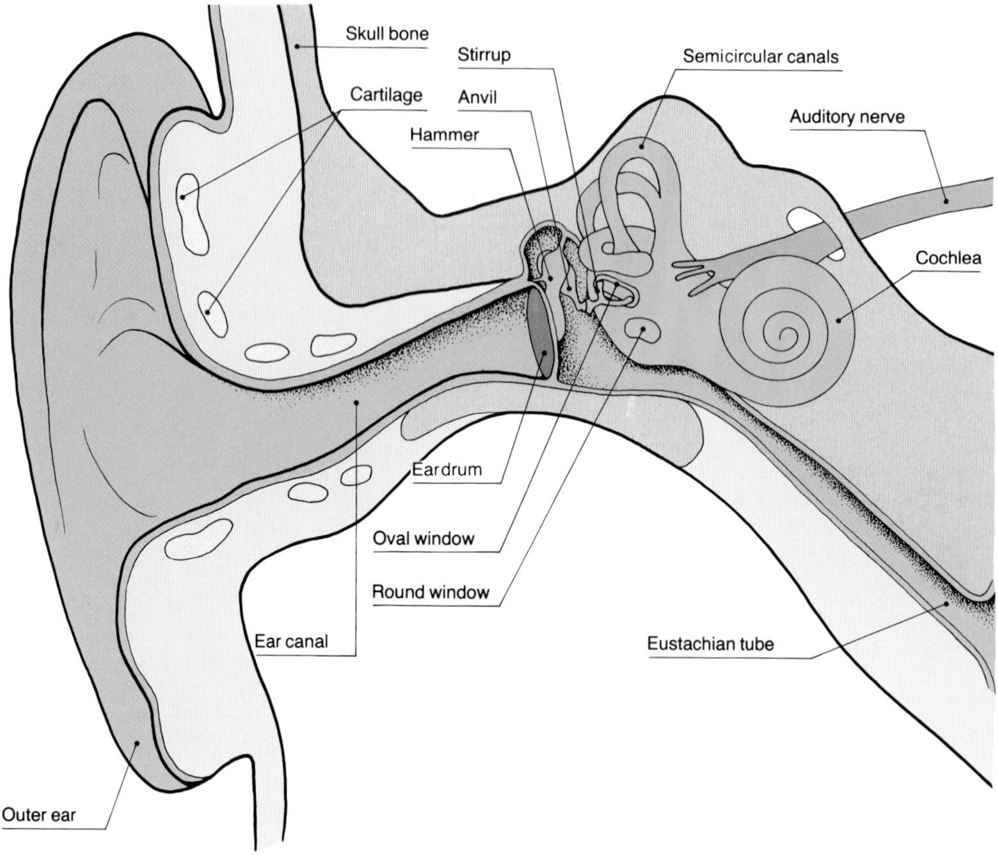

Skull bone
Stirrup
Semicircular canals
Cartilage
Anvil
Auditory nerve
Hammer
Cochlea
Eardrum
Oval window
Round window
Ear canal
Eustachian tube
Outer ear

The ears are responsible for hearing and balance. Each ear has an outer, a middle and an inner part. All three are involved in hearing, but only the inner part with balance.

The **outer ear** (pinna, meaning "wing" in latin) funnels sound down the **ear canal**. This ends at the **eardrum**, which separates the outer ear from the **middle ear**. The lining of the canal produces wax which has a cleansing action and contains natural antiseptics.

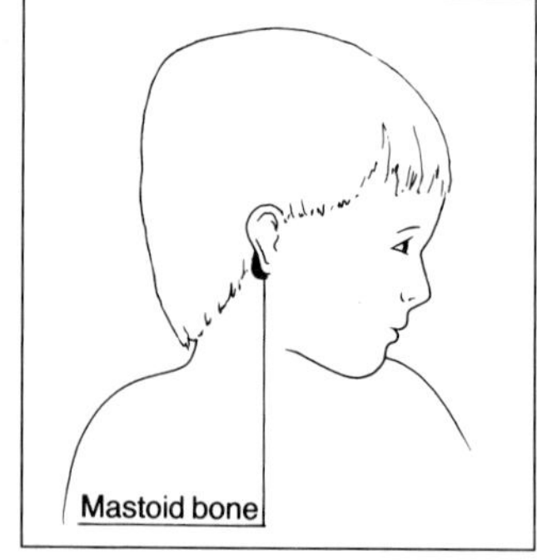

The air-filled cavity of the middle ear is connected to the back of the throat by the **Eustachian tube**. This tube drains fluid from the middle ear to the throat. It also allows the equalization of air pressure between the middle ear and the air outside, so preventing acute earache with changes of atmospheric pressure – for instance when going up or down in an elevator, or when flying. If the tube is blocked, such pressure changes can be painful.

The middle ear cavity is also connected to the air cells of the **mastoid bone**, which is why untreated middle ear infections can

WHEN THINGS GO WRONG

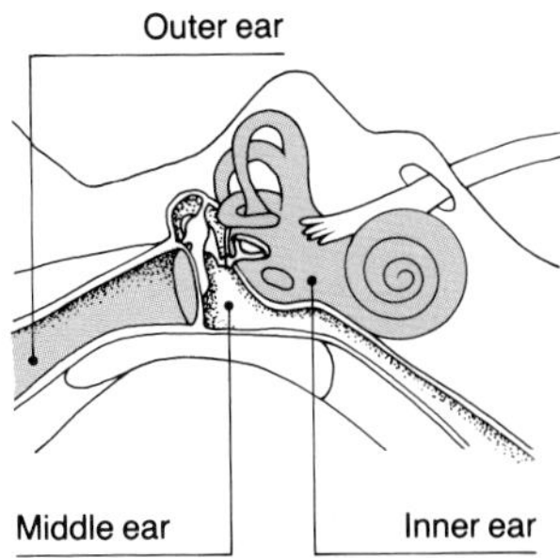

Earache is a common sign that something is wrong with the ear. Pain can arise from the outer ear (perhaps from a boil or a foreign body), the middle ear or the eardrum. It can also be "referred" from areas outside the ear which share a common nerve supply with the outer ear (see When Things Go Wrong, page 101).

However, the commonest cause of earache is inflammation of the middle ear (otitis media) which occurs with many upper respiratory tract infections, such as colds and flu, and with measles, sore throats, whooping cough and infected tonsils and adenoids. Infection spreads from the throat up the Eustachian tube and makes its lining swell. This blocks the tube, causing the absorption of the air normally present in the middle ear, and prevents fluid (formed as a result of infection spreading to the middle ear) from draining out. The child's hearing seems muffled and her own voice sounds different to her.

If there is a bacterial infection, pus forms in the middle ear and its pressure makes the inflamed eardrum bulge outwards into the outer ear canal. The eardrum is relatively thick in babies which explains why even a small amount of fluid or pus in the middle ear can cause such pain. If untreated, the eardrum can eventually perforate, relieving the pain, but causing a discharge from the ear.

ASSOCIATED CONDITIONS

- Deafness
- Earache
- Mastoiditis
- Otitis externa
- Otitis media
- Otitis media with effusion
- Wax

spread and cause mastoiditis.

The middle ear is connected to the **inner ear** by the **oval window**. The inner ear, or labyrinth, which contains the spiral, snail-shaped hearing organ, the **cochlea**, is embedded in bone and filled with a fluid called endolymph. Also in the inner ear are gravity-sensitive cells and three **semicircular canals** at right angles to each other. The fluid inside these canals moves with the body and sends messages to the brain about its state of balance.

The ear is like a microphone. It receives sound waves, converts them into electrical impulses and sends messages to the brain. The sound waves collected by the outer ear make the eardrum vibrate. These vibrations are passed along a chain of three tiny bones – the ossicles – in the middle ear. The bones, known as the **hammer** (malleus), the **anvil** (incus) and the **stirrup** (stapes), are jointed together and their lever action magnifies the vibrations. The hammer is attached to the eardrum and the "footplate" of the stirrup fits into the oval window. Vibrations pass through the oval window into the inner ear, where special cells in the cochlea sense the vibrations as pressure changes and relay them as electrical impulses along the **auditory nerve** to the brain. The brain cuts out unnecessary sounds and focuses on those the child wishes to hear. Sound vibrations finally leave the inner ear via the **round window**.

ASSOCIATED SYMPTOMS

- Deafness
- Discharge
- Dizziness
- Earache
- Excessive wax
- Itching

The teeth and gums

The cutting and chewing action of teeth and gums enable a child to break food down into pieces small enough to be swallowed. Children have two sets of teeth, the first being the milk (deciduous) teeth, and the second, the permanent ones. Tooth formation begins before birth. Hardening with calcium (calcification) starts during the seventh month of pregnancy in the first teeth and shortly before birth in the second teeth.

Each tooth has one or more conical roots embedded in the **jawbone**. The part of a tooth visible in the mouth is called the crown and is protected by a layer of **enamel**, the hardest tissue in the body. Beneath this is **dentine**, which is hard, but slightly elastic. Dentine forms the bulk of a tooth and if exposed by a hole in the enamel, it is sensitive to temperature and various chemicals. In the center of a tooth is soft **pulp** containing a nerve and blood vessels which enter through a narow **canal** in the root. The root is covered by a thin protective layer (**cementum**) which holds the fibers tethering the tooth to the jaw.

There are three types of tooth. **Incisors** are sharp, chisel-like and used for cutting. **Canines** are pointed and used for tearing and gripping. **Molars** and **premolars** are more square and have roundish projections (cusps) for grinding and slicing.

There are twenty teeth in the first set, ten in the upper jaw and ten in the lower, comprising eight incisors, four canines and eight molars. They usually come through in a particular order

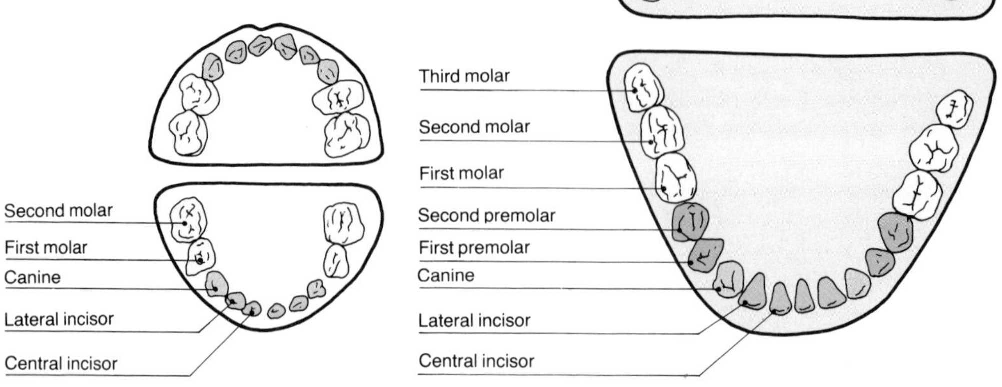

MILK TEETH

PERMANENT TEETH

ASSOCIATED SYMPTOMS

- Gum inflammation and sensitivity
- Toothache

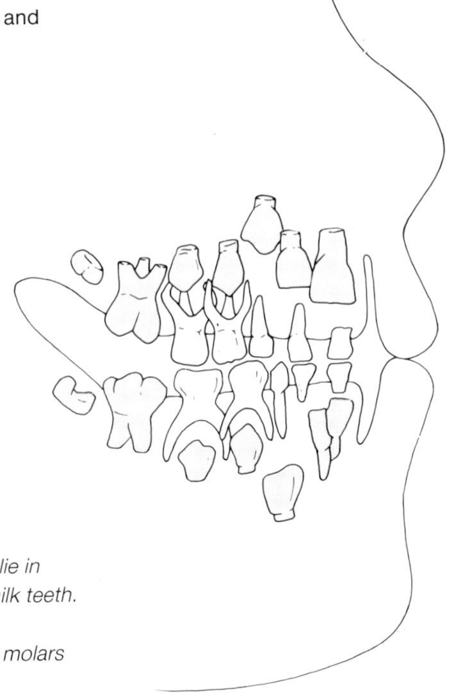

The permanent teeth lie in position behind the milk teeth. At the age of six, as shown here, the third molars are not apparent.

and the lower teeth tend to break through before the corresponding upper teeth. The first tooth to appear is usually a lower central incisor, at between five and seven months, though in some children it erupts at three months and in others not until a year. Next come the upper central incisors (6-8 months), the lower lateral incisors (7-10 months), the upper lateral incisors (8-11 months), the first molars (10-16 months) the canines (16-20 months) and the second molars (20-30 months). At the end of her first year, the average child has six to eight teeth.

There are thirty-two teeth in the second set and these lie in the jaws beneath the gums waiting to erupt. The first through the gums are the "six-year-old" or first molars, and these appear between six and seven years. They grow next to the second molars of the first set, so no first teeth are disturbed. These are closely followed by the lower central incisors which push the central incisors of the first set out of the jaw as they approach the gum. A child usually loses first teeth in the order they will be replaced by the permanent set. The upper central incisors and lower lateral incisors (7-8 years) are followed by the upper lateral incisors (8-9 years), the first premolars (10-12 years), the second premolars (10-13 years), the upper canines (11-12 years), the second molars (11-13 years), the lower canines (12-13 years) and the third molars, or wisdom teeth, in the late teens or twenties.

WHEN THINGS GO WRONG

Tooth decay occurs when the enamal fails to protect the dentine beneath. Normal mouth bacteria help make a gelatinous layer called plaque. The bacteria stick to plaque and ferment sugars from food and drink, so producing acid which strips enamel of calcium. If the acid attack is frequent enough, calcium is lost and a cavity is formed.

To reduce the risk of decay, foods and drinks with added sugar should be eaten only with meals, not on their own. Other foods can then help neutralize and dilute the acid produced from the sugar, besides increasing the flow of saliva which has a similar effect. Removal of plaque by brushing should be efficient and regular. Fluoride supplementation has greatly reduced the incidence of tooth decay.

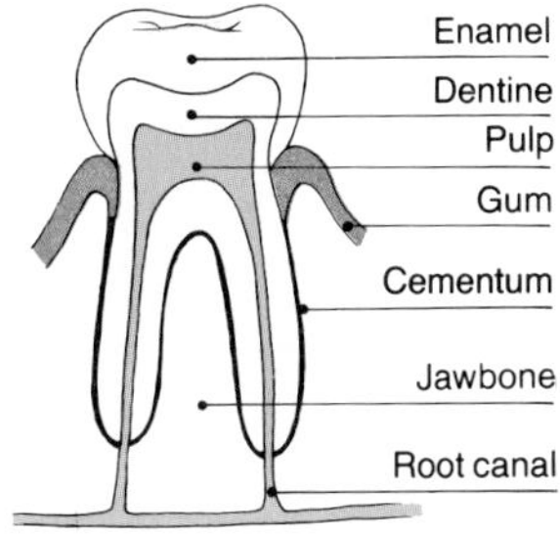

ASSOCIATED CONDITIONS

- Dental caries
- Gingivitis
- Gum abscess
- Gum cyst
- Mouth ulcers
- Toothache
- Tooth discoloration

The upper respiratory tract

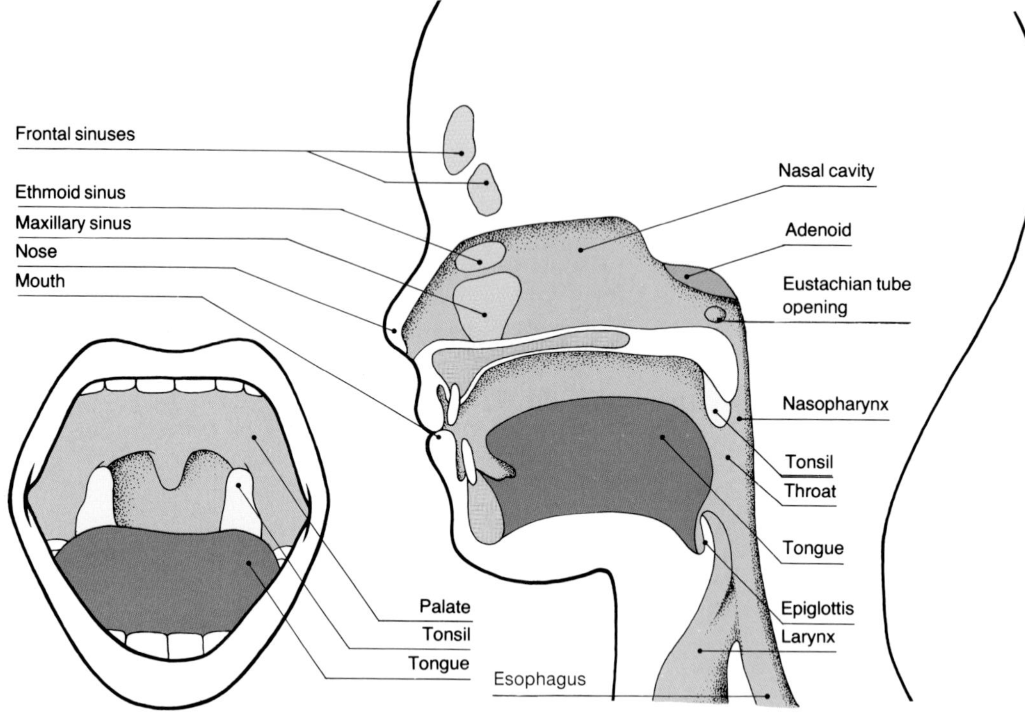

The upper respiratory tract consists of all the spaces and passageways above the voice box (**larynx**) through which air may pass on its way down to or up from the lungs, and it includes the **mouth, nose, sinuses** and **throat**.

Air is inhaled through the upper respiratory tract and taken down into the lungs (see page 90). As air enters the body through the nose, it is warmed and moistened by the mucous membrane lining the nose, sinuses and throat. Large particles of dust and other foreign matter are either filtered out by the hair of the nose or trapped by its mucus. Many smaller particles are caught further back in the nose. Lysozyme, the natural antiseptic in mucus, either destroys or neutralizes many potentially dangerous microorganisms.

Nerve endings in the roof of the **nasal cavity** respond to smells carried in the inhaled air and send signals to the brain. The sense of taste is carried by nerves from the **tongue** to the brain and different parts of the tongue respond to salty, sweet, sour and bitter substances.

The sinuses are air cavities in the bones of the face which connect with the nasal cavity via narrow passages or openings.

Inhaled air circulates through the sinuses and helps give the voice its resonant timbre. The **ethmoid sinuses** above the nose are the only sinuses present at birth. The **maxillary sinuses** in the cheekbones are quite well developed by five, and the **frontal sinuses** in the bone of the forehead, by ten.

Air breathed in through the nose or mouth passes into the **nasopharynx** lying at the back of and above the mouth. Here it comes into close contact with a ring of infection-fighting lymphoid tissue (see When Things Go Wrong, page 103).

As part of this ring, the **tonsils** and **adenoids** filter viruses and bacteria and other microorganisms from the air passing over them and either kill or neutralize them with ready-made antibodies from locally produced lymphocytes (white cells) or respond quickly to produce suitable new antibodies. As they enlarge in their effort to fight infection, the child may have a sore throat, perhaps with tonsillitis. The adenoids are small in young children and reach their peak size in five-year-olds, when they are most active. Enlarged adenoids block the openings of the **Eustachian tubes** and prevent the drainage of fluid from the middle ear (see page 84). This, combined with the ease with which the microorganisms from the air in the throat can travel up the tubes, explains why middle ear infection is so common in children with a sore throat.

The **epiglottis** lies at the back of the tongue and protects the opening of the larynx when swallowing.

ASSOCIATED SYMPTOMS

- Fever
- Mouth breathing
- Nasal discharge
- Nosebleed
- Sneezing

WHEN THINGS GO WRONG

The common cold is an example of how the upper respiratory tract's defenses sometimes fail. With a cold, viruses spread through the nasal passages and throat and usually up the Eustachian tubes into the middle ear. The sinuses are often inflamed too. The infected mucous membranes produce excess mucus (causing a runny or blocked nose) and blockage of the openings of the sinuses (causing discomfort from the accumulation of trapped mucus). Colds are common in children of two or three onwards, partly because they start coming in contact with more people at this age.

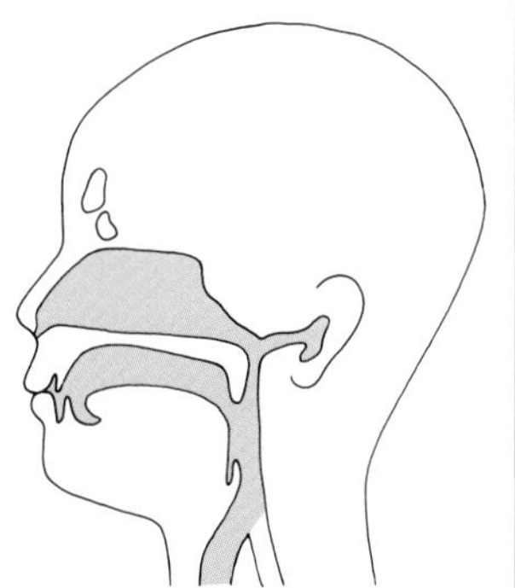

This shows where cold germs can spread to cause infection.

ASSOCIATED CONDITIONS

- Colds
- Hay fever
- Otitis media
- Sinusitis
- Sore throat
- Tonsillitis

The chest and lungs

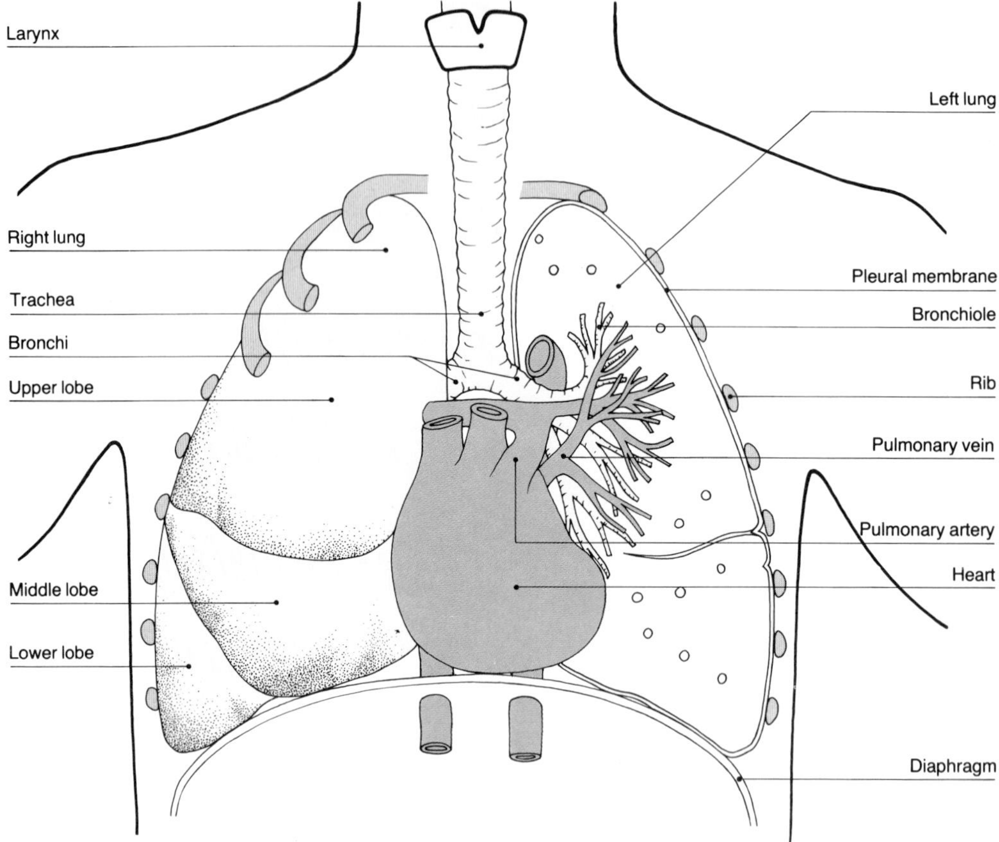

As a child breathes, her **lungs** take up oxygen from the incoming air and get rid of carbon dioxide in the air breathed out. The two pink spongy lungs lie in the chest cavity and are protected by the **ribs**, the chest and back muscles, and the **diaphragm** – the muscular sheet separating the chest from the abdomen. Each lung consists of **lobes**, the right lung having three and the left, two. Before birth the lungs are condensed and airless, and breathing is unnecessary because oxygen from the mother reaches the baby via the blood vessels of the umbilical cord. With the first breath, the lungs expand and fill with air. A baby takes about forty breaths per minute. As a child grows, her breathing rate drops towards the adult rate of twelve to sixteen breaths per minute.

The chest walls and diaphragm are lined with the **pleural membrane** which doubles back on itself to cover the lungs. With each breath in (inspiration), the ribs move outwards and forwards and the diaphragm moves down. Air rushes in through

WHEN THINGS GO WRONG

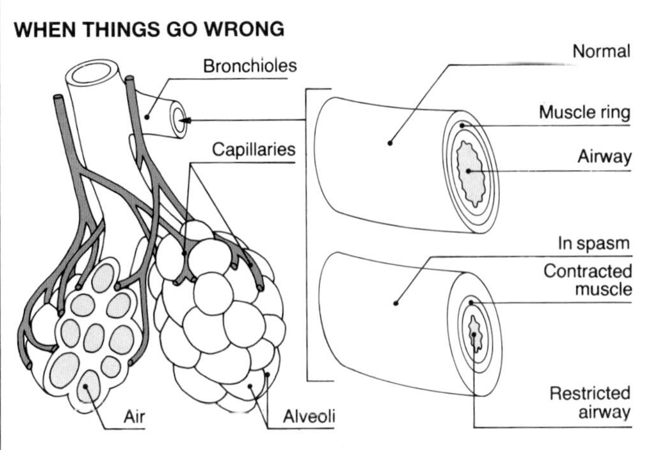

Asthma is one of the commonest disorders of the breathing system. Physical, emotional or environmental factors precipitate the narrowing of the oversensitive airways that is typical of asthma. The small diameter of the airways in children means that the flow of air is reduced relatively quickly by any obstruction. Spasm (tightening) of the muscles in the walls of the airways, together with inflammation of the mucous lining, makes breathing hard work. In severe cases, so little air is moved through the lungs that it's impossible for the child to absorb enough oxygen.

ASSOCIATED CONDITIONS

- Asthma
- Bronchiolitis
- Bronchitis
- Cystic fibrosis
- Laryngitis
- Pneumonia
- Whooping cough

the nose or mouth, then travels through the throat, the voice box (**larynx**) and the windpipe (**trachea**) to the progressively smaller airways in the lungs, the **bronchi** and **bronchioles**. The tiny air sacs at the end of the bronchioles are called **alveoli** and by adolescence there are between 200 and 600 million of them! The moist hot breathing passages warm and humidify the air to prevent it damaging the lungs.

The rich capillary blood supply of the alveoli absorbs oxygen from the inspired air. Red oxygenated blood is taken from the lungs to the **heart** by the **pulmonary vein** and is then pumped round the body. At the same time, carbon dioxide, the body's waste gas, passes from the deoxygenated blood (brought to the lungs from the heart in the **pulmonary artery**) into the alveoli. With each breath out (expiration), the ribs move in and down, and the diaphragm rises. The space inside the chest cavity is decreased and air is forced out. Both inspiration and expiration are automatically controlled by the brain, but breathing can also be consciously regulated, for instance when singing, coughing, laughing, talking, crying or holding the breath. There is always some air left in the lungs after breathing out.

Tiny foreign particles entering the lungs at each breath are normally caught in the fluid produced by the breathing passages. This fluid is wafted up to the throat by the rapid beating of millions of tiny, hairlike cilia in the lining of the larger air passages and is then swallowed. Bacteria and viruses are killed by defense cells and antibodies in the mucus lining the respiratory tract.

ASSOCIATED SYMPTOMS

- Cough
- Coughed-up phlegm
- Hoarseness
- Wheezing

The heart, blood and circulation

The **heart** is situated on the left side of the chest, between the **lungs** and above the diaphragm, and is protected by the ribs. Its strong muscular pumping action works in two directions. It pushes dark-red, deoxygenated blood to the lungs to pick up oxygen and get rid of carbon dioxide, and then pumps this bright-red, newly oxygenated blood round the body.

The right side of the heart is the pump which sends blood to the lungs to be oxygenated and the left side is the pump which supplies the whole body with oxygenated blood. Each separate pump has two chambers, an **atrium** above which receives

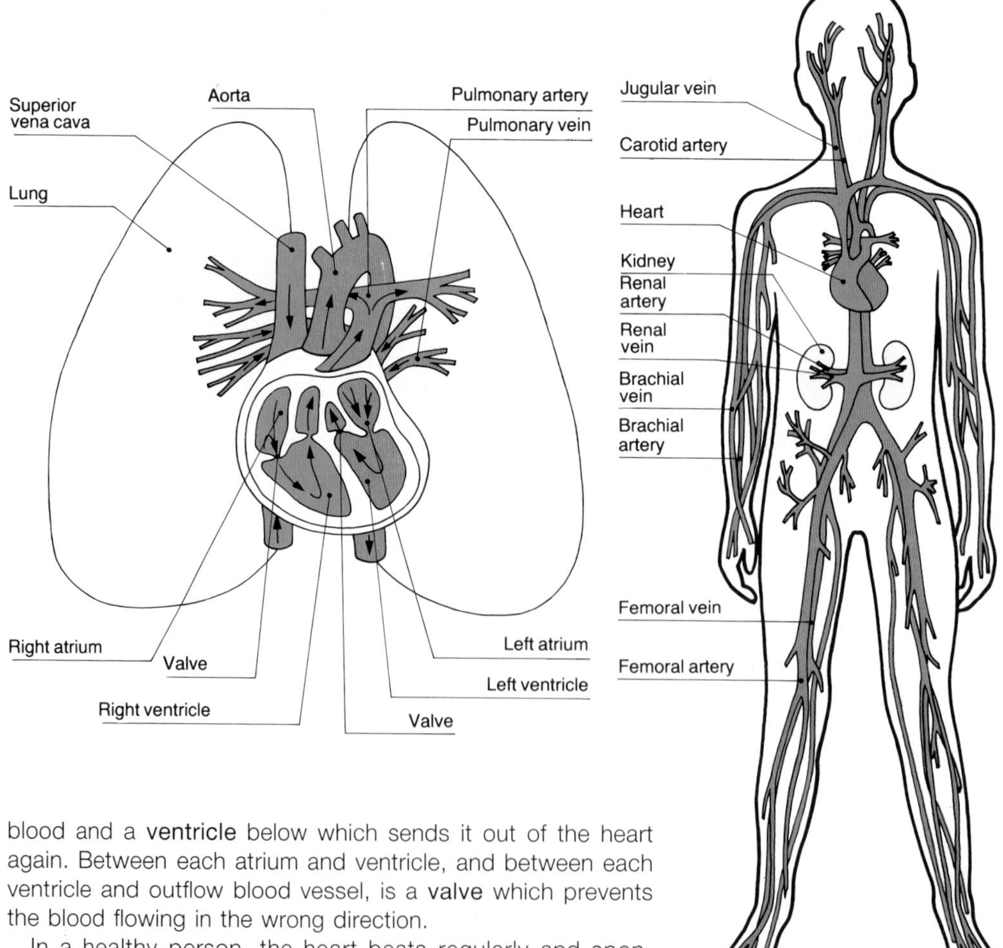

blood and a **ventricle** below which sends it out of the heart again. Between each atrium and ventricle, and between each ventricle and outflow blood vessel, is a **valve** which prevents the blood flowing in the wrong direction.

In a healthy person, the heart beats regularly and spontaneously through life. The heart rate can be altered by such factors as emotion, food, drugs, exercise, altitude and certain illnesses. Normally the beating of the heart is unnoticeable, but sometimes it seems to thump in the chest. With each beat, the whole heart contracts because of a shortening and tightening of its muscle fibers. The two atria contract before the two ventricles, so the atria push blood into the ventricles in time for them to squeeze it out, as they contract, into the outflow vessels. Any turbulence in the flow of blood creates a noise called a murmur.

The blood vessels carrying blood away from the heart are called **arteries**. All the arteries except the **pulmonary artery** carry oxygenated blood. The nearer an artery is to the tissue it supplies, the smaller it becomes. These tiny branches are called arterioles and they eventually become minute capillaries which form a network around the cells and allow oxygen, nutrients and various other substances carried by the blood to diffuse out into the tissue fluid and into the cells.

The blood vessels carrying blood to the heart are called **veins**. All the veins except the **pulmonary vein** carry deoxygenated blood. The nearer the heart, the larger the blood vessels: blood flows from capillaries to venules to veins and back to the right atrium. Veins tend to be larger than arteries and have thinner walls with less muscle in them.

The pulmonary artery carries deoxygenated blood from the heart to the lungs, where carbon dioxide is removed and oxygen added. The oxygenated blood is then returned to the heart by the pulmonary vein, to be circulated round the body.

Nutrients from the food we eat are taken up from the digestive system (see page 94) into the blood and circulated to the tissues. Waste products are carried to the **kidneys**, which filter and remove many of them. Drugs and other chemicals entering the bloodstream after being eaten, breathed in, or taken in through the skin are also carried round and used or eventually removed. Hormones from the endocrine glands (see page 104) are taken by the blood to their various sites of action.

WHEN THINGS GO WRONG

The heart fails to develop normally in some babies and a quarter of these have a hole in the heart – a defect in the muscle separating the right and left ventricles. Small holes rarely cause symptoms. They are usually discovered when a heart murmur is noticed during a routine medical examination and fifty percent close spontaneously within the first year or so. Treatment is not usually necessary for small holes, although antibiotics are given to prevent infection in the heart if the child has to have certain forms of surgery. Larger holes, which are less common, can lead to problems and surgical repair is usually advised.

ASSOCIATED CONDITIONS

- Anemia
- Hemophilia
- Heart disease and abnormality
- Heart murmur
- Leukemia

WHAT IS BLOOD?

Blood is composed of red and white cells and platelets suspended in a straw-colored liquid called plasma. Plasma is mostly water, but also contains nutrients, waste products, blood-clotting factors, antibodies, hormones and various other chemicals. The red blood cells are shaped like round dented discs. They contain the pigment hemoglobin, which gives them their color and carries oxygen and carbon dioxide. Red blood cells are made in the bone marrow. White blood cells are more spherical. They are made in the lymph nodes (glands), spleen, bone marrow and thymus. Different types of white cells manufacture antibodies and destroy bacteria. Platelets are tiny cell fragments made in the bone marrow and are involved in blood clotting.

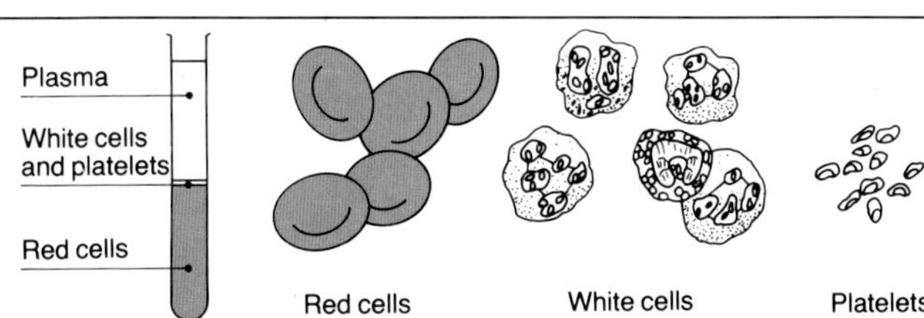

The digestive system

Digestion is the process by which the body takes apart food and drink to supply nourishment in a usable form. The process is carried out in a long tube running from the mouth to the rectum. Food is taken into the mouth and cut up by the teeth. Saliva moistens it and begins to break down starch.

The mixture is then swallowed and passes via the **esophagus** into the **stomach**, a J-shaped container lined with mucous membrane. Glands in the lining produce gastric juice – a mixture of enzymes and acid – whose chemical action, together with the churning action of the stomach, reduces food to a fairly smooth pulp. The stomach acts as a reservoir and regulates the admission of food to the rest of the gut. Every so often the stomach outlet, the **pylorus**, opens and the contents flows into the **duodenum**, the first part of the small intestine.

The duodenum contains bile (made in the **liver** and stored in the **gall bladder**), pancreatic juices (made in the **pancreas**) and a secretion from its own walls. Bile emulsifies fats, and the pancreatic juice contains enzymes that digest protein (into amino acids), fats and carbohydrates. Some food is absorbed into the bloodsteam directly through the walls of the duodenum,

ASSOCIATED SYMPTOMS

- Constipation
- Diarrhea
- Jaundice
- Loss of appetite
- Nausea
- Regurgitation
- Stomachache
- Vomiting

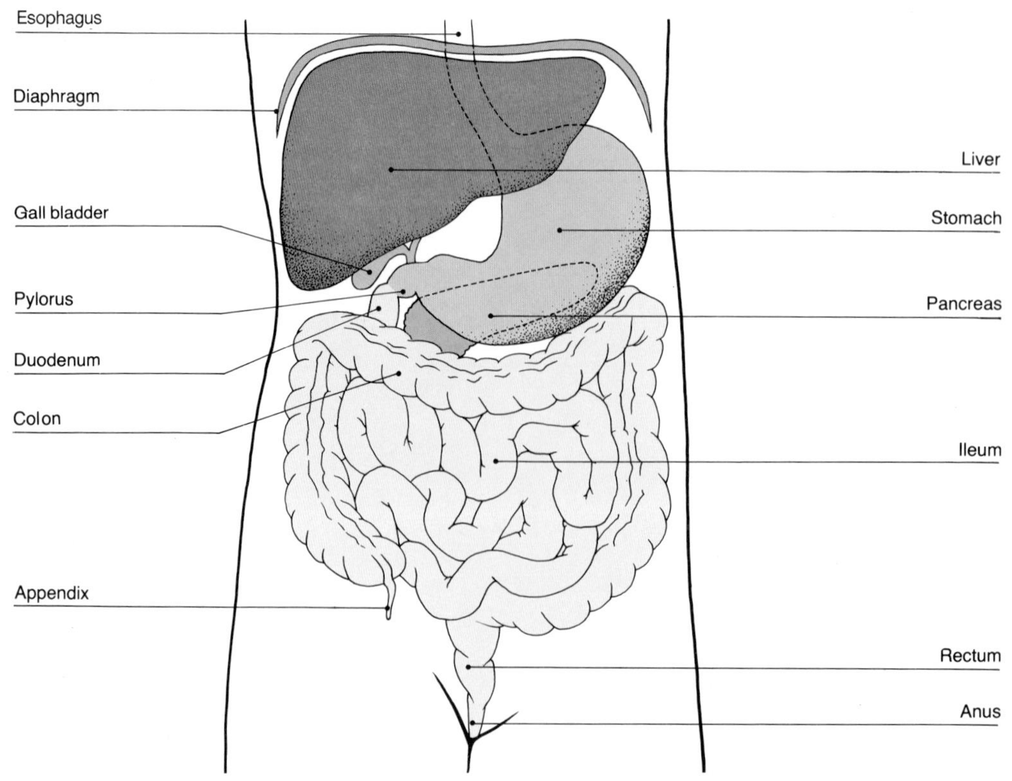

WHEN THINGS GO WRONG

One of the most common signs that something is wrong with the digestive system is diarrhea, when the bowel movements are abnormally frequent, fluid and copious. Diarrhea can begin suddenly and subside just as quickly, with little bodily upset, or it can be more or less continuous.

The wall of the small intestine produces very large volumes of fluid and later reabsorbs much of it. The large intestine also absorbs water, but not in such great quantities. The more watery the diarrhea, the more likely it is that the small intestine is affected.

Whatever the cause of diarrhea, the chemical stability of the body changes because of the loss of water and salts such as sodium in fluid bowel movements. This can lead to dehydration and weakness. It can also lead to poor absorption of nutrients into the bloodstream because of impaired digestion as the food is rushing through. Long-term diarrhea severely depletes the body of essential nourishment and reduces its ability to heal itself.

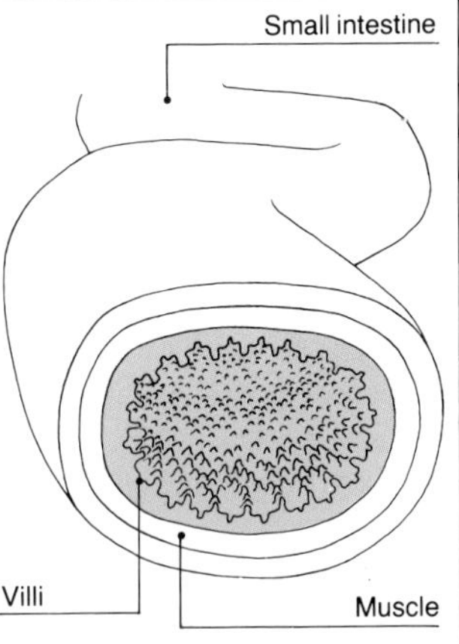

ASSOCIATED CONDITIONS

- Anal fissure
- Appendicitis
- Celiac disease
- Cystic fibrosis
- Diabetes mellitus
- Failure to thrive
- Food intolerance
- Gastroenteritis
- Hepatitis
- Hernia
- Malabsorption
- Moniliasis
- Pyloric stenosis
- Worms

but most is absorbed by intestinal **villi** in the **ileum**, the next section of the small intestine. These villi are minute projections containing blood vessels and lymph vessels that carry nutrients away from the gut.

The portal vein takes blood full of nutrients from the gut to the liver, the largest organ in the body. The liver removes glucose from the blood and stores it as glycogen, which is used for energy. It also converts any amino acids the body doesn't need into urea, which is later passed out in the urine. The liver detoxifies potentially dangerous chemicals and makes the pigments that give bile its color out of the hemoglobin in old red blood cells. This in turn gives bowel movements their color.

The liver is also the main source of plasma proteins, blood-clotting proteins and various enzymes. It stores vitamins A, D, K, and B, helps form vitamin A and plays an important part in maintaining the body's warmth and chemical balance.

Intestinal contents are pushed along by the muscular wave motion of the bowel walls. More water is removed by the large intestine (**colon**), leaving the contents thick and paste-like. The **appendix** is a small, blind-ended tube opening off the colon and its walls produce large numbers of antibodies. Large numbers of bacteria in the colon finish digesting carbohydrates, which pass through its wall into the bloodstream. Bacteria and fibrous food residues give the bowel movements their bulk.

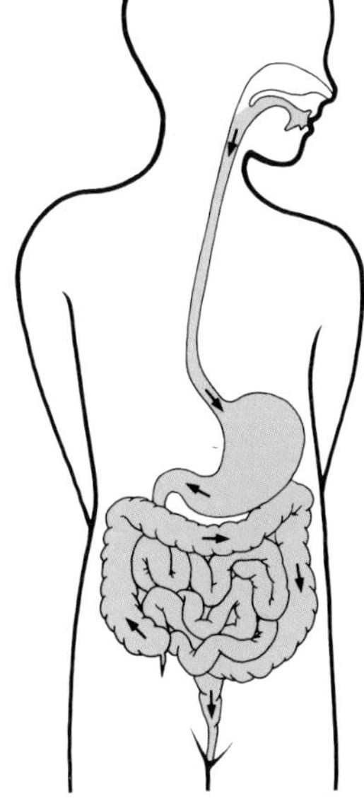

This shows where food progresses during the digestive process

The urinary tract

The urinary tract has the important task of making urine and removing it from the body, Urine consists of ninety-five percent water and five percent solids in solution. The solids include salts and the waste products from various metabolic processes (such as urea from the breakdown of protein). The concentration of urine can be altered by the **kidneys** to keep the composition, volume and acidity of the body's fluids within normal limits. Some drugs and other foreign substances are also disposed of via the urinary tract.

The two bean-shaped kidneys lie in the abdomen on the muscles of the back, one on either side of the spine and roughly at the level of the navel (umbilicus). The right kidney lies slightly lower than the left one. They are well cushioned by fat and are separated from the abdominal organs by a sheet of tissue called the peritoneum. On top of each kidney sits an adrenal gland that produces hormones (see page 104 for the endocrine system). The kidneys have relatively the greatest

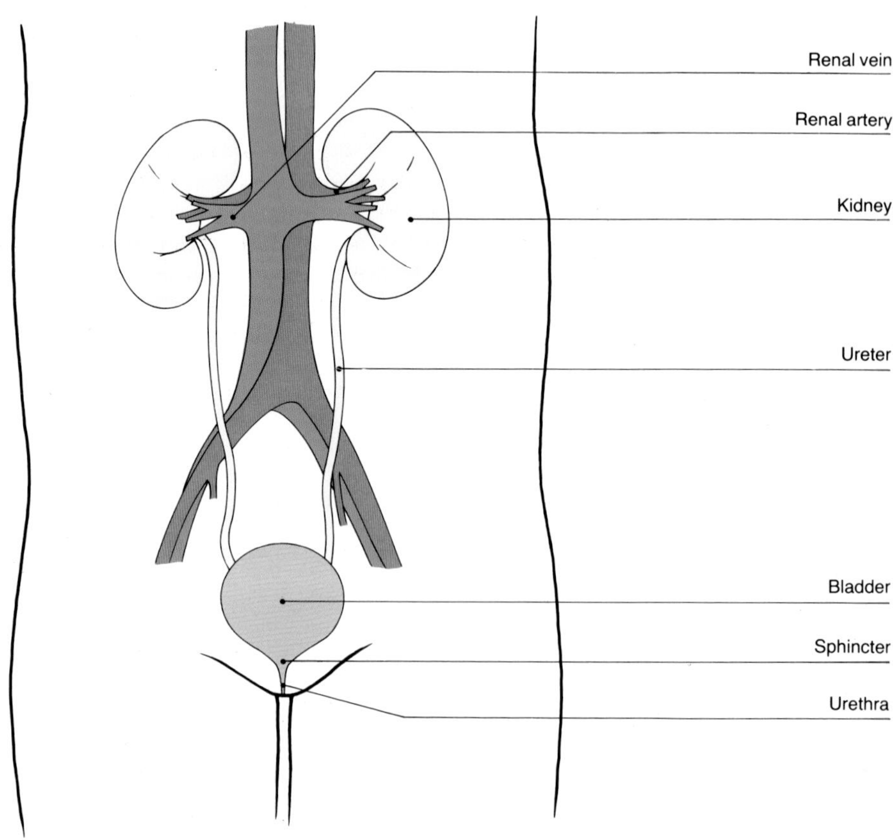

blood flow of any organ – together they receive one fifth of all the blood leaving the heart.

Inside each kidney are about a million minute units called nephrons. These are made up of a series of membranes and little tubes which filter the blood, reabsorb what is necessary and concentrate the urine. Urine collects from these units and runs down the long muscular tube (**ureter**) which empties from the kidney into the **bladder**.

The bladder is a thin-walled muscular container which expands as it fills with urine. Urine is prevented from flowing down the urinary passage (**urethra**) out of the body by a muscular valve, the **sphincter**, at the top of the urethra. This can be relaxed at will to allow urine to be passed. In a baby, urine is passed automatically every so often until she is old enough to learn how to control her bladder.

The urethra is five times as long in boys as it is in girls. It passes through the pelvis to open at the tip of the penis in a boy and in front of the vaginal opening in a girl.

ASSOCIATED SYMPTOMS

- Dribbling urine
- Fever
- Inflammation of the vulva or tip of the penis
- Pain on passing urine
- Smelly/cloudy/dark urine
- Unusual day- or nighttime wetting

WHEN THINGS GO WRONG

A bacterial infection of the urine is a fairly common problem. The infection may affect primarily the bladder (cystitis) or the kidneys (pyelonephritis), but in practice it's often not possible to distinguish one from the other, and urine infections are commonly known as urinary tract infections. Such infections are more common in girls than boys, perhaps because bacteria can more easily travel up their shorter urethra and because infection can easily be passed from the anus forward to the urethral opening. Any abnormality in the urinary tract increases the possibility of infection and boys are more likely to be affected by this. Urinary tract infections in babies can be difficult to recognize because they can't tell you it hurts to urinate. Symptoms can include poor weight gain, vomiting and persistent crying.

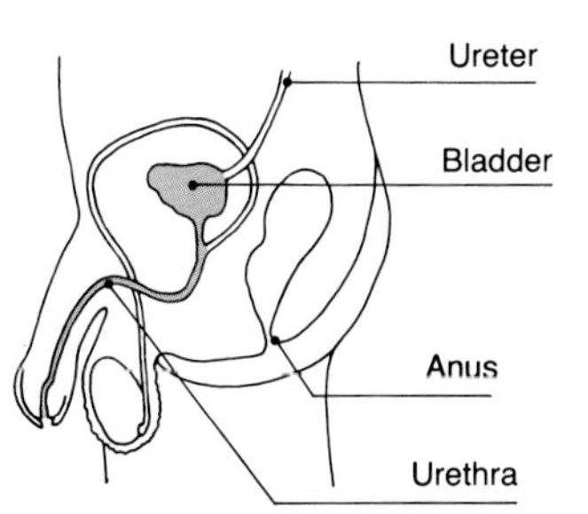

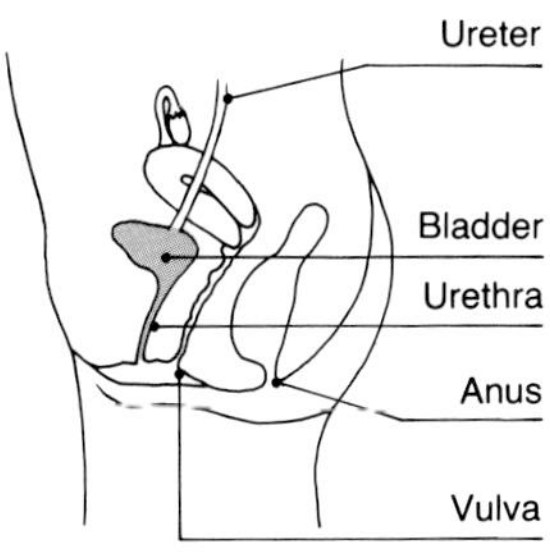

Bacterial infection can spread to the bladder via the urethra. Note the shorter urethra in a girl.

A vaginal infection or a foreign object pushed into the urethra can lead to infection in girls. Poor washing of the area around the vulva makes infection more likely, but some children may simply be more prone to infection than others, however clean they are. Bacteria can also reach the kidneys via the bloodstream from an infection elsewhere in the body, causing pyelonephritis.

Sometimes a throat or skin infection by particular streptococcal bacteria can cause a kidney reaction called glomerulonephritis. The increase in use of antibiotics has helped to control these infections.

ASSOCIATED CONDITIONS

- Bedwetting
- Cystitis
- Glomerulonephritis
- Kidney failure
- Pyelonephritis

The reproductive system

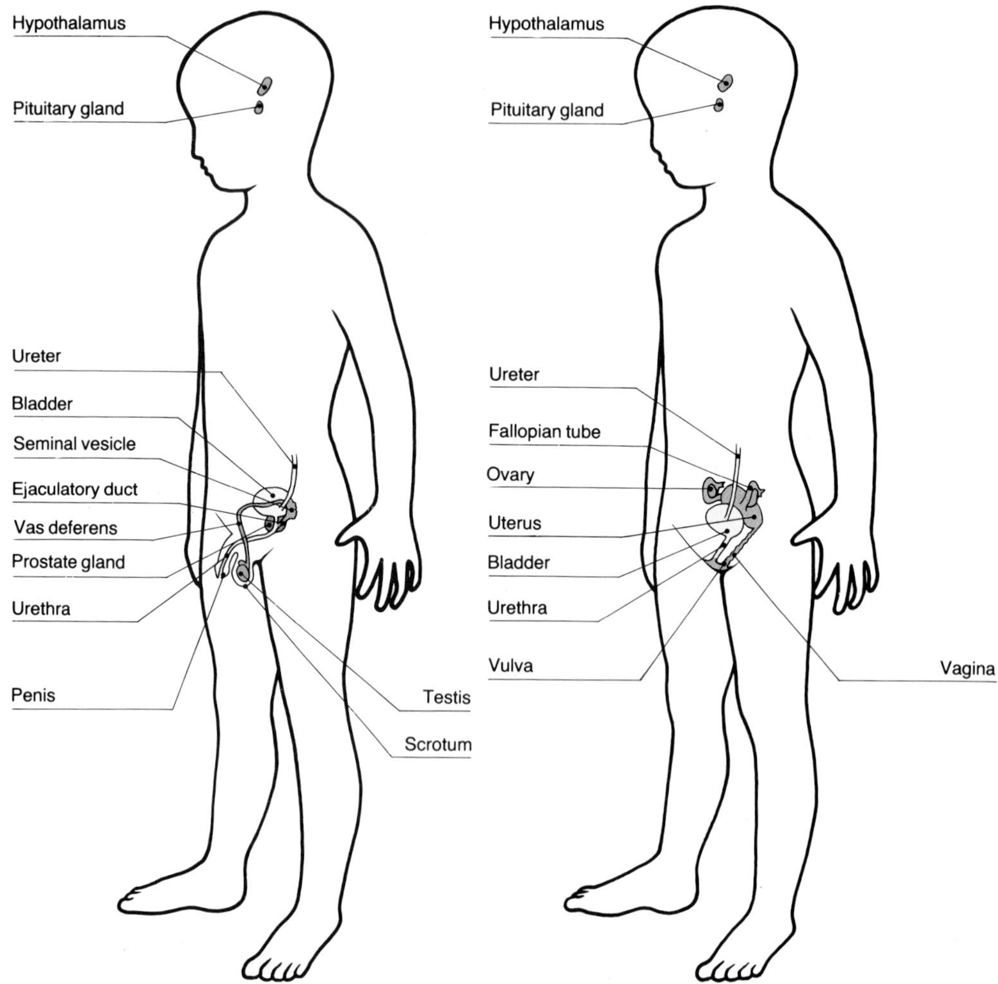

The function of the reproductive system in males is to produce sperm and in females to produce eggs and then to protect and nourish a baby. All the parts of the reproductive system are present in babies although their development is not completed until puberty or later. In the years immediately preceding puberty, the levels of hormones produced by the **hypothalamus** and **pituitary gland** (see page 104 for the endocrine system) gradually rise. These have some effect on hormone production by the testes and ovaries, but it isn't until puberty that the hormone levels surge upward, mature sperm and eggs are made, and sexual development becomes obvious.

In an adolescent boy, sperm are made in the two **testes**, or testicles, which lie one on each side of the **scrotum**. Inside each **testis** there are many tiny coiled tubes and it is in these that the sperm are produced. A larger tube called the **vas deferens** carries sperm from each testis up out of the scrotum into the abdomen, where they are stored in the **seminal vesicles** near the **bladder**. When an adolescent boy has a "wet dream," sperm from the testes and seminal vesicles passes down the **ejaculatory ducts** through the **prostate gland** into the urinary passage (**urethra**). Milky fluid from the prostate mixes with the sperm and the resulting semen passes down and out the penis. The prostatic fluid nourishes the sperm and encourages them to move.

All the eggs (ova) a girl will ever produce are present in her **ovaries** at birth. During puberty a girl's changing hormone levels cause her first menstrual period. After a few cycles she has her first ovulation; an egg ripens and is released into one of the **Fallopian tubes**. The egg is wafted by minute hairs called cilia along the tube into the womb (**uterus**) which has been prepared by the hormones for a possible pregnancy. If the egg isn't fertilized by a sperm, the thick lining of the uterus is shed during menstruation. If fertilization does occur, the egg becomes attached to the lining of the uterus and a pregnancy begins.

Each individual egg and sperm contains minute strands called chromosomes. These carry genetic material vital for the programming of every part of the body. An egg and a sperm contain only twenty-three chromosomes, half the number found in every other body cell. When they join, the fertilized egg has a full complement of forty-six chromosomes – half from each parent. Each cell formed by the continuing division of the fertilized egg during the development of the baby will have forty-six chromosomes too.

SIGNS OF PUBERTY

Puberty signals the maturing of the reproductive system in children and is accompanied by physical changes that can lead to emotional turbulence.

Girls

- First period may occur between 9 and 17 years (average 12-14 years)
- Growth of pubic and underarm hair begins between 11 and 13 years
- Height spurt, usually before the breasts grow
- Breast development
- Slight lowering of voice
- Acne and greasy hair
- Rounding of the hips

Boys

- Enlargement of penis and testes starts between 9 and 13 years
- Pubic hair growth begins around 11 years
- Underarm, chest and facial hair growth starts
- Breaking of the voice
- Acne and greasy hair
- Broadening of the shoulders
- Height spurt when genitals are well developed

WHEN THINGS GO WRONG

During the development of a baby boy in the womb, the testes begin their journey from near the kidneys in the abdomen down into the scrotum. Normally they are in the scrotum at birth, but occasionally they get stuck on the way and the boy has an undescended testis on one or both sides. An operation is usually done when the boy is between one and two to bring the testis into the scrotum and secure it there, so that it can develop normally.

ASSOCIATED CONDITIONS

- Hernia
- Hydrocele
- Hypospadias
- Phimosis
- Torsion of the testis
- Undescended testes
- Vaginal discharge

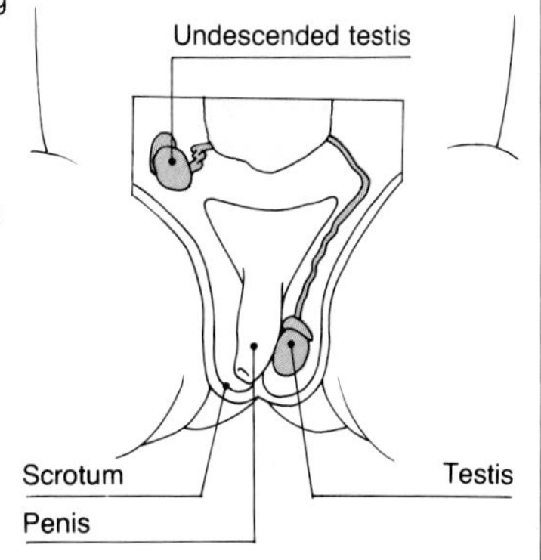

The nervous system

The nervous system has two main parts: a **central** one consisting of the **brain** and **spinal cord**, and a **peripheral** one composed of the nerves connecting the various parts of the body with the brain and spinal cord.

The peripheral nerves receive information about events both inside and outside the body and relay reports to the brain or spinal cord. From the latter, quick reflex commands can be transmitted back along the nerves to instruct a part of the body to respond. Alternatively, the information can be transmitted to the brain where it is interpreted, considered and acted upon. Some information is stored for future reference.

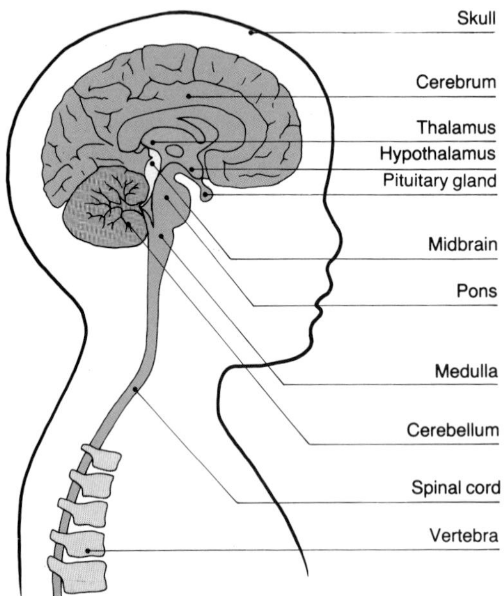

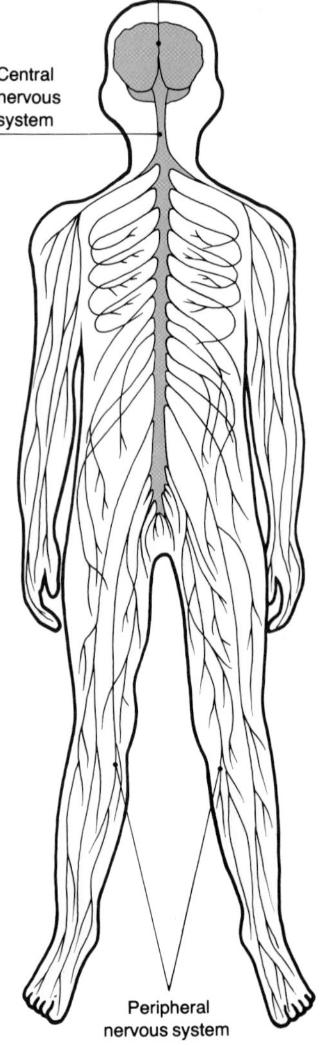

Tiny nerve endings from specific tissues in each area join to form bundles of white nerve fibers. Information travels along nerve fibers in the form of electrical impulses at a speed of 160-260 feet (50-80m) per second. There are separate fibers to carry messages to and from the central nervous system.

The brain is protected by the hard rigid **skull**. The spinal cord runs through a canal in the vertebral bones in the spine. Both brain and spinal cord are covered with three layers of tissue called the meninges. Between two of these layers is cerebrospinal fluid which cushions the underlying nervous tissue and acts as a reservoir to maintain normal pressure in the brain.

The brain is the main coordinating center of the nervous system. It has sensory input from the twelve pairs of cranial nerves (which receive information from the head, including the ears, eyes, nose and mouth) and also from the spinal cord, which relays messages from the rest of the body.

The bulkiest part of the brain is the **cerebrum** in the front, top and back of the head. The human cerebrum is proportionately larger than that in other animals and this accounts for the difference in intelligence. The cerebrum is composed of two halves, the cerebral hemispheres. These are concerned with the control of voluntary movement, consciousness, memory, learning, reasoning, judgment, emotions, dreaming and creativity. The right hemisphere controls the muscles of the left side of the body and vice versa.

Inside the cerebrum lies the wedge-shaped **thalamus** which conveys incoming sensory messages to the cerebral hemispheres. The **hypothalamus** is connected to the underside of the thalamus and makes several hormones which regulate the production of hormones by the **pituitary gland** (see page 104 for the endocrine system). It also functions as an integrating center for all the involuntary or automatic activities of the body which are normally not under conscious control, such as breathing, the heartbeat, the regulation of blood pressure and the movements of the gut.

The **midbrain** connects the cerebrum with the **cerebellum**, which is responsible for balance and the coordination of movements, the **pons**, the junction box of all the nervous pathways of the brain, and the **medulla**, which is the continuation of the spinal cord into the brain.

ASSOCIATED SYMPTOMS

- Behavioral problems
- Headache
- Hyperactivity
- Lack of coordination
- Numbness
- Pins and needles
- Tremor
- Twitching

WHEN THINGS GO WRONG

Sometimes pain isn't felt in the part of the body it comes from, but is felt in the skin somewhere else. This is known as referred pain, because the body "refers" the pain from the injured or diseased part to a specific area of skin elsewhere. This happens because the body of the fetus develops in segments. The skin, organs and other structures in each segment share a common sensory nerve supply. As the baby grows, the organs and structures may move to occupy positions far away from the skin originating from the same segments, but pain may be interpreted by the nervous system as coming from the area of skin which developed from the same segment.

One of the most common examples of referred pain is earache. The skin of the outer and middle ear is supplied by six different nerves, each of which also carries sensory information from other areas to the brain. Pain in one of these areas may be referred to the part of the ear which is supplied by the same nerve. Three to six days after a tonsillectomy, pain is often referred to the middle ear and to the crease behind the ear. The same can happen with tonsillitis, an abscess in the back of the throat or with something stuck in the throat. Dental decay in the lower molars can cause pain in the ear and pain from mumps, wounds or swollen lymph nodes (glands) in the neck may also be felt there. In early appendicitis, pain may be felt around the navel.

ASSOCIATED CONDITIONS

- Autism
- Brain tumor
- Cerebral palsy
- Encephalitis
- Epilepsy
- Hydrocephalus
- Meningitis
- Mental retardation
- Spina bifida

The immune system

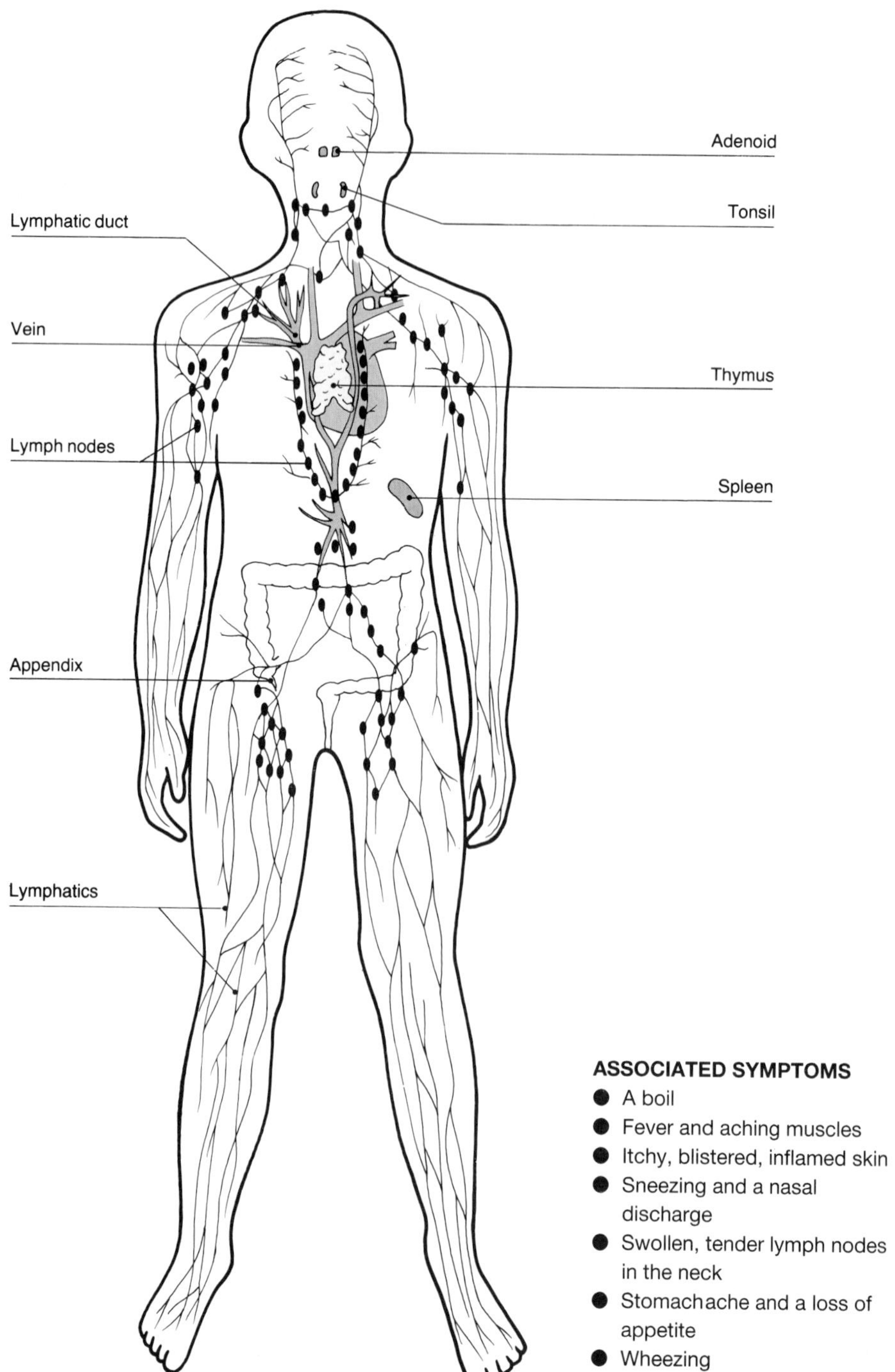

ASSOCIATED SYMPTOMS

- A boil
- Fever and aching muscles
- Itchy, blistered, inflamed skin
- Sneezing and a nasal discharge
- Swollen, tender lymph nodes in the neck
- Stomachache and a loss of appetite
- Wheezing

The body constantly protects itself against invasion by microorganisms (bacteria, viruses, fungi and protozoa) and damage by chemicals and other substances. The first line of defense is the physical barrier of the skin (see page 108). Sweat and tears contain natural antiseptics, the skin itself has an oily barrier and wax protects the ear canals. Swallowed germs are attacked by the stomach's acid.

The upper respiratory tract has especially good defenses. The hair and mucus in the nose discourage the entry of foreign organisms and substances, but the strongest defenses are provided by the lymphoid tissue of the **tonsils** and **adenoids** which form a ring-shaped trap for germs at the back of the throat (see right, When Things Go Wrong). Patches of pus on the tonsils or anywhere else in the body are evidence of an active fight against infection.

The lymphatic system is particularly important in the body's fight against infection. It drains fluid called lymph from every part of the body (except the heart and the brain) via a series of progressively larger lymphatic channels (**lymphatics** and **ducts**) to one of the large **veins**. The lymph from each main area passes through a collection of **lymph nodes** (glands) which contain the white cells known as lymphocytes. Lymphocytes are also found in the lymphoid tissue of the tonsils and adenoids, gut lining, bone marrow, **thymus, spleen** and **appendix**, and they circulate around the lymphatic system and the blood system. When foreign matter such as microorganisms comes into contact with lymphocytes, it stimulates the production of proteins known as antibodies. These are secreted into the lymph and carried round the body in the blood to fight the threatened invasion by foreign matter. Lymph nodes swell as they are producing antibodies and this is a sign that the immune system is working properly. Swollen lymph nodes can sometimes be felt in the neck, under the arms and in the groin. Other white cells and substances in the blood and in the tissues help destroy foreign matter without making antibodies.

A baby is born with some natural immunity and can be further protected by infection-fighting cells, antibodies and other substances in breast milk. The child's own experiences of infection boost her immunity. For some infections, immunity is life-long while for others it is short-lived. Some illnesses, such as the common cold, are caused by one of several strains of virus, which is why having one cold doesn't necessarily prevent another later.

Immunization renders a child immune without having the illness itself. Measles, mumps, whooping cough, tetanus, polio and German measles immunizations are routinely offered.

Sometimes the immune system dosen't work properly, as with AIDS and some rare conditions, and sometimes it overworks and causes allergy. It can also be affected by emotional distress and physical exhaustion.

WHEN THINGS GO WRONG

The ring of lymphoid tissue in the throat is made up of the tonsils, the adenoids and patches of lymphoid tissue on the tongue. Together these trap viruses and bacteria as they are inhaled and prevent them passing down into the lungs. Enlarged red tender tonsils are a sign that the local lymphoid tissue is working overtime to produce lymphocytes with their antibodies against whichever germ is responsible for the infection. In some children, repeated infection eventually wears the tonsils out and they become either chronically enlarged or small and useless. If the tonsils are so large that they prevent a child from eating properly for a long time, they may have to be removed.

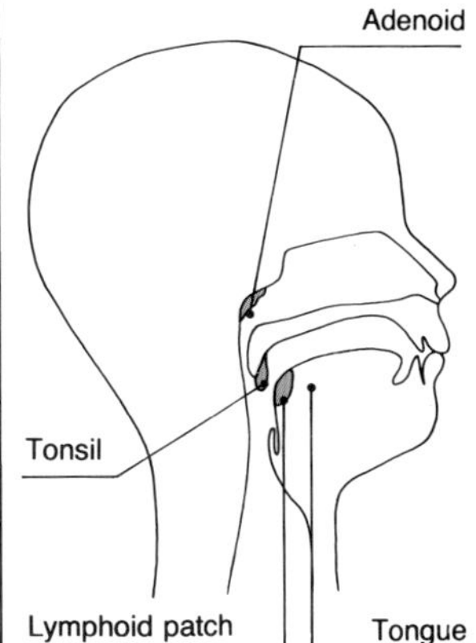

ASSOCIATED CONDITIONS

- AIDS
- Any bacterial, viral or fungal infection
- Allergies, such as asthma, eczema, hay fever
- Arthritis
- Rheumatic fever

The endocrine system

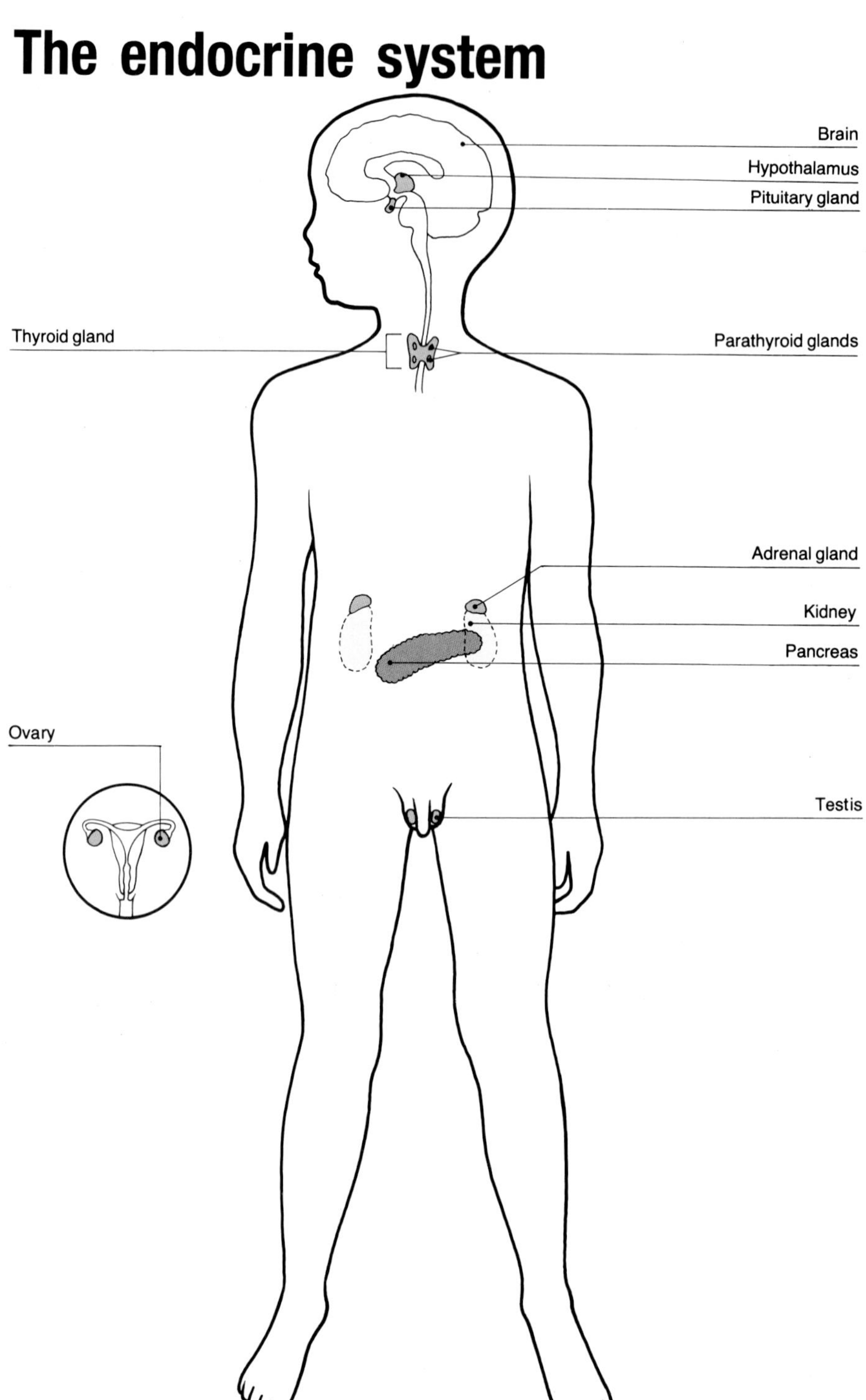

The endocrine system is the name given to the glands and other tissues in the body that produce hormones. Hormones are the body's chemical messengers and are sent to the various parts of the body to help maintain its activities and chemical balance within safe limits. They are vital to the healthy functioning of every cell. They also have an important part to play in the emotions and moods – this effect is particularly noticeable during puberty and adolescence (see page 98 for the reproductive system).

Conducting the whole system are the **hypothalamus** (a part of the brain) and the pea-sized **pituitary gland**, which lies just under the **brain** and is connected to the hypothalamus by a short stalk. Hormones from the hypothalamus instruct the pituitary gland to pour out more, or less, of its hormones according to their levels in the blood. Many of the pituitary hormones regulate the hormone production of other endocrine glands, as well as directly affecting functions such as bone growth and water levels in the body.

The action of the hypothalamus is affected by environmental factors such as light and darkness, by sleeping and waking, and by stress and excitement.

The **thyroid gland** is shaped like a butterfly and lies across the voice box in the throat. Its hormones, one of which is thyroxine, affect the body's energy level, metabolic rate, rate of growth and sexual development.

The **parathyroid glands** next to the thyroid make a hormone which, together with vitamin D and one of the thyroid hormones, calcitonin, promote calcium balance.

The **adrenal glands** lie on top of the **kidneys**. They produce several important hormones including androgens, the male sex hormones, and adrenaline, which affects blood pressure, the release of glucose from the liver and the movements of the intestine.

Insulin and glucagon are made in the **pancreas**, a long thin gland lying behind the stomach. Insulin is the most important of the hormones regulating the use of carbohydrates and fats by the body, and it maintains the blood sugar within normal levels. Glucagon stimulates the breakdown of glycogen (part of the body's energy store in the liver and muscles) and the release of glucose from the liver.

Several important hormones come from the secretory cells in the kidney; they include renin, which helps control the blood pressure, and erythropoietin, which stimulates red blood cell production.

Both the **ovaries** and the **testes** manufacture increased levels of sex hormones at puberty. Hormones made by the intestine have a variety of local actions. Prostaglandins are hormones made by various organs on site which are important in many processes including inflammation, fever, blood pressure control, stomach secretions and blood clotting.

WHEN THINGS GO WRONG

Illness or abnormality follow if an endocrine gland produces too much or too little of one of its hormones. Diabetes mellitus (sugar diabetes), for example, is caused by a lack of the pancreatic hormone insulin. All the body's cells need insulin so they can take up glucose from the blood. Normally, a rise in the blood sugar after a meal stimulates insulin production. Without enough insulin the blood sugar level rises abnormally high.

Large amounts of urine are made in order to try to get rid of this sugar load and the child has to drink much more than usual to keep up with his thirst. The body uses its fat deposits for energy and there is rapid weight loss and a fruity smell to the breath.

Treatment involves balancing the amount of exercise, food and injected insulin.

ASSOCIATED CONDITIONS

- Diabetes mellitus
- Goiter

The bones and muscles

The skeleton acts as a framework to shape, support and move the body. The bones of the **skull, ribcage** and **pelvis** protect vital organs and the movement of the ribs allows the lungs to expand and contract during breathing. Bone is an important factory for the production of red and white blood cells and platelets, and a storehouse for mineral salts.

Bone is one of the hardest tissues in the body. Its density and strength come from calcium, phosphate and carbonate – crystalline salts deposited in the **cartilage** of the soft bones during infancy and childhood. Healthy bones need an adequate supply of these salts in the diet, as well as the right level of acidity, the hormone calcitonin (from the thyroid gland) and vitamin D in the blood.

Special areas in bones act as hardening and growth centers and in long bones these are at one or both ends. The process of calcification (hardening of the bones) continues until the age of twenty-five. Whatever the age of a child, bone tissue is never static, but constantly being remodelled by two groups of bone cells responsible for breakdown and renewal. Some bones, such as those in the skull, fuse together as a child grows.

Bones can be flat (as in the skull), irregular (in the face and

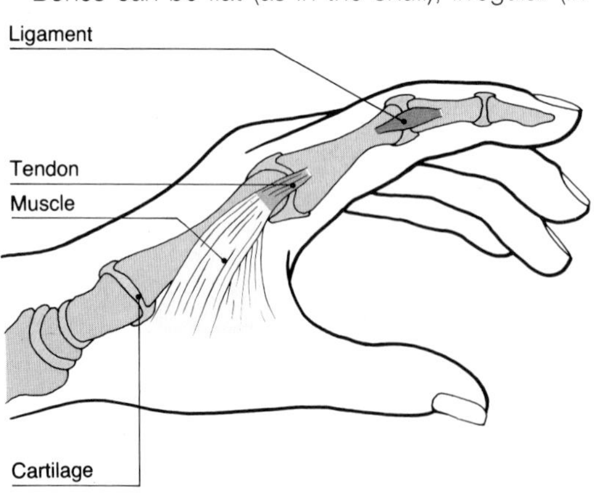

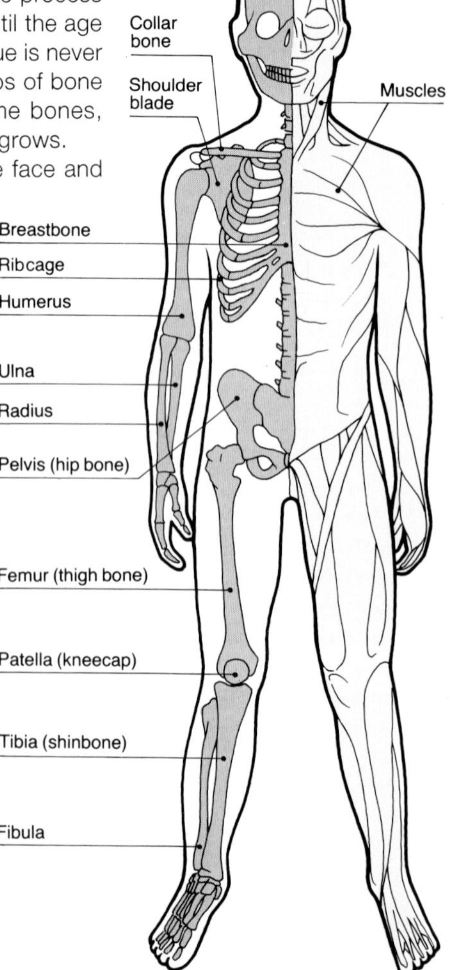

pelvis), long (in the limbs) or short (in the fingers). On the outer surface of any bone is a membrane called the periosteum. Beneath this lies a harder layer and the innermost part is like a honeycomb. Many bones have a central canal containing bone marrow, blood vessels and tiny lymph channels.

The skeleton is made up of many bones jointed or fused together. **Ligaments** are bands or sheets of strong, relatively rigid, fibrous tissue that bind bones together and so strengthen joints and help prevent dislocation. Skeletal or "striped" **muscles** are attached to bones either directly or by **tendons** and help give the body its contours. They are made of bundles of elastic fibers lying close together which are able to contract or shorten in length. This contraction and relaxation enables the bones to be moved. Muscles have an extremely good blood supply to give them enough energy and oxygen for the work they do, and also to dissipate some of the heat they produce.

Different joints allow various forms of movement or none at all. The elbow and knee joints are hinges; the hip and shoulder joints function like a ball and socket, with a wider range of movement; the neck joint is a pivot; and the joints of the skull bones allow a gliding motion over each other in a young baby, but no movement in an older child after they have fused. Many joints are separated by a thin layer of fluid which lubricates the surfaces of the bones as they move against each other.

ASSOCIATED SYMPTOMS

- Awkward gait from pigeon toe
- Cramp
- Pain from a pulled muscle
- Swelling, pain, hotness and limitation of movement from a sprain

WHEN THINGS GO WRONG

The skeleton can only do its job well if it is undamaged. Fractures are a relatively common result of accidents involving children. Sometimes a fracture is obvious, with pain, tenderness, swelling, loss of movement, bruising and deformity. At other times, a broken bone may go unnoticed for several days because there are so few symptoms. A bone can break right across or it can splinter. "Greenstick" fractures (where the bone is bent and partly broken) are often seen in the limb bones. If the skin remains intact after a fracture, it is said to be a "simple" or "closed" fracture; if there is a wound it is called "open." If a broken bone has damaged an internal organ, the fracture is known as "complicated."

If a child can't move a fractured limb, the bone is probably damaged enough to make movement extremely painful. Any attempt to move the bone by using the muscles attached to it alters the position of the broken ends and hurts the surrounding tissues.

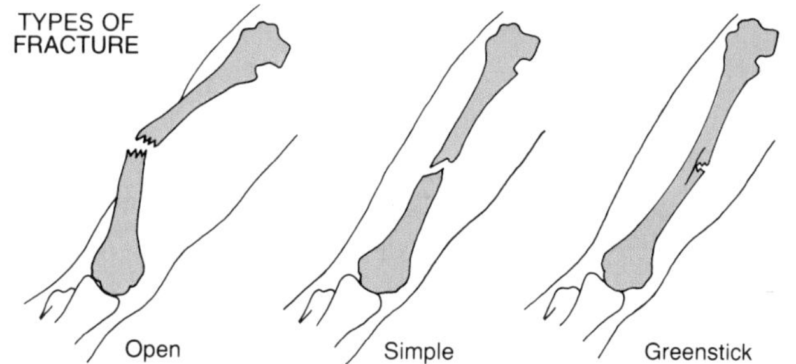

ASSOCIATED CONDITIONS

- Back problems
- Bowlegs
- Clubfoot
- Growing pains
- Hip dislocation
- Knock knees
- Muscular dystrophy
- Perthes' disease
- Pigeon toe
- Rickets
- Sprains (see Emergencies and first aid, page 213)

The skin, nails and hair

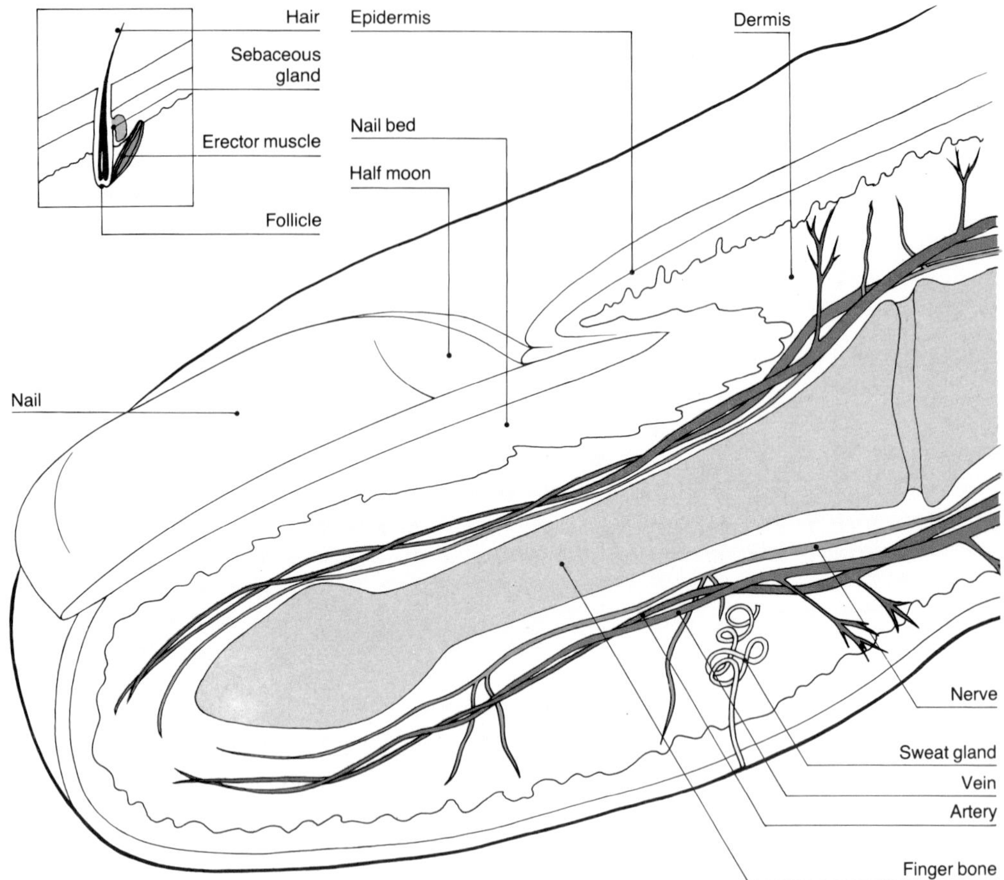

The skin protects the body against physical injury, infection and the weather. The outer part, the **epidermis**, is made of dead flattened cells which are constantly produced by the underlying layer. Each cell lives for about twenty-eight days before being shed. Epidermal cells called melanoblasts make the brownish-black pigment melanin that gives skin its color. The amount of melanin is determined by inherited factors, but ultraviolet rays in sunlight stimulate melanin production, so darkening or tanning the skin.

Beneath the epidermis is the thicker **dermis**. This contains a protein, collagen, and elastic fibers which make it tough, pliable and supportive. Skin has a very rich **nerve** supply and can sense touch, pain and temperature. It's also responsible for making vitamin D from sunlight.

The body is cooled by the evaporation of sweat from the **sweat glands**, which lie in the dermis. Sweat contains natural antiseptics and waste substances. The palms of the hands and soles of the feet have the most sweat glands, and these are especially active during stress. Sweat doesn't usually develop its characteristic smell until around puberty.

Hairs are rooted in small sacs in the dermis called **follicles**. **Sebaceous glands** supply sebum (oil) to the hair and skin, and **muscles** attached to the hair shafts can lift the hairs slightly up from the skin. This latter action traps warm air next to the skin when it's cold, causing the raised skin bumps known as goose pimples. The color and thickness of the hair, the number of hairs and their degree of curl are largely inherited. A hair grows from its root in the follicle at a rate of about one-half inch (1.25cm) a month. After a phase of growth lasting several months or years, a hair rests, then loosens and falls out. About a hundred hairs fall out each day.

The **nails** are convex, translucent plates of dead cells containing the tough protein, keratin. A nail grows from its **nail bed**, which is partly visible as the **half moon**. Nails protect the sensitive fingertips and grow about one-twentieth of an inch (1mm) every ten days.

ASSOCIATED SYMPTOMS

- Blisters
- Flaking
- Itching
- Rash
- Sunburn

WHEN THINGS GO WRONG

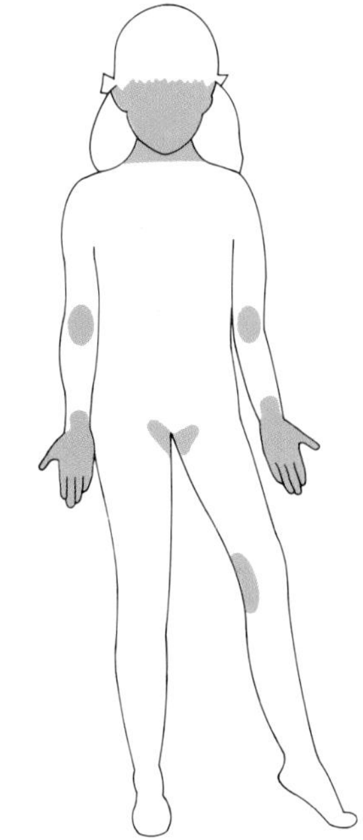

These are the areas of the body most commonly affected by eczema.

A rash is an important sign that something is wrong with the skin or with the body generally. It can be composed of flat discolored spots or patches; red, round, raised pimples with or without a head; blisters of varying sizes; or combinations of these three. Small purple spots, weals, ulcers or small solid lumps are other variations. A rash may be characteristic of a particular disorder or may be common to many. The history of the accompanying illness, if any, together with an accurate description of the rash can often lead to the correct diagnosis, but sometimes it's impossible to be sure without special tests. Causes of a rash include heat, bacterial or viral infection, allergy and insect bites.

Some common rashes in children are those associated with infectious diseases such as measles and chickenpox. The rash in each of these conditions has a characteristic pattern of onset, duration, appearance, area first affected and final distribution about the body.

ASSOCIATED CONDITIONS

- Birthmarks
- Chickenpox
- Chilblains
- Cold sores
- Eczema
- Fifth disease
- German measles
- Impetigo
- Measles
- Milia
- Prickly heat
- Psoriasis
- Ringworm
- Roseola infantum
- Scarlet fever
- Urticaria
- Warts

Part Three

A–Z OF ILLNESSES AND COMPLAINTS

Most children experience some or many of the more common childhood complaints, such as colds, sore throats and ear infections, and some may suffer from more unusual conditions, such as appendicitis, bronchiolitis or a squint. It is therefore highly likely that you as a parent will at some time find yourself caring for a child who is sick.

All parents worry when their child is ill, but if you understand something of the nature of your child's illness you will have more confidence in looking after him and knowing when to seek professional help from your doctor.

In this section you will find an alphabetical list of many of the more common problems of childhood, both physical and emotional, together with helpful cross-references. Also included are some of the rarer complaints that you will hear about in the routine treatment of your child, for example, phenylketonuria for which your child is tested soon after birth. The nature, cause and treatment of each problem is discussed and guidance is given as to what can be done by parents. There is also an informative symptoms guide at the beginning of the section which indicates some of the possible disorders that might be responsible for any one common symptom.

Medi-Kit

SYMPTOMS GUIDE

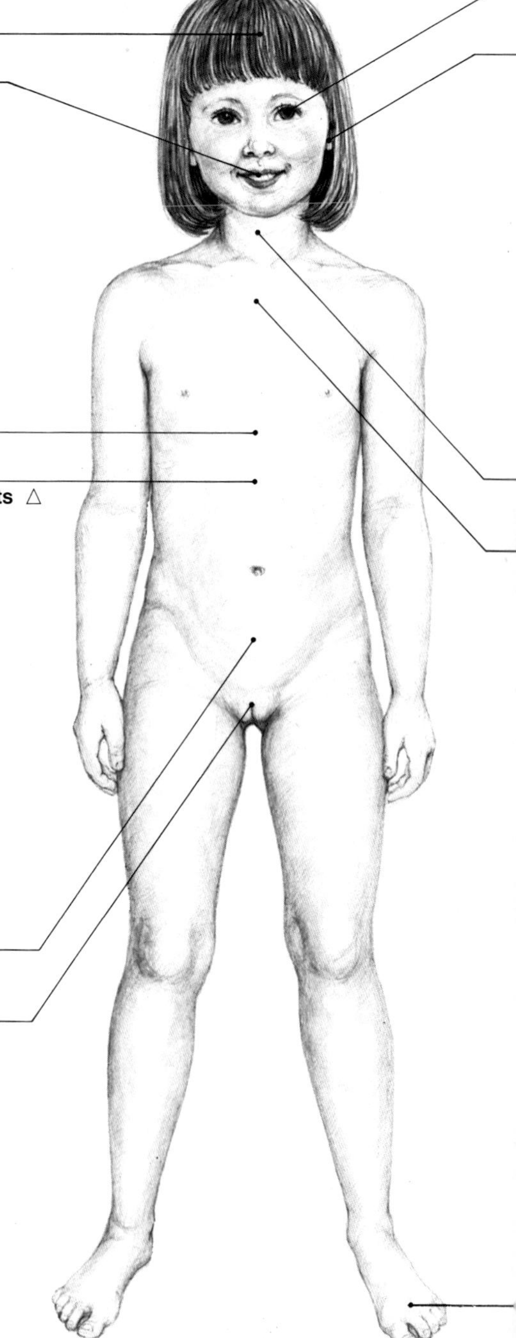

HEAD

Headache △
anxiety
astigmatism
farsightedness
fever
food allergy
glomerulonephritis
hay fever
low blood sugar
migraine
sinusitis

MOUTH

Sore gum
gingivitis
gum abscess
herpes
scurvy

Sore mouth
chapping
cold sores
fever
herpes
moniliasis
mouth ulcers

Toothache △
dental caries

STOMACH

Tummy ache △
anxiety
appendicitis
colic
encephalitis
food allergy
food intolerance
food poisoning
glomerulonephritis
hepatitis
indigestion
intestinal obstruction
malabsorption
mesenteric adenitis
pneumonia
sore throat
urinary tract infections

Swollen tummy
intestinal obstruction
malabsorption

DIGESTIVE SYSTEM

Blood in bowel movements △
anal fissure
diarrhea
food allergy

Constipation △
anal fissure
appendicitis
intestinal obstruction

Diarrhea △
anxiety
appendicitis
constipation
food allergy
food intolerance
food poisoning
gastroenteritis
malabsorption

URINARY SYSTEM

Excessive urine
diabetes mellitus

Scant urine
dehydration
glomerulonephritis

REPRODUCTIVE SYSTEM

Sore penis
balanitis

Vaginal discharge △
moniliasis
worms

This guide indicates some disorders that may be associated with common symptoms. It should not be used for diagnosis. Always consult your doctor if you are worried about any symptoms your child is showing.

EARS

Earache △
dental caries
otitis externa
otitis media
otitis media with effusion
sore throat

Hearing difficulty
deafness
otitis media with effusion
wax

CHEST AND LUNGS

Breathing difficulty △
anemia
asthma
bronchiolitis
bronchitis
croup
heart disease and abnormality
laryngitis
pleurisy
pneumonia

Cough △
allergy
asthma
bronchiolitis
bronchitis
croup
influenza
laryngitis
measles
pneumonia
sinusitis
whooping cough

Wheezing △
allergy
asthma
bronchiolitis
bronchitis

FEET

Itchy toes
athlete's foot

EYES

Blurred or distorted vision
astigmatism
farsightedness
migraine
nearsightedness

Red, itchy, sticky or watery eyes
allergy
blepharitis
blocked tear duct
conjunctivitis
German measles
hay fever
influenza
measles
stye

UPPER RESPIRATORY TRACT

Blocked or runny nose
colds
hay fever
influenza
sinusitis

Sneezing △
colds
hay fever

Sore throat △
colds
German measles
infectious mononucleosis
influenza
laryngitis
roseola infantum
scarlet fever
tonsilitis

GENERAL SYMPTOMS

Appetite loss
anemia
fever
mesenteric adenitis
sore throat
urinary tract infections

Blisters △
allergy
chickenpox
cold sores
eczema
herpes

Fever △
appendicitis
arthritis
bronchiolitis
chickenpox
colds
encephalitis
food poisoning
hepatitis
herpes
infectious mononucleosis
influenza
laryngitis
measles
meningitis
mumps
osteomyelitis
otitis media
pneumonia
rheumatic fever
roseola infantum
scarlet fever
tonsillitis

Itching △
allergy
chilblains
eczema
fifth disease
prickly heat
ringworm
scabies
urticaria
worms

Nausea and/or vomiting
anxiety
appendicitis
encephalitis
food intolerance
food poisoning
gastroenteritis
glomerulonephritis
intestinal obstruction
meningitis
migraine
otitis media
peritonitis
pyloric stenosis
recurrent abdominal pain syndrome
tonsillitis

Painful and/or swollen joints
allergy
arthritis
Perthes' disease
rheumatic fever

Rash △
allergy
chickenpox
dermatitis
eczema
German measles
impetigo
measles
purpura
rheumatic fever
roseola infantum
scarlet fever
seborrheic dermatitis

Swollen lymph nodes △
chickenpox
German measles
herpes
infectious mono-nucleosis
measles
mesenteric adenitis
scarlet fever
sore throat
tonsillitis

Weight loss △
diabetes mellitus
malabsorption
pyloric stenosis
urinary tract infections

The various disorders listed under each symptom (shown in **bold** type) – and information on the symptoms marked △ – can be found in alphabetical order on the following pages.

A

Abdominal pain – *see* Tummy ache, Recurrent abdominal pain syndrome

Abscess

A collection of pus which shows that the body has been fighting infection locally. The pus usually contains infectious organisms as well as infection-fighting cells.
Symptoms: Local symptoms include swelling, pain and tenderness, and there may be a general feeling of being sick.
What can be done: The pus has to be let out and this is best done by your doctor who may want to check whether there's an underlying problem.

Aggression

Some degree of aggression is essential for self-preservation. Harnessing this natural behavior so that it can be a useful force is something we learn from babyhood onwards.

Aggressive behavior arises when a child's needs or desires are thwarted. A baby screams and kicks if the breast or bottle isn't offered when wanted. If a child's needs are consistently not met, the agression may be directed inwards, leading to depression or failure to thrive, or outwards, leading to behavioral problems such as bullying or spitefulness. Some agressive behavior in older children can be a normal part of development, but it may indicate an emotional reaction to underlying family problems.
What can be done: Try not to respond in an angry way, but rather to understand why your child is behaving like this. Your doctor may be able to help you, but in the most complicated situations family therapy may be advisable.

AIDS

The acquired immune deficiency syndrome is a potentially fatal disease caused by infection with the human immunodeficiency virus (HIV). Not everyone carrying the virus has the disease, though they may develop it in time. HIV is spread by sexual contact and by infected blood (for instance, in a blood transfusion or from shared syringes, needles or mixing bowls used by drug addicts). Ordinary contact is currently thought to be safe. A newborn baby of an infected mother has a 50 percent chance of being infected.
Symptoms: These may include weight loss, fever, enlargement of the lymph nodes (glands), decreased resistance to infection, blood disorders, and unusual malignant growths.
What can be done: As yet there is no cure for AIDS, and problems are treated as they occur.

Allergic rhinitis – *see* Hay fever

Allergy

As the immune system of the body develops, it protects a child against "foreign" proteins which enter the body via the digestive tract, the respiratory tract and the skin. In about 1 in 5 children the immune system overreacts and causes allergic symptoms in response to certain of these foreign proteins. Such allergic disorders include eczema, asthma, hay fever, allergic conjunctivitis and some sorts of diarrhea. Migraine and celiac disease may have an allergic basis, and some children develop an allergic reaction (such as blisters) to certain drugs, insect bites and foods.
Symptoms: Allergy should be considered if a child wheezes, has diarrhea, tummy ache, a frequent runny nose, a cough, an eczematous rash, conjunctivitis, or suffers from repeated ear infections.
What can be done: Try to establish the cause of the allergy, with the help of your doctor, or a specialist if necessary, so this can be avoided. Antiallergy medicines and applications are sometimes helpful.

see also **Asthma, Celiac disease, Conjunctivitis, Eczema, Food allergy, Hay fever, Migraine,** *and p. 102 for* the immune system.

Alopecia – *see* Baldness

Anal fissure

This is a crack in the skin round the opening of the rectum.
Symptoms: The fissure is painful and bleeds when your child has a bowel movement. The pain may make him reluctant to defecate, leading to constipation.
What can be done: Lubricate the skin around the fissure with petroleum jelly to make defecating easier. Make sure your child's diet contains plenty of fiber to keep the stool soft, and give him plenty to drink.
see also **Constipation,** *and p. 28 for* diet

Anemia

An anemic child has either too few red blood cells, too little hemoglobin in each cell, or both. The three basic causes are poor production of red blood cells, excessive breakdown of these cells and blood loss.

Iron-deficiency anemia is the commonest problem and can be caused by a diet low in foods containing iron (necessary for the production of red blood cells) or by long-term blood loss. About 1 in 3 children with this condition has microscopic and invisible bleeding from the gut caused by cows' milk intolerance. Inherited disorders such as sickle cell disease and thalassemia can cause red blood cells to be destroyed. Anemia that develops gradually is easy to miss without a blood test because symptoms tend to appear only when the anemia is severe.
Symptoms: These include paleness, irritability, weakness, fast breathing, shortness of breath on exertion, a rapid pulse, loss of appetite, and possibly dirt-eating.
What can be done: Your doctor will order blood tests to help find out the basic cause of your child's anemia, so that this can either be eliminated or helped as much as possible. He may prescribe iron supplements for iron deficiency and will advise you on your child's diet.
see also **Sickle-cell anemia, Thalassemia,** *and p. 92 for* the blood

Anger

Anger is a normal feeling in response to certain situations and is often better expressed rather than repressed. Hidden unrecognized anger can cause long-term emotional problems, but there are many situations in life when it is inappropriate to be outwardly angry and a child has to learn how to cope with them.
What can be done: If the situations making your child angry are unavoidable, you can help by simply being there to understand and listen, and to teach how and when to express anger. A child will learn how to cope with anger to a large extent by your example.

Anxiety

Some degree of anxiety is normal, but too much can cause problems. The level of anxiety felt by an individual child depends on his personality, past experience, and parental or other example, as well as his current emotional and physical state. Anxiety can lead to behavior problems (such as excessive fear of the dark), constipation, eating problems, recurrent tummy aches and vomiting.
What can be done: You can help by trying, perhaps with professional help, to understand the cause of your child's anxiety, and by giving him as much emotional support and security as you can.

Appendicitis

An infection thought to be caused by inflammation produced by hard pellets of food becoming lodged in the appendix (the narrow blind tube off the large bowel).
Symptoms: These include a tummy ache which often starts in the center of the stomach and later shifts to the right, fever, vomiting, and perhaps diarrhea or constipation.
What can be done: The appendix is removed under a general anesthetic. It's sensible to consult your doctor if you're worried about your child's tummy ache, because neglected appendicitis can quickly lead to peritonitis if the appendix bursts. Appendicitis is less likely if your child has plenty of fiber in his diet.
see also **Peritonitis,** *and p. 28 for* diet

Arthritis

Arthritis (inflammation of one or more joints)

has many possible causes. Arthritis associated with an infectious fever is rarely serious. Bacterial infection in the joints (septic arthritis) sometimes occurs after an upper respiratory or skin infection, and arthritis can also be associated with an injury, allergy, rheumatoid arthritis or rheumatic fever.
Symptoms: The joints are painful and may be stiff and swollen, and the pain is worse when the child wakes or moves. The first signs of rheumatoid arthritis may be a fever and rash.
What can be done: Arthritis is always best taken seriously, so talk to your doctor, who will look for the cause and either treat it himself or refer your child to a specialist. Work with your doctor to get the most benefit for your child from the drugs, physiotherapy and special equipment available.
see also **Allergy, Rheumatic fever**

Asthma

A narrowing of the lung passages usually caused by an allergy or an infection. Allergic asthma can be provoked by insects present in dust (house dust mites), grass pollen, animals and foods. Emotional stress, exercise, fumes and extremes of temperature can provoke asthma too. Infectious asthma is caused by a respiratory infection.
Asthma is a common condition, affecting about 1 in 20 children, twice as many boys as girls, and is more likely if there is eczema, asthma, hay fever or urticaria in the family. It tends to improve with age: half of all asthmatic 7-year-olds are clear by the time they're 11, and only half of all asthmatic children become wheezy adults.
Symptoms: Your child may cough and breathing – particularly breathing out – is difficult which can make the child (and the onlookers) frightened. It can start quite suddenly or it may gradually develop.
What can be done: Your doctor will treat any infection and may give medicines to increase the diameter of the breathing passages. An antiallergy drug taken between attacks may help prevent asthma. During an attack, a calm reassuring atmosphere is helpful. However, it is sometimes also necessary to seek medical help during an attack.
see also **Eczema, Hay fever, Urticaria,** *p. 90 for* **the chest and lungs,** *and p. 216 for* **useful addresses**

Astigmatism

A condition in which light entering the eye is distorted by a faulty curvature of the lens or cornea. Some degree of astigmatism is quite common.
Symptoms: Your child may have headaches, pain, tiredness, redness of the eyes and problems with reading.
What can be done: If necessary, glasses can be prescribed to help the condition.
see also p. 82 for the eye

Athlete's foot

A contagious fungal infection of the skin between the toes, spread by an infected person walking around barefoot.
Symptoms: It commonly affects the skin between the little toe and its neighbor, and is identified by cracked, peeling, itchy skin with raw areas underneath.
What can be done: Keep the skin as dry as you can, and use an antifungal powder between the toes after washing and drying them thoroughly. Wash the socks daily and sprinkle them inside with the antifungal powder. Prevent the infection spreading within the family by giving your child his own towel, getting him to step straight out of the bath onto his towel, and by making him wear shoes or slippers everywhere except in the bath or bed. Buy cotton moisture-absorbing socks, and shoes with leather soles and uppers to avoid trapping sweat.
see also **Ringworm**

Attention seeking

The love and attention of parents are essential for a child. If there isn't enough, the child may try to get more by asking for it or, more often, by behaving in such a way as to attract it. The trouble is that any response is better than none, and many a child prefers an adult to be angry with him than to ignore him. Antisocial behavior, such as bullying, is often a hidden cry for attention.
What can be done: It's always better to acknowledge and attend to a child's demands for attention, even if the demand isn't necessarily met in the way the child wishes, as the theory is that behind every

demand there's a real need. If the demands seem too much, it may be sensible to talk it over with your doctor. Adults have needs too, and you might benefit from more emotional and practical support yourself.

Autism

This condition affects 4 or 5 children in every 10,000, boys more than girls. It is sometimes caused by a birth complication or epilepsy.
Symptoms: Speech delay may be the main problem in a young child and 1 in 3 autistic children never learns to talk. Looking back to babyhood there may have been trouble with feeding and a general development delay. Autistic children appear not to make sense of the world around them and don't communicate normally. They are withdrawn and don't form normal relationships. Overactivity, repetitive movements and the bizarre use of words are common. About half of all autistic children are mentally retarded, but a few are very able in some areas.
What can be done: It can be frustrating for parents when their autistic child doesn't respond, but the best thing is for them to persevere in trying to communicate and help the child make sense of the world. The family may benefit from general social help, support and encouragement. The child will probably need special education with backup and assessment from a skilled team. Some children become more socially competent as they grow older, while others will need special care and sheltered jobs as adults.
see also **Epilepsy,** *and p. 216 for* useful addresses

B

Back problems

Structural abnormalities of the back include a sideways curve (scoliosis) and a hump back (kyphosis), either of which may be present from infancy or may develop later.
What can be done: Ask you doctor to refer your child to a specialist who will see if there is any underlying cause and will treat the problem if necessary. Backache should be taken seriously because it may indicate a disorder which could be treated.

Bad breath – *see* Halitosis

Balanitis

An inflammation of the skin covering the end of the penis. It comes from infection of, or irritation by, secretions under the foreskin.
Symptoms: The end of the penis looks red, painful and slightly swollen.
What can be done: Pull the foreskin back very gently as far as it will easily go and wash the area thoroughly. Apply a little antiseptic cream and pull the foreskin down again. Do this several times a day and, with a baby, make sure that his diaper is changed as soon as it is wet, so the penis doesn't chafe. If the inflammation is severe, or doesn't clear up, your doctor may recommend antibiotic cream or medicine. Circumcision is rarely necessary even for repeated infections.

Baldness

The commonest form of patchy baldness in children is caused by ringworm, a fungal infection of the skin and hair. Alopecia areata is a longer-lasting type of baldness which can be patchy or total. Some children develop a nervous habit of pulling their hair out, while many babies rub their heads against the bedclothes and create a bald patch.
What can be done: Ringworm of the scalp is easily treated by your doctor. There is no known cause and as yet no effective treatment for alopecia areata, but the hair may regrow in time. If your child is pulling his hair out, try to find out what is upsetting him, with help from your doctor or a child psychiatrist if necessary.
see also **Ringworm**

Bed wetting

Most children are dry by day before they are at night. The majority are dry at night when they

are two or three, but 1 in 4 three-year-olds, 1 in 5 five-year-olds and 1 in 20 eleven-year-olds still wet the bed. The commonest causes are sleeping too deeply to be woken by a full bladder, feeling too tired or too frightened to get up, and not being old enough to cope with getting up alone to use the potty or toilet.
What can be done: Bed wetting can be a sign of an emotional or even a medical problem, so if you are worried, or if your previously dry child starts wetting at night, consult your doctor.

Making sure the child is warm in bed may help, and some parents like to put their child on to the toilet before they go to bed. Older children often respond well to a system of rewards for dry nights. Drug treatment and alarms are occasionally recommended.

Behavioral problems

No child is perfect, just as no adult is perfect, and it's often not possible to control the circumstances in which we live. This explains why few families escape behavioral problems in one form or another. Also, the behavior of each member of a family is influenced not only by his own personality, but also by that of the other members of his family, and personalities and behavioral patterns can clash.
What can be done: If your child has a problem, try to discover the cause and deal with it early, before it becomes deeply rooted. Children respond well to praise, so remember to use this to encourage the sort of behavior you want to see. Children also do best with a clear idea of what their "house rules" are. They need clear instructions that are followed through, less indiscriminate punishment issued in a moment of irritation, and plenty of attention, interest, joint decision making (when appropriate), and shared activities with their parents. Sometimes behavioral problems are the result of a physical disorder. Talk to your doctor and never be ashamed to ask for professional help if you want it.

Bereavement

Children vary in their response to death, depending on their age, how close the person was to them, on their own personality, their past experience, and the example of those around them. They may accept the loss stoically, or may go through stages of numbness, sadness, anger and depression as a necessary part of their own response.
What can be done: It's much more helpful to a child if you are open about death and grief, rather than trying to hide your feelings. Talking about the dead person can help a child accept death as a natural event, and also helps the normal process of mourning. Some children feel guilty, as though they had in some way caused the person to die by any negative feelings they might ever have had about them. Discussing such ideas helps allay their fears.

Birthmarks

Usually present at birth, these marks on the skin are harmless. There are several different types. A stork's bite mark is a small red or pink mark on the head, neck or face of a newborn baby. A strawberry nevus is raised and red, and may not appear until a few days after birth. A port wine stain is darker colored and permanent. Some babies have a bluish patch at the base of the spine known as a Mongolian blue spot.
What can be done: Stork's bite marks disappear within a year or so, and Mongolian blue spots fade in time as well. Most strawberry nevi disappear within two years, but often enlarge a few months before they go. A port wine stain does not fade, but can be covered with cosmetics if it is on the face and the child is self-conscious about it.

Bites and stings – *see* Emergencies and first aid p.207

Blepharitis

An eye condition caused by infection, allergy, irritation by dust, fumes, smoke or seborrhea.
Symptoms: The edges of the eyelids are inflamed and itchy, and the eyelashes may be matted together with discharge.
What can be done: Consult your doctor who will decide if your child needs treatment.
see also **Allergy**

Blindness

Few children are totally blind but a large number are partially sighted. Causes of blindness include injury, infection of the eyes and an untreated squint.
What can be done: It's important to discover any impairment of vision as soon as possible because early treatment can prevent certain conditions getting worse. Ensure your child has regular checkups and report anything you're worried about to the doctor.
see also **Cataract, Squint, Worms**

Blinking

Repeated blinking is usually a nervous habit (tic) which first shows up when a child is anxious about something. Sometimes blinking is caused by itchiness from allergic conjunctivitis or blepharitis.
What can be done: Telling your child not to do it may stop the blinking, but the worrying may come out in another way, so the best thing is to try and discover the cause of the problem and help the child deal with it. In some instances, it is best not to draw attention to the blinking.
see also **Blepharitis, Conjunctivitis**

Blisters

Blisters may have an obvious cause such as repeated friction from a badly-fitting shoe. Other causes include sunburn, burns and scalds, chickenpox, allergic skin conditions and cold sores.
Symptoms: Small or large fluid-filled blebs on the skin. Blisters have very thin walls and are easily broken by scratching or rubbing.
What can be done: If you're not sure why your child has blisters, consult your doctor. Leave blisters unbroken if possible because of the risk of infection of the raw skin beneath.
see also **Chickenpox, Cold sores, Eczema,** *p.202 for* burns and scalds, *and p.210 for* sunburn

Blocked tear duct

Tear ducts drain tears from the inner corners of the eyes into the nose. Sometimes a duct becomes blocked, making the eye water.
What can be done: Usually it clears spontaneously or with gentle massage, but if not, a minor surgical procedure will unblock it.

Blood in stool

The color of blood in the stool can be red or black, depending on where it comes from and how much there is. If you can see a crack in the skin around the anus (an anal fissure), then the blood is almost certainly coming from that. Other causes can include severe diarrhea or a small harmless growth. Newborn babies may have blood in their stool from swallowing maternal blood.
What can be done: If you are at all worried, or if your child is ill, consult your doctor.
see also **Anal fissure**

Blood in vomit

Severe retching can cause bloodstreaking and breastfed babies may have blood-flecked vomit if the mother has a cracked nipple. Blood in the stomach looks like coffee grounds.
What can be done: Report what you have seen to your doctor.

Blueness of the skin

Blueness of the skin is usually caused by too little oxygen in the blood. The causes include a knot in or pressure on the umbilical cord; delayed breathing at birth after the placenta has separated; and some congenital heart defects. Anything interfering with lung function can also cause blueness. Many young babies have blue fingers and toes even though they are kept warm. This is caused by immaturity of the tiny blood vessels.
What can be done: If you notice that your baby or child looks blue, tell your doctor at once. He will examine your child, and be able to reassure you if all is well.
see also **Heart disease**

Boasting

Children are normally open about their pride and pleasure in their possessions and

achievements, but a problem arises if in comparing themselves and what they have with others, they belittle them. Boasting can be a sign that a child is not getting enough love and emotional attention – the things he needs and unconsciously wants most.
What can be done: Give your child more of your time, boost his confidence that he is valued for himself, and teach by example that it's unacceptable to be pleased that someone else hasn't got, or can't do, something.

Boils and pimples

These local infections of the skin usually start in a hair follicle, especially in areas rubbed by clothes.
What can be done: Let the pus come to a head and burst of its own accord, then keep the area covered to avoid spreading the infection. Don't squeeze a boil or pimple as this can force the infecting organisms deeper and make the condition worse. Large or repeated boils may be a sign of chronic illness or malnutrition, so consult your doctor.

Boredom

Many children learn to expect ceaseless amusement or occupation. Left to their own devices they may not know what to do and find it impossible to be content with doing nothing. A child's boredom threshold also depends on his personality and position within the family. First-borns often learn to amuse themselves early on and so may be less prone to boredom, though others may be very reliant on adult company. Later-born children can become so used to having older siblings around that they find it difficult to cope when alone. Both very bright children and very slow children tend to be easily bored, and almost all under-fives become bored when they are with adults who talk only to each other!
What can be done: Because boredom can be so frustrating, it's helpful if you and your child work out ways of coping with time when there is nothing obvious to do. Unfortunately, many adults have so little unpressured time that they have lost the knack of being content with idleness, and as a result their children have no example to copy.

Bossiness

Personality differences show up very early, and some children naturally like to tell others what to do and when, but aren't equipped with the sophistication to get what they want by leading and instructing tactfully. Sometimes bossiness is a sign of an underlying emotional problem (such as a fear of not belonging to the peer group), or it can reflect family problems at home.
What can be done: A child's bossiness is usually quickly ironed out at school. Check whether your child is simply copying the way you speak at home. It may be worth considering – with the help of your doctor if necessary – whether your child is being bossy because something is upsetting him.

Bowlegs

It's normal for newborn babies to have bowlegs, and it's quite safe for a child to bear weight on the legs as soon as he wants to, provided the routine developmental hip tests have been done. Sometimes, however, severe bowlegs can be a sign of rickets.
What can be done: By the age of 5, most children's legs have straightened out, though overweight children may remain bowlegged for longer. If only one leg is bowed, or if you are worried, consult your doctor.
see also **Rickets**

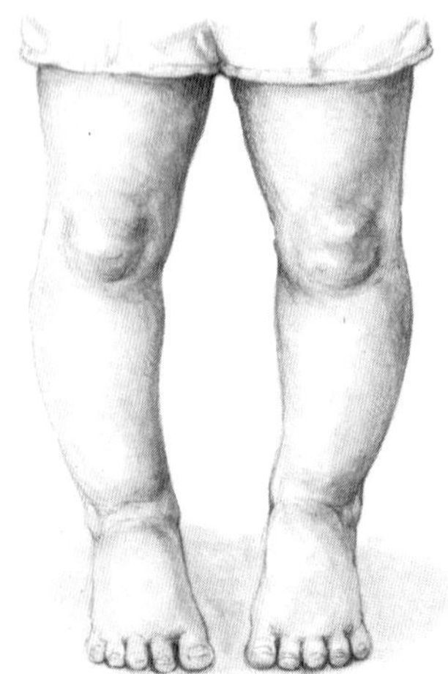

Slight curving of a young child's legs is usually perfectly normal and should straighten in time.

Brain damage

Brain damage may happen before, during or after birth, or may occur later. Depending on how bad the damage is, when it happened, and whereabouts in the brain it is, a child may develop cerebral palsy, epilepsy, clumsiness, mental retardation, or behavioral problems.
What can be done: Any treatable cause must be dealt with. It's difficult to predict the result of brain damage, but severely affected children need special schooling and their parents need loving and effective support.
see also **Cerebral palsy, Epilepsy,** *and p. 216 for* useful addresses

Brain tumor – *see* Cancer

Breathholding

Breathholding spells are a dramatic way for a child to demonstrate frustration or anger.
Symptoms: Depending on how long the breath is held, the child's face turns first red, then blue. Unless a breath is taken, there is either a convulsion or the child faints.
What can be done: An attack can be interrupted by hooking the tongue forward (take care not to get bitten!) or by startling the child, and recovery is immediate with no permanent damage.
see also **Anger, Frustration**

Breathing difficulties

The breathing passages may be obstructed by mucus, pus, a foreign body (such as a bead or peanut), or by a narrowing of their diameter (caused by muscle spasm or swelling of the lining). If the obstruction is in the nose or at the back of the nose, then the child breathes through his mouth. Problems start when the obstruction is lower down. Laryngitis, croup, bronchiolitis, pneumonia, asthma and a foreign body can all prevent enough air getting in and out of the lungs. Heart defects can cause problems as the child struggles to improve the oxygenation of the blood.
Symptoms: A child with breathing difficulty is a distressing sight. His breathing is fast, noisy and labored, the neck muscles may stand out and there are hollows between the ribs. Such a baby becomes breathless when feeding.
What can be done: Any disturbance in the normal breathing pattern must be taken seriously, especially in a young child who may not be able to tell you how he feels. Unless you are confident in coping (for example, if your child regularly has asthma), call your doctor.
see also **Asthma, Bronchiolitis, Croup, Heart disease and abnormality, Laryngitis, Pneumonia**

Bronchiolitis

A viral infection of the small air passages in the lungs mainly affecting children under two. It is commonest in winter and spring. Attacks of wheezing may persist through childhood.
Symptoms: Breathing difficulty, a cough, wheezing and perhaps blueness of the skin.
What can be done: Consult your doctor. Because bronchiolitis is potentially serious, hospitalization may become necessary.

Bronchitis

A viral or bacterial infection of the large air passages of the lungs. It is more common in older children, many of whom wheeze as well as cough. Overweight children tend to wheeze more. A damp cold climate and air pollution encourage this infection, and it's more common with tonsilitis, sinus infection, congenital heart disease and cystic fibrosis.
Symptoms: An initial cold is followed in 3 to 4 days by attacks of coughing, pain in the chest, and sometimes shortness of breath. After a few days the child starts coughing up phlegm.
What can be done: Cough medicines are of little use and antibiotics aren't generally prescribed. Chest physical therapy is helpful, and parents can be taught what to do at home. Encourage your child to spit out any phlegm rather than swallow it. Watch your child for other symptoms, because sometimes "bronchitis" turns out to be measles, influenza or whooping cough.
see also **Cystic fibrosis, Heart disease and abnormality, Influenza, Measles, Sinusitis, Tonsillitis, Whooping cough**

Bruises

An injury hard enough to damage small blood vessels, but not break the skin itself, causes a bruise which is simply an accumulation of blood. Easy or frequent bruising can also be caused by a blood disorder, such as leukemia or hemophilia, and unexplained bruising may be the result of child abuse.

What can be done: An ice pack left on for 15 minutes helps prevent or reduce bruising. It generally takes about 7 days for the blood to be absorbed. If your child seems to bruise easily, consult your doctor.

see also **Hemophilia, Leukemia,** *and p.205 for* bruising

C

Cancer

Cancer is rare in children, and for those who develop this disease the outlook has improved considerably over recent years because of more effective treatments. Tumors of the brain and kidney, leukemia and lymphoma (cancer of the lymph nodes) are some of the forms most frequently found in children. Hodgkin's disease is also a type of lymphoma.

Symptoms: A persistent headache (worse in the morning and on moving the head) and vomiting may be among the first signs of a brain tumor, followed by increasing sleepiness and tiredness. In lymphoma, symptoms include painless swelling of the lymph nodes (glands), usually in the neck, night sweats, loss of appetite, weight loss, tiredness, fever and itching. Enlarged nodes elsewhere cause problems according to where they are. A tumor of the kidney (nephroblastoma or Wilm's tumor) may be felt as a hard lump on one side of the abdomen and there may be blood in the child's urine.

What can be done: A headache in a child should be taken seriously, especially if it is persistent. Early diagnosis, improved drugs and skilled surgery have greatly improved the treatment of brain tumors. In lymphoma, radiation therapy, with or without drug treatment (chemotherapy), leads to a prolonged remission or a cure in many children. A nephroblastoma can usually be cured by surgery, followed by radiotherapy and chemotherapy.

The medical care of children with cancer is very skilled, and experienced counseling to help prevent and cope with emotional problems is available in most areas. It rarely does any good to keep the nature of the child's illness secret. Children tend to manage better if they know the facts and are prepared for what may happen to them as a result of the treatment and progression, remission or cure of their illness.

see also **Leukemia,** *and p. 216 for* useful addresses

Cataract

Cataracts are sometimes present at birth and they can also result from an injury to, or inflammation of, the eye.

Symptoms: There is a mistiness in the lens of the eye which is usually only apparent to the doctor through a special instrument. An older child may have obvious difficulty in seeing.

What can be done: If a cataract is causing a serious visual problem, an operation can be done to remove the lens. Afterwards, glasses or contact lenses have to be worn.

Celiac disease

A rare condition also known as gluten enteropathy, in which a baby can't tolerate gluten, the cereal protein found in wheat, rye, barley and oats.

Symptoms: When one of these cereals is given, the baby stops eating, is irritable, passes pale, bulky, smelly stool and may vomit. As time passes the baby stops gaining weight, his tummy looks swollen, and he develops anemia and other nutritional deficiences.

What can be done: Treatment involves removing all gluten from his diet, perhaps for a long time, and your doctor will advise you on this. If a gluten-free diet is carefully followed, your child will completely recover.

see also **Anemia**

Cerebral palsy

This is due to brain damage before, during or after birth. Certain groups of high risk newborn babies have a higher than normal incidence of cerebral palsy and they need to be followed closely for early signs of the disease.
Symptoms: Stiffness of one or more limbs (spasticity), paralysis, involuntary writhing or jerky movements, lack of coordination, or a loss of balance are each a form of cerebral palsy. Often an affected child may show a combination of these forms. The degree of disability depends on the site and extent of the damage and is often difficult to predict in a baby. In a child with mild cerebral palsy, there is a 1 out of 3 chance that he will "outgrow" his cerebral palsy.
What can be done: Cerebral palsy is not a progressive disease. However, if it is left alone, certain physical conditions will become worse. A great deal can be done to improve the function of the child's body while he is growing and maturing.

As soon as the diagnosis is made, your doctor will refer your child to a special cerebral palsy clinic. A pediatrician who is specially trained will design a treatment program for your child. Normally many disciplines are involved, including occupational therapy, physical therapy, biomedical engineering, speech pathology, audiology, psychology, special education, nutrition and social work. To look after a handicapped child, you as parents will need both practical and emotional support from the professionals and the community.

see also p. 66 for **caring for a handicapped child,** *and p. 216 for* **useful addresses**

Chapping

Upper respiratory tract infection or a fever can lead to chapping, as can sensitivity to sunlight or to certain foods, toys, or anything else touching the lips.
Symptoms: Dryness, soreness, cracking and flaking of the lips, most often seen in cold windy weather and made worse if the lips are licked a lot. Other areas of the body can also become chapped – most often the hands.
What can be done: Protect your child's lips with petroleum jelly or lip balm. A high protection factor suncream will filter ultraviolet rays if your child is sensitive to the sun. Prevent chapping of the hands by drying them well after washing.

Chapped lips can be very painful and may even bleed. It helps to keep them as dry as possible and protect them by applying lipsalve in cold weather.

Cheating

Disobeying rules in order to do well at an activity – whether it's a game of Monopoly or a school exam – can be a warning sign that a child is worrying about something. Perhaps there is a lack of self-confidence or a fear of being looked down upon, laughed at, punished, or even not loved, for not succeeding. Many young children cheat for fun and learn to go along with the rules only as they grow older and understand their significance. Some children experiment with cheating temporarily to discover the limits set by others and by themselves.
What can be done: Try to work out why an older child is cheating and, if necessary with the teacher's or family doctor's help, discover how he is feeling by talking over any worries he has.

Chickenpox

A viral infection easily spread by touch or by droplets from coughing, sneezing or speaking. The incubation period is between 13 and 17 days.
Symptoms: The first symptoms are a headache, feeling ill, swollen lymph nodes (glands), a fever and a blotchy rash. This is

when the illness is at its most infectious. The blotchy rash is replaced within a day or two by the classic chickenpox rash of little pimples which develop into blisters. The pimples come in crops over the first 3 or 4 days, are most profuse on the trunk, and develop in a few hours into blisters which gradually dry and scab over. An infected child remains contagious until *all* of the lesions are scabbed over. The scabs fall off after about 10 days, unless they've been scratched and infected. The rash is seen mainly on the trunk, face, scalp and palate.

What can be done: There is no specific treatment, but lotions such as calamine can help soothe the itching. An oral antihistamine may also help relieve the irritation. Aspirin should *never* be given to a child with chickenpox because of the risk of Reye's syndrome (see page 163); use acetaminophen instead for the relief of pain or fever. Encephalitis is a rare complication. If you're pregnant and haven't had chickenpox, but have been in contact with it, your doctor may want to give you an injection of immune globulin.

see also **Encephalitis,** *and p. 177 for* infectious illnesses chart

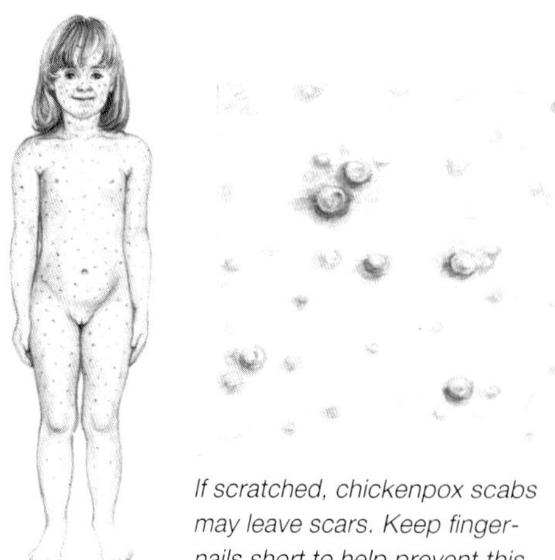

If scratched, chickenpox scabs may leave scars. Keep finger-nails short to help prevent this.

Chilblains

Chilblains are thought to be caused by narrowing of the small arteries of the skin. This is brought on by wearing insufficient warm clothing, or flimsy or wet footwear in cold weather.

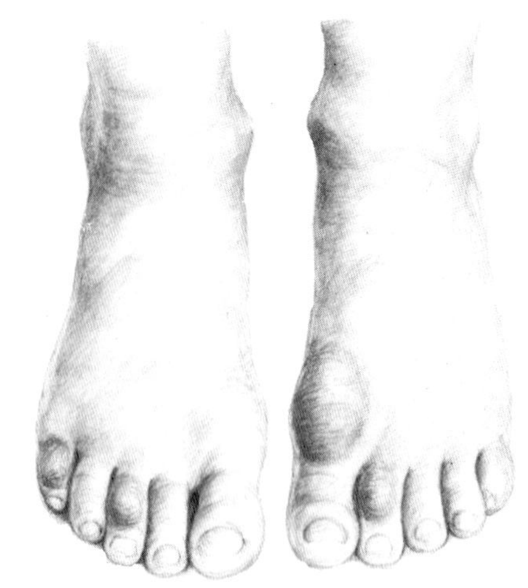

Regular exercise to improve circulation and wearing warm gloves and socks may help prevent chilblains.

Symptoms: Red, itchy, swollen, painful areas show up on the child's toes or fingers, or, less often, on legs or ears. His skin may ulcerate.

What can be done: If the skin is kept warm enough, the chilblains clear up in a week or two. Extra protection against cold is the best prevention.

Cleft lip and palate

Faulty joining of the palate and/or lip of a baby during early pregnancy causes a "cleft" or split in 1 out of every 600 to 1250 babies born in the US. The reasons are rarely clear, although X-rays, German measles and steroid drugs during pregnancy have all come under suspicion. It isn't an hereditary condition as such, though 12 per cent of affected children have an affected relative.

What can be done: The timing of the necessary surgery depends on the individual child, but a cleft lip is often repaired by 3 months. Another cosmetic operation may be done when the child is older. An operation for a cleft palate is usually delayed until after 6 months. An orthodontic "feeding plate" can help a baby with a cleft palate to suck. Breastfeeding may be difficult, but is certainly not impossible, and many mothers discover the trick of moulding the breast to fit the shape of their baby's lip to prevent air leaking during sucking. Complications include

speech, hearing and dental problems, and there may be other developmental abnormalities.
see also p. 216 for useful addresses

Clinginess

Every child has a favorite person and understandably wants to be with that person when tired, sick, unhappy or uncertain. Clinginess is normal and to be expected at such times. A baby starts being particularly dependent on his favorite person at about 6 months, and cries if he or she goes out of sight. A young child gradually learns independence, but likes to explore from a safe base.
What can be done: Trying to force his normal developmental process can lead to undue clinginess resulting from a real fear of being abandoned to strangers or left alone. Some children need to be gently encouraged to venture away, but a child who is forced to leave before he is ready may react with anxiety, sadness or even anger. Patience during this clinging period will lead to a more secure child later.

Clubfoot

A baby may be born with a foot pointing up or down and perhaps twisted so that the sole faces in or out.
What can be done: The treatment of a clubfoot may involve repeated manipulation, followed by plaster casting or adhesive strapping, bracing, exercises, or even surgery. Mild degrees of clubfoot get better spontaneously.

Clumsiness

It is quite natural for children to vary widely in their coordination, but undue clumsiness may be a result of minor brain damage before, during or after birth. A very clumsy child may not be able to tell the difference between right and left, or judge distances accurately.
What can be done: Be tolerant with your child. Clumsiness can improve as the child grows older. If you are worried, consult your doctor.

Colds

The average child in the US between the ages of 4 months and 2 years has from 6 to 7 colds a year! They are caused by a viral infection of the mucous membranes of the nose, ears, throat and sinuses.
Symptoms: These include a runny nose, sore throat, sneezing, and – in babies – irritability and restlessness. Very young babies don't usually have a raised temperature, but in children between 3 months and 3 years, one of the first signs of a cold may be a sudden fever. Older children may or may not have a low fever. Some children swallow their nasal discharge and so feel sick, actually vomit, or have diarrhea. Coughing results from the tickling of this "post-nasal drip" of discharge running down the back of the throat.
What can be done: Colds last up to 10 days, unless complicated by a bacterial infection that causes a greenish-yellow nasal discharge and possibly infection of the ear, throat, sinuses or even the lungs. Such an infection is best treated with antibiotics, but these do not cure the uncomplicated cold because they do not kill viruses. There is no way of preventing a cold other than by avoiding infected people and improving the child's general health.

A baby with a cold may not suck efficiently because of nasal congestion and may benefit from saline nose drops and suctioning before a feeding. Dehydration and overheating should be avoided. A cool mist humidifier or vaporizer may make the room more comfortable. Petroleum jelly will protect the skin under the child's nose, and an oral decongestant may help an older child to breathe more easily.

Teach an older child to blow his nose gently and to put a hand in front of his mouth when sneezing or coughing.
see also p. 61 for how to give nose drops

Cold sores

Cold sores appear on the face, typically around the mouth and lips, and are caused by the herpes simplex virus. After the first infection, the viruses lie dormant. A fever, cold weather, sunlight, and physical or emotional stress can reactivate them.
Symptoms: Cold sores start off as blisters

which burn and itch. If they are scratched, they can become infected with bacteria.
What can be done: Treatments vary in effectiveness, and what helps one child may not help another. Putting an ice cube on the lips at the very first sign prevents cold sores in some children. Creams, lotions and sticks are available from pharmacies to ease burning and itching, and reduce the chance of bacterial infection. A very successful new antiviral agent called acyclovir is available as a cream and lotion on prescription from your doctor. Uninfected cold sores heal within a week or two.
see also **Herpes**

Cold sores may be made less painful by applying drying agents such as calamine lotion or glycerine with carbamine peroxide.

Colic

This is a tummy ache which comes and goes and is caused by spasm (muscle tightening) of a hollow organ in the abdomen, usually the intestine. "Infantile" colic tends to be a problem in the baby's first 3 months, and also tends to happen in the evening. It is often difficult to pin down the cause of the baby's discomfort, and a lot of what is called "colic" isn't due to actual colic at all, but has other causes, such as emotional tension.

Possible causes of colic include sensitivity to traces of undigested foods in breast milk (more likely if there is a family history of allergy); sensitivity to the breakdown products of foods the mother has eaten and which are in her milk (such as onions, beans, cabbage and alcohol); and hunger. Cows' milk formula produces colic in some babies and bottlefed babies are just as likely to get colic as are breastfed ones. Older children can get colic from eating certain foods, such as green apples. The pain that many children have just before they defecate is a type of colic too.
Symptoms: A baby is restless, irritable, cries a lot, is difficult to comfort and may draw his legs up towards his stomach. This can go on for several hours at a stretch, and it may bear little relation to feedings. An older child will either complain of tummy ache or will be irritable and apathetic.
What can be done: Discuss the problem with your doctor if you are worried. He will help you sort out the possible cause and put it right. Some breastfeeding mothers find that if they eat little and often, their babies are happier. With many babies, there's nothing for it but to comfort them by holding and perhaps keeping them on the move while they are in distress.

Color blindness

This is 20 times more common in boys than in girls, and up to 8 per cent of boys are affected to some degree. An inability to distinguish between reds and greens is the most common type.
Symptoms: Unless the difficulty is pronounced, you may not notice that your child has any trouble until his color vision is tested during a routine medical examination. A few children who are slow at learning the names of colors have a degree of color blindness, but many eventually learn to distinguish shades of the colors in question.
What can be done: There is no cure for color blindness, but, although there are a few occupations in which it may be a problem, it is not a handicap in adulthood.

Coma

A state of unconsciousness from which the child cannot be roused. A child may go into a coma after an accident, or it may follow an epileptic fit or be due to diabetes.
see also p. 200 for unconsciousness

Comfort habits – *see* Habits

Concussion – *see* Emergencies and first aid p.200

Congenital malformations

Four percent of babies are born with some sort of abnormality, usually minor. Babies with very severe malformations are usually miscarried spontaneously in early pregnancy. Sometimes there is no apparent reason for the abnormality, and sometimes the cause is genetic. A genetic abnormality in one or both parents may mean that their baby inherits the disorders itself, a tendency to develop it in later life, or the ability to pass it on to the next generation. Examples include color blindness, phenylketonuria, hemophilia and cystic fibrosis. Some conditions affecting the mother and known to be associated with malformations (though not invariably) are German measles, herpes simplex infection, certain drugs and – in some circumstances – X-rays.
What can be done: Prenatal testing is available for some disorders and malformations, for example, spina bifida. Genetic counseling is helpful if you have already had a baby with a genetic abnormality, or if you are concerned that you might.

Conjunctivitis

This is inflammation or irritation of the conjunctivae (the membranes lining the inside of the eyelids and the exposed part of the eye) and can be a result of infection, a foreign body (such as dust), chemical irritation, or an allergy. It is sometimes known as pink eye.
Symptoms: The whites of the eye are pink and the eye feels gritty and sticky, especially first thing in the morning. The eye may water or there is a yellowish discharge making eyelashes mat together.
What can be done: Wash out any irritating chemical, such as soap, with plenty of warm water. Ask your child to look up and down and from side to side while you check whether there's anything in the eye. With a young baby, gently wipe each eye in turn with a clean absorbent cotton swab, moistened with warm water, from the nose to the outside of the eye. Allergic and infectious conjunctivitis can be treated with special eye drops or ointment, so consult your doctor to find out which form it is. If it is infectious, take precautions not to spread the infection to the rest of the family by giving your child his own washcloth and towel and keeping them separately from the others.
see also **Allergy,** *and p. 61 for* how to give eye drops

Constipation

This can be caused by a diet low in fiber. Some children are reluctant to use toilets away from home, and this can also lead to constipation. Overenthusiastic potty training may make a child refuse to go to the bathroom at all. The infrequent bowel movements of some breastfed babies are quite normal, provided they are getting enough milk.
Symptoms: There is difficulty or delay in going to the bathroom. Constipation can also cause an anal fissure (crack) which may be so painful that the child is afraid to defecate.
What can be done: Make sure your child is eating a high-fiber diet containing whole flour, wholegrain cereals, beans and other seeds, and fresh fruit and vegetables. Encouraging him to drink more water or other fluids may help too. Try to allow time in the morning for your child to go to the bathroom unhurriedly before leaving home for daycare, shopping or school, if this is the time he usually chooses. Over-strict potty training techniques for young children often cause more trouble than a calmer, more relaxed approach.
see also **Anal fissure, Diarrhea, Soiling,** *and p. 28 for* diet

Contrariness

A contrary under-five-year-old is not trying deliberately to annoy, but is learning how to make choices and become independent. Contrariness in older children is sometimes a signal of anxiety or unhappiness. It can also be a way of testing you, as most children

prefer to know how far they can go.
What can be done: If your child always wants to do the opposite to what you want, try giving him one or two choices, rather than saying what he must do. Being patient and allowing enough time for the child to do things are also sensible measures.

Convulsions

A convulsion is a series of muscular spasms caused by a spontaneous outburst of electrical activity in the brain. The commonest cause of convulsions, or seizures, in children under five is a fever of over 102°F (38.9°C). These are called febrile convulsions. If the temperature is normal, epilepsy is the most likely culprit.
Symptoms: An older child may first complain of a headache or strange sensations, such as a feeling of fear or an hallucination of sight, sound, smell or touch. This "aura" is followed by stiffness of the legs and arms, and then repeated jerky movements. Finally the child will often go to sleep.
What can be done: Consult your doctor, who may advise a lumbar puncture to see if the child has meningitis. If your child's temperature is high, it's sensible to bring it down, through tepid bathing, even though it's not certain whether it's the fever or the infection itself that causes convulsions. Simple febrile convulsions do not require anticonvulsant medicine. Whooping cough immunization may not be advised if your child has had a convulsion.

see also **Epilepsy, Meningitis,** *p. 63 for* **bringing down temperature,** *p. 77 for* **lumbar puncture,** *and p. 200 for* **seizures**

Cough

Any irritation of the throat, windpipe, or main airways in the lungs can cause a cough. The irritation can be productive or dry. The commonest cause of a productive cough is a cold infecting the nose, throat or sinuses, when the discharge runs down the back of the throat and tickles it. The discharge can arise from infection of the lower breathing passages too, but, either way, coughing brings up the irritating material into the mouth. The younger the child, the more likely he is to swallow the discharge and so develop tummy ache, vomiting or diarrhea. Other causes of coughing include allergy, cystic fibrosis, an inhaled foreign body, such as a small toy or peanut, or a smoky atmosphere.
What can be done: A cough should only be suppressed with cough medicine if it is making the child uncomfortable or waking him from his sleep. It's sensible to let a child cough up and spit out the discharge from a "productive" cough. Most coughs are caused by viruses, so antibiotics are of no use. A few children develop a "nervous" cough, sometimes because the habit of coughing is difficult to break after an infection.

see also **Allergy, Cystic fibrosis**

Cracked lips

This can be caused by a sensitivity to various substances (such as toys and foods) or to the sun's rays, by repeated licking of the lips, and by a fever. Cracked skin at the corners of the mouth is sometimes associated with an infection with the thrush fungus. Cracked lips can also indicate a deficiency of riboflavin (one of the B vitamins).
What can be done: Help your child avoid any food or substance which seems to cause irritation when eaten, sucked, or put to the lips. Licking the lips is a habit that can be hard to give up. Protect the lips with petroleum jelly or lip balm, and use a high protection factor sun cream if the sun is a problem.

If anyone in the family has thrush or any other monilial infection, tell your doctor. Nystatin ointment can be prescribed to heal the lips, and the person who initially had the infection should be treated too. If riboflavin deficiency is the cause, this can be treated by your doctor with B-complex vitamins.

see also **Moniliasis**

Cradle cap

Some babies and young children have particularly oily skins. This is known as seborrhea and is often associated with cradle cap.
Symptoms: A yellowish-brown crusting on the top of the head, particularly over the soft spot (fontanelle). Sometimes the child has

seborrheic dermatitis as well.
What can be done: Cradle cap eventually disappears by itself, but you can help it to disappear by softening the crusts (with baby oil or baby shampoo), then gently removing them with a soft toothbrush. There are also special shampoos available, so ask your doctor or pharmacist for advice about these.
see also **Seborrheic dermatitis**

Cretinism – *see* Hypothyroidism

Crib death

The cruel reality of a crib death (sudden infant death syndrome or SIDS) strikes 1.6 to 2.3 in every 1000 live births in the U.S. Incidence peaks at 2 to 3 months of age; few occur before 2 weeks or after 6 months of age.

Most babies who die of crib death appear healthy prior to death. However, there is some question of existing abnormalities in these children. The cause of SIDS has not yet been found.
see also p.216 for useful addresses

Crib rocking – *see* Habits

Croup

A barking, or "croupy," cough together with noisy and difficult breathing. Croup may be caused by inflammation or other obstruction of the larynx (and sometimes the trachea or epiglottis), usually from an acute viral infection, which may extend down to the lungs. Other causes may be an allergic response, an inhaled foreign body (such as a peanut), emotional upset or excitement, or there may be no apparent reason.
Symptoms: Infectious croup often begins with a cold, which progresses to a harsh barking cough, noisy wheezy breathing and perhaps also to breathing difficulties, which may be bad enough to make the child short of breath or turn blue. The child is anxious and restless, and may have a fever and a sore throat. The symptoms of allergic croup are similar, but without the fever, and they can come on suddenly. A foreign body may cause croup at once, or only when it has set up an inflammation in the larynx. Some young children have recurrent bouts of croup with no obvious signs of infection or allergy. This tends to start during the night and may follow excitement or emotional upset.
What can be done: Stay calm; try to find out whether a toy or nut or other foreign body has been inhaled; make the air humid (with a cold steam vaporizer, steam from a running shower or bath, or with a kettle boiling in a safe place); and open the window slightly, but keep the room warm. If your child is very distressed, if he is fighting for breath, if his lips look blue, if he looks very pale, if he has a high fever, if he is obviously very ill, or if you are worried, call your doctor. Antibiotics are only used for the few cases of croup which are caused by bacterial infection. Antiallergy medicine will be prescribed if there is thought to be an allergic basis. Some children suffer from croup frequently, and their parents get used to calmly humidifying the room and waiting with the child until the symptoms subside.
see also **Allergy,** *and p. 88 for* the upper respiratory tract

Crying

Crying is an expression of emotional or physical discomfort, and can act as a valve for the release of feelings at the same time as alerting others to the fact that help is needed. Humans – and mothers especially – are programmed to respond to tears of distress, so it's almost impossible for most mothers to ignore their crying child.
What can be done: A child who can explain the problem is obviously easier to help than a baby or young child who can't talk, and it's sometimes very frustrating to try and comfort a baby who continues to cry even though you've done all you can. However, don't be afraid of comforting him – you can't spoil a baby or child by responding to his cries for help, even if the only help you can give is your presence.

Cystic fibrosis

One white baby in 2,000 live births and one black baby in 17,000 live births in the U.S.

inherits a tendency to make an excess of sticky mucus in the lungs, bowel, pancreas, and sweat and salivary glands.
Symptoms: The condition can lead to an obstruction of the bowel, failure to thrive, diarrhea, prolapse of the rectum and repeated chest infection.
What can be done: Efficient treatment with a special diet, antibiotics, enzymes, inhalations and physiotherapy for chest infections has greatly improved the outlook for such children.
see also **Prolapse of the rectum,** *and p. 216 for* useful addresses

Cystitis – *see* Urinary tract infections

D

Dandruff –*see* Scurf

Deafness

Deafness can be temporary or permanent, and may be complete or, more frequently, partial. Causes include congenital malformations (rare), German measles during pregnancy, severe jaundice of the newborn, brain damage, mumps, meningitis, encephalitis, wax or a foreign body, such as a bead, in the outer ear, and – most common – fluid in the middle ear, often combined with inflammation (otitis media).
What can be done: Deafness can be quite difficult to spot, which is why routine hearing tests are carried out. The sooner treatment is started the better, especially with regard to the child's learning to listen and hence to speak. Even temporary deafness can cause speech problems and is best taken seriously. Treatment ranges from antibiotics for acute otitis media to a hearing aid and special help from a teacher of the deaf.
see also **Congenital malformations, Encephalitis, Jaundice, Meningitis, Mumps, Otitis media, Wax,** *and p. 216 for* useful addresses

Defiance

With a defiant child, the first thing to do is to try to understand the cause of this behavior. Possible reasons include testing you to discover the limits you set; resentment at supposed unfairness; fatigue; feeling sick; unhappiness; and attention-seeking.
What can be done: Defiant children tend to lack confidence and do best with loving, firm consistency, positive encouragement of good behavior, and understanding guidance rather than punishment.

Dehydration

Drinking too little fluid or losing too much (by vomiting, sweating, or diarrhea), or both, can lead to a potentially dangerous water deficiency. The younger the child, the more likely it is that dehydration will be a problem, so watch a young baby very carefully.
Symptoms: If your child is ill, look out for him not wanting to drink, vomiting and diarrhea, sunken glazed eyes, a dry mouth, and scanty urine production.
What can be done: If your child won't or can't drink more, or if you are at all worried, consult your doctor. Never put extra scoops of milk powder in a bottlefed baby's formula, as the kidneys may not cope with this extra load.
see also p. 58 for looking after an ill child

Dental caries

After eating, a sticky layer (plaque) coats the teeth. Bacteria break down sugar in the plaque and acid is formed as a by-product. The acid eats into the enamel and leads to dental caries or decay. Some children are naturally less prone to dental decay, perhaps because they form less plaque, have different bacteria, more resistant enamel, a better diet, or take in more fluoride.
Symptoms: Once the decay is through to the tooth's nerve, the child develops toothache. Pain from decay in the lower molar teeth can sometimes be felt as earache.
What can be done: Help prevent decay by reducing the amount of sugar in your child's diet and by brushing the teeth with a fluoride toothpaste. Never let your baby go to sleep

while drinking a bottle of milk or juice. Talk to your dentist or doctor about giving your baby or child extra fluoride in drops or tablet form if your water supply is not fluoridated.

see also p. 37 for caring for teeth, *and p. 86 for* the teeth and gums

Depression

Children can become depressed and, in a sense, this is more of a problem than in adults because children are less able to control their environment. Children of depressed parents are more likely to suffer from depression, both as children and later as adults.

Symptoms: Depression can show up as failure to thrive, anxiety, apathy, irritability, a short attention span, sleep difficulties, temper tantrums, bed-wetting, and learning and behavioral difficulties.

What can be done: Depressed children usually need more love, security, stability and attention than they are getting. Family therapy can be a great help because the problem is rarely that of the child alone.

see also **Bed wetting, Temper tantrums**

Dermatitis

This is any inflammation of the skin and can be provoked by chronic skin irritation (for example, from rubbing), by chemicals, or by allergy. Eczema is a form of dermatitis, as is diaper rash.

see also **Allergy, Eczema, Diaper rash, Seborrheic dermatitis**

Diabetes mellitus

In diabetes mellitus (sugar diabetes), the pancreas doesn't make enough of the hormone insulin, which regulates the amount of sugar in the blood. As a result, the blood sugar is too high and overflows into the urine.

Symptoms: If your child loses weight, drinks more than usual and passes large quantities of urine, diabetes must be suspected and you should consult your doctor. Very occasionally the first sign is a diabetic coma which needs urgent medical attention.

What can be done: Your doctor will confirm the diagnosis by taking blood and urine tests. Treatment is with insulin by injection, which most parents learn to do until their child can manage it himself. He should be encouraged to carry sugar with him to eat if he feels faint, and your doctor will give guidance on his diet which must be carefully controlled.

see also p. 104 for the endocrine system, *and p. 216 for* useful addresses

Diaper rash

An inflammation of the skin in the diaper area which can be caused by irritation from a wet chafing diaper; seborrhea (excessive skin oil production); being in a dirty diaper too long; diarrhea; allergy; sensitivity to chemicals; psoriasis; and moniliasis.

Symptoms: Reddening of the skin is followed by raised, red, sore, broken patches. Weeping, crusting, bleeding, flaking and ulceration can follow.

What can be done: Change the diaper (especially if dirty) much more often; wash the skin at each diaper change with soap and water (unless the skin is very dry, in which case use just water); dry the skin well, and use a protective cream, such as zinc oxide or a silicone barrier cream. If there is much irritation, an antiseptic cream containing benzalkonium chloride is useful. Let your baby go without a diaper whenever you can to allow air to get to the skin. Sterilize terry diapers by boiling them or soaking them in a special sanitizing solution and then rinsing or washing them thoroughly. Seborrheic or monilial rashes will probably need medical treatment, so consult your doctor if the rash persists or gets worse.

see also **Allergy, Moniliasis, Psoriasis, Seborrheic dermatitis**

Diarrhea

A child has diarrhea if he is passing abnormally frequent, watery bowel movements. Diarrhea can be caused by irritation from, or sensitivity or allergy to, certain foods; by irritation from chemicals in the diet or from medicines; by irritation from chemicals produced by the body (for example, in jaundice); by infection in the bowel; by catarrh or phlegm from a

respiratory infection being swallowed; by the excess mucus produced in cystic fibrosis; by emotional factors, such as anxiety; and by watery bowel movements leaking around a constipated mass of bowel movements.
Symptoms: The movements become looser, often paler, and are passed more often. In severe diarrhea, the movements have a watery consistency. Often there is soreness of the skin around the anus.
What can be done: If your child is ill, or if the diarrhea is persistent and you are worried consult your doctor. Because of the danger of dehydration, it's important to give plenty of fluid and your doctor may suggest clear liquids or oral electrolyte solution.
see also **Allergy, Dehydration, Soiling, Sugar intolerance**

Diphtheria

Routine immunization has all but eradicated diphtheria, which is a potentially serious bacterial infection spread by airborne droplets from coughing, sneezing or even talking. Diphtheria vaccine is given with tetanus and whooping cough vaccines in the DTP vaccine.
see also p. 53 for immunization

Dirt eating

When a child eats dirt it is usually done as a form of experimentation. Occasionally it is a symptom of anemia. Emotionally disturbed or mentally retarded children sometimes develop the habit of dirt eating or eating unsuitable things, such as their own hair. Physical side effects can arise if a child eats old paint, containing lead, or if substances such as hair form a ball and obstruct the gut.
What can be done: If a child is emotionally disturbed, try to find out why, with the help of your doctor if necessary, and try to resolve the problem. Otherwise, simply watch him and intervene when he begins to eat dirt.
see also **Anemia, Lead poisoning**

Dizziness

Children don't often complain of dizziness, but if they do, the most common cause is infection or injury of the ear.
Symptoms: A young child may become unsteady on his feet, and an older one may describe the sensation of going round and round. Ringing in the ears sometimes accompanies infection, and rapid jerking of the eyes (nystagmus) is a sign of problem with the inner ear.
What can be done: Report the symptoms to your doctor who will treat any infection.
see also **Nystagmus**

Down's syndrome

A genetic condition, also called mongolism, in which each cell in the body of a Down's child has an extra chromosome number 21.
Symptoms: These children have a characteristic physical appearance and are usually mentally retarded to some degree. They may have other congenital abnormalities and are more likely to suffer from cataracts, respiratory infections and leukemia.
What can be done: Make the most of the support, encouragement and advice offered by your health and social work professionals, by the parents of other Down's children, and by your local community to help you give your child the time and attention he'll need as he learns to cope to the best of his ability in society. Down's children are increasingly being educated at ordinary schools for as long as possible.
see also **Cataract, Leukemia,** *and p. 216 for* useful addresses

Dying

It is generally agreed that it is better to be open and honest about the subject of death to a terminally ill child. There will be fears and concerns not only about real or imagined pain and discomfort, but about parents' and friends' unhappiness and about leaving loved ones behind. Talking about these worries can help, as can discussing what happens after death, and it's surprising how positive a dying child can be over what's happening. Don't forget that the brothers and sisters of a dying child can harbor all kinds of fantasies, such as that they are the cause of the death. They also need to be helped to get their feelings into perspective.
see also **Bereavement**

Dyslexia

Dyslexic children aren't as capable as other children of making sense of symbols or understanding the rules of language. They may be bright or dull, but their literary ability always falls far short of their ability in other areas. About 4 per cent of the population have dyslexia, but the diagnosis is rarely made before the age of 5.

Symptoms: There is difficulty in learning to read and perhaps also with writing, spelling, arithmetic, memory, recognizing sequences and learning about direction.

What can be done: Your child should be offered help from a special education teacher trained to work with dyslexic children. Expert help enables a child to cope much more easily with his problem and he may eventually learn to read fairly well.

see also p. 216 for **useful addresses**

E

Ear infections – *see* Otitis externa, Otitis media

Earache

This is most often caused by infection of the middle ear (otitis media), but infection of the outer ear canal (otitis externa), dental decay, disorders of the jaw and a sore throat can also be responsible.

What can be done: A source of heat, such as a warm hot water bottle held against the ear, and some acetaminophen if necessary, will help ease the pain. If the pain is bad, or if it doesn't get better, consult your doctor.

see also **Dental caries, Otitis externa, Otitis media**

Eating problems

The meal table can become an emotional battlefield if a child is forced into eating patterns which are not natural to him. Any problems in the family may become focussed on what the child does or does not eat, and a sense of proportion is easily lost. Some children like to eat little and often, while others are content with the more adult pattern of two or three meals a day. Some children naturally need much more, or less, food than others. Sickness or changes in the family can easily affect eating patterns. Flexibility and a sense of humor are essential if you're dealing with a child who doesn't eat when or as you'd like him to. It is also important to be consistent, so that the child knows what you will and won't allow.

Loss of appetite is common in many young children who from time to time go through phases of eating very little or only accepting a few foods, and gaining little or no weight. Less frequent causes include infection, diseases of the thyroid gland, kidney, liver or intestine, and emotional problems.

What can be done: Never force your child to eat, but make sure that the food you offer is as attractive and nutritious as possible. Unless the child is ill, there's little danger from not eating, although it is always important to have enough to drink. However, if you are worried, ask your doctor for advice.

Eczema

Eczema is a form of dermatitis or inflammation of the skin. The commonest type is atopic eczema, which is one of a group of conditions (including asthma and hay fever) that runs in families. About 3 percent of children suffer from atopic eczema and sometimes this is followed by asthma. Certain foods trigger it in some children, but often no cause is found.

Contact eczema (allergic or caused by a "primary" irritant) is also common, and is provoked by prolonged or repeated contact with various substances including bubble bath, saliva, citrus juice, detergent, sap, nickel (in jewelry), and a wet or dirty diaper; by plants such as chrysanthemums and primroses; by some drugs used on the skin, such as neomycin, and some antihistamines and local anesthetics; and by skin infections such as ringworm and impetigo.

Symptoms: Redness and itching are quickly followed by tiny blisters. Scratching makes the skin swell and itch more, and yellowish crusts are formed from oozing blister fluid. As the skin heals it flakes, and in chronic eczema it thickens, cracks and bleeds.

Atopic eczema usually begins in the first few months and tends to be gone by 5 years. It frequently coincides with the introduction of certain foods into the baby's diet and may be heralded by colic, urticaria and flushing. Typically it affects the cheeks, ears, neck, fronts of the legs and arms, and finally the insides of the wrists, elbows and knees. A severely affected child can be almost covered in eczema, and this is very distressing both to the child, who is irritable because of the itching and the resultant lack of sleep, and to the parents who feel helpless and are often short of sleep themselves.

Contact eczema affects the area of contact with the irritating substance.

What can be done: If the precipitating factor is obvious, try to remove it or find a way of protecting the skin from it. For instance, a teething child with eczema from dribble could be laid to sleep with his face on something soft and absorbent, such as an old cotton diaper, and nonperfumed moisturizing cream or petroleum jelly could be put on the skin around his mouth. Patch testing isn't very reliable, nor are blood tests. It's worth trying to discover whether anything in the diet could be responsible for atopic eczema. Tests should be carried out under the guidance of a dietician unless you or your doctor have specific nutritional expertise, because an elimination diet is very restrictive and food avoidance tests usually involve commonly eaten foods such as milk, eggs, wheat and citrus fruits. In both cases it's essential that the child has adequate nourishment.

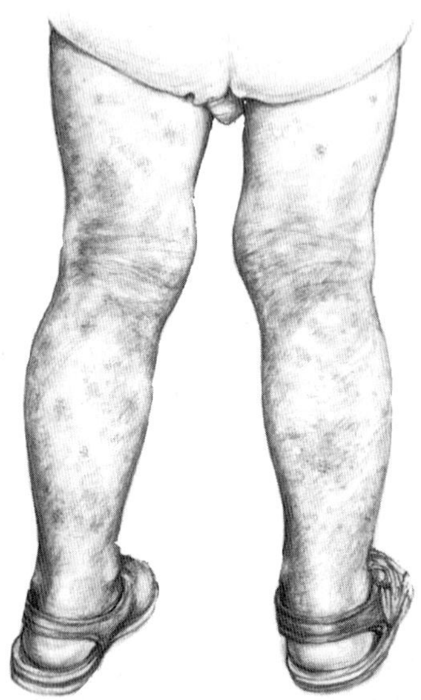

Itching from eczema is worse when the skin is warm.

Sunlight and salt water often help the condition. Smooth-textured clothing is advisable, but wool should be avoided and babies should not be allowed to crawl on a wool carpet. Bathing should be kept to a minimum. When you do bathe your child, let him soak in the water for 20 minutes, then add some nonperfumed bath oil or emulsifying ointment. This helps seal moisture into his skin and so combats dryness which can lead to cracking. Soap and detergents are best avoided. Moisturizing creams and lotions should be applied to his skin after bathing. Keep his fingernails short and clean to minimize damage from scratching and to prevent the skin becoming infected. Cotton scratch mitts are useful for babies.

Special steroid creams or ointments may be prescribed to alleviate itching and inflammation, and are best used after a bath. The stronger ones are rarely used because of the risk of thinning and stretching the skin with long-term use.

see also **Asthma, Hay fever, Impetigo, Ringworm, Seborrheic dermatitis,** *and p. 216 for* useful addresses

Emotional deprivation

Love, physical affection and attention are essential for emotional and physical health, and without enough of these precious commodities a child literally fails to thrive. Each child, each parent and each situation is different, so it's not sensible to make rigid rules. What might suit one child might be far too little for another. Emotional deprivation can show up as depression, apathy, behavioral problems, abnormal dependency, sadness or unconscious idealization of the parents. Because children learn about parenthood from their parents, a cycle of emotional deprivation may continue from generation to generation unless interrupted.

see also **Behavioral problems, Depression**

Encephalitis

An inflammation of the brain usually caused by viral or other infection. When encephalitis follows a general infection, but there is no evidence of direct infection of the brain, it has been suggested that it may be caused by an allergic reaction to the infection. It can also be a rare side effect of some vaccines.
Symptoms: Most commonly there is a fever, perhaps a mild cold, a headache, tummy ache, nausea and vomiting, and mental dullness, perhaps progressing to confusion and finally coma. There may be strange movements, neck stiffness, convulsions, emotional outbursts, incontinence, and signs of involvement of the nervous system, such as unsteadiness or even paralysis.
What can be done: Consult your doctor immediately. If encephalitis is suspected, he will arrange for your child to have a lumbar puncture in the hospital.

see also p. 77 for lumbar puncture

Epilepsy (Seizure disorder)

Many disorders of the brain can be associated with epilepsy, but often there is no known cause. Epilepsy frequently begins in infancy, and a small proportion of children with febrile convulsions go on to develop it.
Symptoms: There are two main types of epileptic seizure. In *petit mal* epilepsy, a child has transient losses of consciousness (he may just stare or stiffen momentarily), but not long enough to make him fall down. These may happen many hundreds of times a day. In *grand mal* epilepsy, there is a recognizable seizure: the child loses consciousness, falls to the ground, shakes, wets or soils himself, goes rigid, and often sleeps afterwards.
What can be done: Modern drug treatment ensures that most of those with epilepsy lead a normal seizure-free life.

see also **Convulsions,** *and p. 216 for* useful addresses

Eye infections – *see* Blepharitis, Conjunctivitis

F

Failure to thrive

A term used to describe those babies or children who don't gain as much weight as they should over a period of weeks or months. In a looser sense, the term could be applied to any child who is unhealthy or unhappy. Causes of failure to thrive include inadequate nutrition, emotional neglect and underlying physical disease.
What can be done: Your family doctor or pediatrician will help you sort out the reasons for your child's failure to thrive, and suggest a suitable plan of action.

Fainting (Syncope)

A temporary loss of consciousness caused by insufficient blood reaching the brain. Breathholding during crying can lead to a fainting spell. The child holds his breath and turns blue, and his arms and legs become rigidly extended. He then becomes limp, resumes breathing and, after a few seconds, returns to full alertness. This type of fainting spell occurs commonly in young children between the ages of 6 months and 4 years. It disappears spontaneously before school age.

Some fainting may follow a bump on the head or other sudden, minor injury. The child may start to cry, holds his breath momentarily and turns pale. He then collapses, but recovers rapidly.

In older children and adolescents, fainting can occur when they move suddenly from a lying position to a standing one. It may also happen when they are just standing still. They quickly regain consciousness when they are in a horizontal position (that is, when they fall down).

see also **Breath holding** *and p. 200 for* **unconsciousness**

Fantasies

Imaginary ideas which help a child to puzzle out and make sense of the world. Relationships and activities can be explored safely by acting them out in play, by painting, modeling, or other creative activities, or by story-telling. Games of "doctors and nurses," "mommies and daddies," or "school" enable children not only to pretend to be a variety of people and to experience what it feels like, but also to express and work out in play some of the feelings they have about real or imagined situations, instead of bottling up their emotions. Daydreaming is another avenue through which desires, fears and ideas can unfold. A child's fantasy life is potentially both healing and creative.

Farsightedness

A child is said to be farsighted if he is unable to see near objects clearly. This may be because the eyeball is too short, or the refractive power of the lens or cornea isn't strong enough, and rays of light entering the eye can't be properly focussed on the retina.
Symptoms: A farsighted child may have blurred vision, eye strain and headaches. You may notice that he screws up his eyes to see close things, rubs his eyes, has inflamed eyelids and is uninterested in reading.
What can be done: Routine developmental testing for young children by pediatricians and at school includes simple tests for farsight and other visual problems. However, if you suspect that your child may be farsighted, ask your doctor to refer him to an optometrist or an ophthalmologist.

see also p. 82 for the eye

Fat child – *see* Obese child

Fear

Fear is a natural and essential emotion for survival. It's impossible to prevent a child from feeling afraid sometimes, but it's important to recognize what makes a child fearful and to minimize it if possible, if only to reduce distress. Pain, frustration, separation from the mother, the possibility of rejection or failure, darkness, fairy stories and even their own fantasies can all make children afraid.
What can be done: Fear should be taken seriously and never ridiculed, however silly the cause may seem to you. Irrational fear doesn't just disappear, but may go "underground" into the child's unconscious, only to surface at another time. Fear calls for recognition, acceptance and understanding, and the child needs reassurance and love.

Feeding problems

Problems with breastfeeding, bottlefeeding, and giving a baby foods other than milk are common and have many causes, so it's sometimes difficult to sort out exactly what's wrong.
What can be done: Your pediatrician or the LaLeche League (if you are breastfeeding) will be able to give you advice and reassurance.

Fever

Any rise above the normal body temperature (98.4°F/37°C). In young children, a fever is usually the result of an infection.
Symptoms: These include feeling ill, a loss of appetite, fitful sleep, a headache, pain behind the eyes, and perhaps, if the child's temperature is high enough, a febrile convulsion.
What can be done: A high temperature can be lowered by removing your child's clothes and sponging him with tepid water; by giving acetaminophen in the recommended dose for his age; and by giving lots to drink to replace fluid lost as sweat. If the fever is the result of a bacterial infection, your doctor may prescribe antibiotics. If the child is very sick, he may have to be cared for in the hospital.

see also **Convulsions,** *p. 58 for* looking after an ill child, *p. 62 for* taking your child's temperature, *p. 63 for* cooling your child, *and p. 64 for* going into the hospital

Fifth disease

So-called because it was once placed fifth in a list of common infectious illnesses with a similar rash, fifth disease is presumed to be viral. The average incubation period is 16 days (but can range from 7 to 28) and the rash lasts on average 11 days (but can range from 2 to 39).
Symptoms: The cheeks look as though

they've been slapped (hence its other name, slapped cheek disease), and there may also be a blotchy rash on the forearms, lower legs and slightly on the trunk. The rash may itch and it feels worse when the skin is hot. Other symptoms may include a cold, sore throat, headache and diarrhea.
What can be done: No specific treatment exists and your doctor probably won't advise isolating your child. Calamine lotion may sooth the itching and acetaminophen can be given for the headache if necessary.
see also p. 177 for infectious illnesses chart

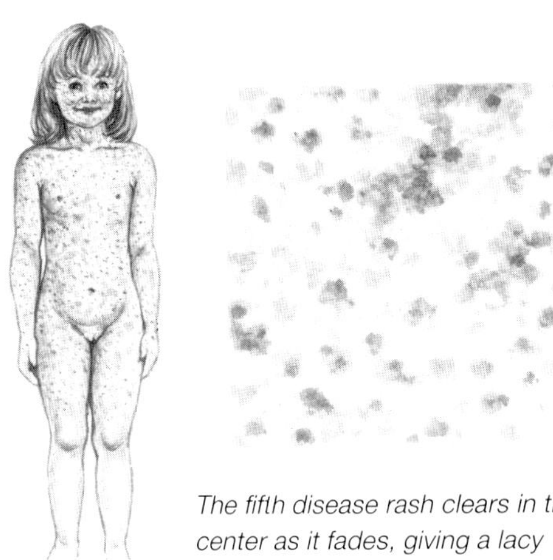

The fifth disease rash clears in the center as it fades, giving a lacy effect.

Flat feet

A condition in which the lengthways arch along the inner side of the foot is flattened. Flat feet are normal in babies, as their feet have pads of fat along the inner sides of the soles. Some children appear to be flat-footed, but when they stand on tiptoe the arches of their feet can be seen.
What can be done: Exercises are of no proven value for flat feet. If your child's feet hurt during exercise, your doctor may suggest that he should see an orthopedic surgeon. Shoes with special supports may be recommended.

Flu – *see* Influenza

Food allergy

Food allergy can give rise to hay fever, eczema, asthma, migraine, celiac disease, milk intolerance and urticaria. It may also lead to such conditions as behavioral disorders and epilepsy. Food allergy is more likely if there is a family history of allergy.
Symptoms: These include a runny nose (hay fever); wheezing (asthma); a cough, fever and shortness of breath (inflammation of the lung); failure to thrive (celiac disease or milk intolerance); diarrhea, blood in the stool, tummy ache with a swollen stomach (celiac disease, milk intolerance or inflammation of the colon); red itchy skin (urticaria or eczema); headache (migraine); and convulsions. Arthritis, earache and behavioral disorders may also be caused by food allergy.
What can be done: Babies in families with an allergic history are best given only breast milk until six months. It is sensible to delay giving the child wheat until at least 8 months, citrus fruit until 9 months, fish until 10 months, cows' milk until 11 months and eggs until 1 year. Nuts, and any food with pips or seeds, are best delayed longer still.

The diagnosis is made by removing the suspect food from the child's diet to see if the symptoms subside. Usually if they're going to they'll clear up in a few days, but sometimes it takes up to three weeks. The elimination and subsequent reintroduction of that food have to be repeated several times to be sure. This is best done under medical supervision, as sometimes several foods are responsible and sometimes reintroducing the suspect food can produce much worse symptoms than before. After a long period of not eating the food that causes the allergy, the child may be better able to tolerate that food in the future.
see also **Asthma, Celiac disease, Eczema, Epilepsy, Food intolerance, Hay fever, Hyperactivity, Migraine, Milk intolerance, Urticaria**

Food intolerance

By no means do all adverse reactions to food indicate an allergy. Some children have an "idiosyncratic" response caused by the lack of an enzyme (for instance, in phenylketonuria or some forms of sugar intolerance). Others are frankly intolerant of certain foods or substances such as cereals (gluten), fish, cheese, tomatoes, strawberries, one of the ingredients in curry powder, green apples, caffeine, and traces of toxic substances. Temporary intolerance to a food can follow gastroenteritis, jaundice or malnutrition. Cows' milk is an example of a food that can cause not only an allergic or an idiosyncratic reaction, but also intolerance.

What can be done: If you are worried about your child's adverse reaction to a food, or foods, discuss it with your doctor.

see also **Allergy, Celiac disease, Food allergy, Milk intolerance, Phenylketonuria, Sugar intolerance**

Food poisoning

An infection of the intestine caused by infected food or drink. Infection with salmonella bacteria is the commonest sort of food poisoning.

Symptoms: Within 8 to 24 hours of eating contaminated food there is a fever, tummy ache, nausea and vomiting, aching limbs and diarrhea. Staphylococcal food poisoning comes on quicker (within 2 to 6 hours).

What can be done: It's very important to give your child plenty to drink. If he won't or can't drink and is becoming dehydrated, call your doctor urgently. Food poisoning can be prevented by scrupulous attention to hygiene during food preparation and storage, and by washing the hands well and drying them with a clean towel after using the bathroom.

Frustration

Being hindered or prevented from doing or having something is a common experience from babyhood onwards. There is always the danger that repeated and unreasonable frustration can lead to feelings of anger which, instead of being expressed, are turned inwards, leading to emotional and perhaps behavioral disorders.

What can be done: Meeting a young baby's needs as soon as possible is sensible. When an older child's desires or actions have to be thwarted, it's best to explain simply why this is so. Children have to learn to cope with frustration as it is a normal part of life.

G

Gastroenteritis

Infection of the gastrointestinal tract, causing inflammation of the small or large intestine and sometimes the stomach. A viral or bacterial infection affects the intestine either primarily or as a complication of infection elsewhere in the body, for example, in the ear of the urinary tract. Rotavirus infection is the commonest cause and is responsible for up to 8 out of 10 cases of severe gastroenteritis in babies in the winter.

Symptoms: Sudden diarrhea, low fever and possibly vomiting which can last from 1 to 7 days. Sometimes there is blood in the stool and tummy ache. Most young children with rotavirus infection have (or have recently had) a respiratory infection. There may be other symptoms specific to the particular infecting organism.

What can be done: In babies, breastfeeding offers some protection, but however a baby is fed, dehydration is the main potential problem and medical help may be necessary. There's no need to encourage a child to eat if he doesn't want to, though recovery from mild gastroenteritis may be quicker if some food is eaten. With severe gastroenteritis, your doctor may suggest giving only clear fluids or an oral electrolyte solution. Some children continue to have diarrhea after the initial illness, and this can be due to damage to the inflamed intestine by sugar or protein, especially milk protein.

see also **Dehydration, Milk intolerance, Sugar intolerance**

German measles

A viral infection, also called rubella, which is mild in young children, but in a nonimmune pregnant woman can kill or damage her baby (with deafness, cataracts or a heart disorder). The incubation period after contact is between 14 and 21 days.

Symptoms: Initially there is a runny nose, sore throat, conjunctivitis, a slightly raised temperature, loss of appetite, swelling of the lymph nodes (glands) behind the ears and at

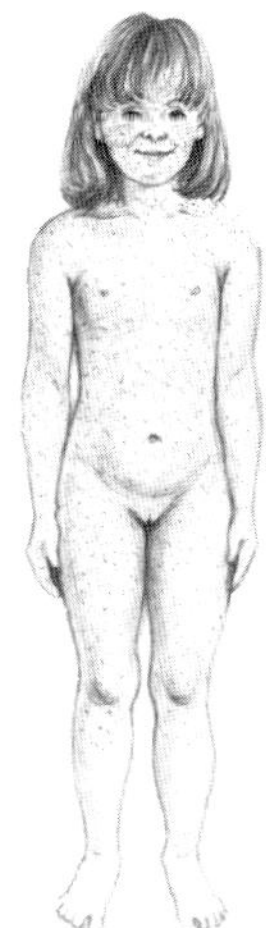

The German measles rash may be fading on the face by the time it reaches the chest.

the back of the neck, and – 24 hours later – a rash on the face which spreads over the body, but spares the feet and ankles and around the mouth. The flat pink spots may converge so that the skin looks red all over; they may itch; and they usually disappear within 3 days.
What can be done: If you know your unimmunized child has been in contact with German measles, keep him away from any woman who may be pregnant for up to 21 days afterwards, by which time either the rash will have come out or you'll know it isn't going to. If an unimmunized pregnant woman is exposed to German measles, an antibody test should be done urgently.

A child with German measles doesn't usually feel too bad and needs no specific treatment, except perhaps something to soothe the sore throat. He could theoretically be infectious from 7 days before the rash appears and for up to 8 days after it has gone. However, once the rash appears, the child will probably only be infectious for up to 5 days.

Preventive immunizing is routinely required at 15 months for all children.

see also **Cataract, Conjunctivitis, Heart disease and abnormality,** *and p. 177 for* infectious illnesses chart

Gingivitis

Inflammation of the gums which can be caused by poor dental hygiene, mumps, herpes infection, the antiepileptic drug phenytoin, and – rarely – by bacterial infection in a chronically malnourished child.
Symptoms: The gums are swollen, spongy, reddish-blue, tender and liable to bleed.
What can be done: If the gum disease is caused by too much plaque on the teeth, alter your child's diet so it contains less added sugar and fewer refined white flour products. Regular efficient toothbrushing helps remove plaque. A child with mumps will benefit from frequent antibacterial mouthwashes to prevent gingivitis.

see also **Herpes, Mumps,** *and p. 37 for* caring for teeth

Glomerulonephritis

This is an inflammation of the kidney, caused by an immune reaction following a streptococcal sore throat. Boys are affected more often than girls.
Symptoms: There is blood in the urine, swelling of the face and ankles, high blood pressure, a headache, fever and tummy ache.
What can be done: Your doctor will advise you about treatment. Glomerulonephritis sometimes needs treatment in the hospital, but most children recover within 3 weeks.

Gluten enteropathy – *see* Celiac disease

Goiter

A swelling of the thyroid gland in front of the neck, for which there are many possible causes in a baby. Children over the age of 6 can develop a goiter known as lymphocytic thyroiditis. This is thought to be an auto-immune disorder and is more common in girls than in boys.
Symptoms: These vary, depending on whether the thyroid gland is over- or under-active. Sometimes, however, a child with a goiter has a normally active thyroid gland.

An underactive gland in a baby causes hypothyroidism. An underactive goiter that develops in an older child results in less disturbance of growth and development, but can cause skin and hair changes, constipation, sleepiness and mental slowing.

An overactive gland (hyperthyroidism) is less common and is associated with emotional disturbances, irritability and excitability, shaking of the fingers, a large appetite but no increase in weight, protrusion of the eyes, a flushed sweaty skin, weakness and heart problems.
What can be done: Some goiters present at birth disappear spontaneously, while others need treatment. Lymphocyctic thyroiditis may have to be treated with thyroid hormones. Other sorts of goiter need regular expert assessment to determine whether the child's thyroid hormones need to be boosted with additional thyroid hormone, or suppressed by surgery, radioactive drugs or with antithyroid medicines.

see also **Hypothyroidism**

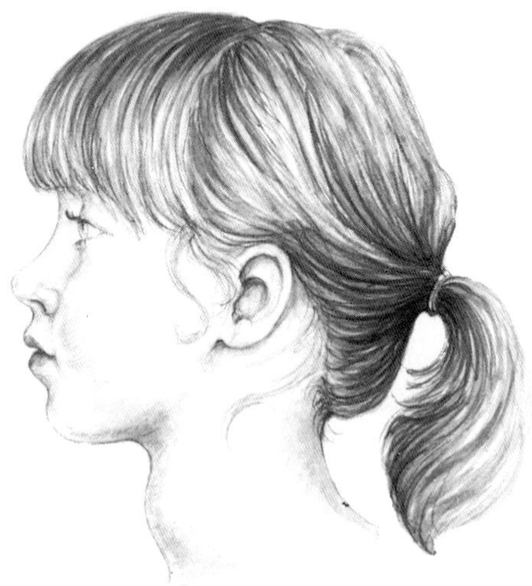

A main cause of goiter is lymphocyctic thyroiditis.

Growing pains

These vague aches and pains in the legs are quite common in childhood.
Symptoms: The aches usually occur in the evening or at night, and may be bad enough to wake the child. Moving the legs makes no difference.
What can be done: Massage and keeping the legs warm sometimes help. It has been suggested that growing pains happen after a lot of exercise, but whatever the cause, they always disappear in time.

Gum abscess

A contained collection of infected pus usually around the root of a tooth.
Symptoms: There is nearly always decay in, or damage to, the tooth, and it hurts when it is tapped or pressed, or when there are temperature changes in the mouth as with hot or cold drinks or food. The pus in the abscess may find its way out by pointing through the gum, in which case you may notice that the gum becomes progressively more red, tender and swollen until a head of pus appears and then breaks. Alternatively it may point through the bone and cause deeper-seated pain.
What can be done: Take your child to the dentist as soon as you can, so that the pus can be safely let out. The dentist may remove the tooth if it's a baby tooth and badly decayed, or carry out a root canal treatment during a series of visits.

Gum cyst

A small pearly-white swelling on a baby's gum which looks as though it may be the tip of a tooth about to break through, but isn't. Such a cyst is painless and disappears spontaneously.

H

Habits

Comfort habits and "nervous" habits have a variety of underlying causes. Some start as a comforting mechanism during a time of anxiety, fear, loneliness or boredom, while others are the result of imitating another child or adult. Some children discover the activity by chance and continue simply because they enjoy it, and an initial illness may spark off certain habits, such as repeated coughing and sniffing. Thumb sucking, nail biting, rocking, crib rocking, head banging, hair twirling or pulling, nose picking, rubbing the nose and blinking are some of the more common habits.

Sometimes a child may behave in a certain

ritualized way, such as chewing his food many times before swallowing it, or putting his shoes into a neat pair at night and rechecking several times that they are tidy. This type of behavior can be a way of preventing unpleasant feelings from surfacing in the child's mind.

What can be done: Whatever the original cause of a long-standing habit, you can't automatically assume that it continues to hold true. It's sensible to look out for an underlying emotional problem, just in case, as otherwise the trouble may surface in another way. Make sure that your child is getting enough time, affection and attention, but try not to focus this on the habit itself, or he will use it to gain attention. Praising him for not doing whatever it is is much more helpful than nagging.

If your child's obsessional behavior is worrying you, seek help from your family doctor who may refer you to a specialist if necessary.

see also **Blinking, Nail biting, Thumb sucking**

Hair twirling or pulling – *see* Habits

Halitosis

Poor dental hygiene or actual dental decay are the commonest causes of halitosis (bad breath), though a dry mouth during a fever and conditions such as tonsilitis, appendicitis, hepatitis and pneumonia can be the cause. Constipation doesn't cause bad breath, but the sort of highly refined diet that leads to constipation is likely to be associated with bad teeth. Some children have bad breath for no apparent reason.

What can be done: Consult your doctor if your child is sick and you want advice. Check on the child's teeth and take him to the dentist regularly. The dentist or dental hygienist will teach your child how to clean his teeth more efficiently if necessary. It's sensible to change your child's diet to one high in fiber and low in refined carbohydrates (including sugar) and fat.

see also **Appendicitis, Dental caries, Hepatitis, Pneumonia, Tonsillitis,** *and p. 37 for* caring for teeth

Hay fever

Hay fever itself is caused by an allergic response to certain pollens, but the term is loosely applied to allergic rhinitis (inflammation of the nasal passages caused by allergy) which can also be the result of other triggers, or allergens, such as house dust, certain foods and drugs, animal fur and carpet underlay. This is why so-called hay fever may be present at any time of year.

Symptoms: The mucous membranes lining the nose are inflamed, with swelling and a discharge causing a blocked nose, redness, itching, sneezing, itchy and watery eyes, and a headache. The symptoms last for hours or days at a time, depending partly on the pollen count or on the proximity of the allergen. Some children also have earache and deafness if the allergic swelling affects the Eustachian tubes. Secondary bacterial infection can complicate the picture because allergic inflammation seems to make the child more vulnerable to infection.

What can be done: If possible, keep the child away from the source of the allergy. Drugs, such as cromolyn sodium, help prevent allergic rhinitis, and antihistamines and decongestant nose drops are useful during an attack.

see also **Allergy**

Headaches

Pain in the head isn't a common complaint in young children and must always be taken seriously. Possible causes include fever, dehydration, emotional problems such as anxiety or depression, eyestrain or stormy weather. Other reasons may be a head injury, meningitis, an epileptic seizure (the headache comes before or after the seizure), some drugs (such as antihistamines), or a brain tumor.

What can be done: If there seems to be nothing to worry about, simply make sure your child has enough to drink, let him be quiet, and give him some acetaminophen if necessary. Tell your doctor if your child's headache is persistent, sudden, severe, present on waking, or repeated. Any headache associated with unexplained or worrying symptoms, or signs such as vomiting, a stiff neck, a bulging fontanelle (soft spot) in a baby, visual problems, or an unaccountable change in mood or behavior needs medical help urgently.

see also **Cancer, Epilepsy, Fever, Meningitis,** *and p. 200 for* head injury

Head-banging – *see* Habits

Heart disease and abnormality

The major routine well-child checkups after birth and during the first years of a child's life include an examination of the heart for abnormality. This means that any condition which is present at birth, or develops early on, is likely to be detected quickly. Heart disease is unusual in children, but the two conditions most often seen are a narrowing of one of the heart valves and a hole between the two sides of the heart. In a very few babies, the heart is in the right side of the chest instead of the left.

Symptoms: Any severe disorder of the heart produces rapid breathing, a poor color and perhaps swelling of the limbs.

What can be done: Modern surgical techniques can overcome many of even the most serious heart defects, and children are often able to lead a normal active life.

Heart murmur

This is a noise made by blood flowing through the heart or larger blood vessels. A murmur of some sort is present in nearly half of all newborn babies. Most of these murmurs are innocent, but are followed up routinely in order to pinpoint those few children who have a heart defect. Certain murmurs are strongly suggestive of a heart abnormality and further tests are then done as soon as possible.

see also **Heart disease and abnormality**

Heat rash – *see* Prickly heat

Heatstroke – *see* Emergencies and first aid p.210

Hemophilia

An inherited disorder of blood clotting affecting males almost exclusively, but passed on by females.

Symptoms: These include easy bruising, often first noticed as a toddler learns to walk, with difficult-to-stop bleeding on injury. Bleeding into the joints is one of the worst problems as it is not only painful, but also causes swelling, reduces movement and can lead to long-term joint damage unless the child has expert and immediate treatment.

What can be done: Consult your doctor. Children with hemophilia need sensible protection against everyday injury and good preventive dentistry. Bleeding episodes are treated with transfusions of blood or of the specific missing clotting factors. If you have a family history of hemophilia, or already have a child with this disorder, you may wish to consult a genetic counselor before having another child.

see also p. 216 for useful addresses

Hepatitis

The usual cause of hepatitis (inflammation of the liver) is a viral infection. Infectious hepatitis (hepatitis A) and serum hepatitis (hepatitis B) are the two main types. Infectious hepatitis is spread by fecal contamination, and serum hepatitis by contaminated syringes or needles or by blood contact. A mother can pass hepatitis to her unborn baby.

Symptoms: There is enlargement and tenderness of the liver, jaundice, dark urine, pale bowel movements, bad breath and a general feeling of being ill. Symptoms of serum hepatitis are usually milder than infectious hepatitis and may be associated with arthritis and a rash. (After-effects can also be more serious and longer lasting.)

What can be done: There is no specific treatment apart from rest and diet high in protein and calories. Immune globulin injections are sometimes given to protect children who have been in contact with hepatitis or to reduce the risk of catching it in areas where it is prevalent. There is now a vaccine available to protect against hepatitis B.

see also **Arthritis, Jaundice**

Hernia

A muscular weakness which allows the abnormal protrusion of part of the body. The two most common hernias (ruptures) in childhood are umbilical and inguinal hernias.
Symptoms: An umbilical hernia can be seen and felt as a soft lump at the belly button (umbilicus) and can be pushed back gently into the abdomen, though it will come out again right away. A large hernia can contain both intestine and fat, and is fairly common in black children.

An inguinal hernia is usually felt as a soft lump in the groin, though it may go down into the scrotum or vulvar lip on one side. A hernia gets bigger when the child coughs, cries or strains, but isn't usually painful or tender.
What can be done: An umbilical hernia is best left alone as the weak area is likely to close spontaneously. An operation is done for the few children who have a persistent hernia after the age of about 5. An inguinal hernia is repaired surgically because of the risk of complications. If your child's hernial lump begins to hurt, changes color, can't easily be pushed back, or becomes swollen or tense, consult your doctor urgently.

Herpes

Herpes simplex is the virus that causes primary herpes infections (including neonatal herpes and – in adults – genital herpes) and cold sores. The infection is caught by contact with an infected person, for instance, by kissing someone with a cold sore, or during birth if the mother has genital herpes.

Herpes zoster is the virus that causes chickenpox and shingles.
Symptoms: The first infection with herpes simplex is common, nearly always very mild, and most often affects the mouth. Small blisters in the mouth and on the lips may ulcerate. The gums are inflamed and there may be a fever, a coated tongue, bad breath, swollen lymph nodes (glands) in the neck and a feeling of being ill. In newborn, severely malnourished, or eczematous babies, the primary infection can be much more serious.
What can be done: A mild primary infection clears up in a few days, but the viruses lie dormant and can be reactivated later to produce cold sores. An antiviral drug has been used with some success to treat neonatal herpes and severe cases of herpes.
see also **Chickenpox, Cold scores, Gingivitis**

Hiccups

Hiccups are repeated, uncontrollable contractions of the diaphragm. Some babies naturally hiccup more than others, and an overfull stomach, indigestion, and certain minor illnesses may cause hiccups in an older child.
What can be done: They rarely last for long and are not usually harmful. Popular remedies for an older child vary from holding the breath while counting to 10, to trying to drink a glass of water from the far side of the glass. If the hiccups don't stop after a few hours, consult your doctor.

Hip dislocation

Between 4 and 11 babies in every 1,000 are born with an unstable hip joint in which the head of the femur (thighbone) is unstable and may spontaneously dislocate from its socket in the pelvic bone. The condition is commoner in girls, first-born children, winter babies and babies born by a breech birth. It used to be common for the first signs of an unstable hip to be noticed only when a child was learning to walk, and sometimes even later. Routine medical examination of all babies has helped prevent the possible long-term deformity of the leg which can result from bearing weight on an undiagnosed dislocated hip.
What can be done: If you suspect that there is something wrong with your baby's hip (for instance, if you feel a "click" in the hip when playing with your baby or changing a diaper), tell your doctor. Treatment usually involves splinting the hip for 6 to 12 weeks, if the problem is discovered before the baby starts to walk, but may be more complicated if left longer.

Hoarseness

This results from any condition affecting the vocal cords in the larynx (voice box). It can be caused by straining the voice (by screaming,

crying, or too much singing, for example), croup, laryngitis, and allergy. Less common causes include something the child has swallowed stuck in the larynx, injury to the larynx, diphtheria, and a condition present at birth in which the larynx is abnormally soft and tends to collapse with each in-breath. This last problem tends to cure itself within a year or so.
Symptoms: There is distortion and muffling of the voice, and in extreme cases the voice is lost completely.
What can be done: Warm drinks, keeping the neck warm, and humidifying the air are all helpful. The underlying cause should be found and treated if necessary.
see also **Allergy, Croup, Diphtheria, Laryngitis**

Hookworms – *see* Worms

Hydrocele

A harmless collection of fluid around the testis, most commonly present at, or soon after, birth.
Symptoms: One half of the scrotum looks and feels slightly swollen.
What can be done: It gets better by itself, usually within the first year. A hydrocele which tends to enlarge towards the end of the day is likely to be associated with an inguinal hernia. If a hydrocele hasn't gone by the age of 4 to 5, it can be removed by a minor operation.
see also **Hernia**

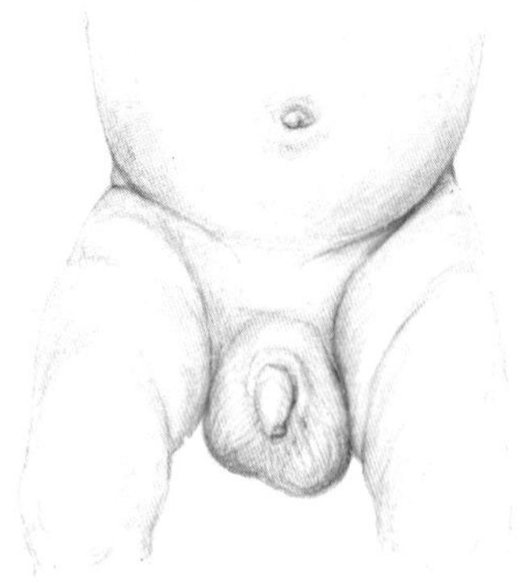

The doctor may shine a light behind the scrotum, which glows through the fluid in the hydrocele.

Hydrocephalus

An excess of cerebrospinal fluid in and around the brain, also known as water on the brain. The commonest reason is a congenital malformation of the brain that blocks the normal flow of the fluid. Congenital hydrocephalus is sometimes associated with spina bifida. Sometimes the condition can be diagnosed during pregnancy, but usually it isn't apparent until the baby is a few weeks or months old. Hydrocephalus appearing later may be caused by meningitis or a tumor.
Symptoms: There is abnormal skull growth which can be detected early by routine head measurement during checkups. Other signs include a bulging fontanelle (soft spot), a shiny thin scalp, a bulging forehead, and whites of the eyes which are clearly visible above the iris.
What can be done: Surgical treatment involves the insertion of tiny drains (shunts) to reroute the fluid round the blockage. The outlook for children with hydrocephalus varies, but many suffer from associated mental or physical handicap.
see also **Cancer, Meningitis, Mental retardation, Physical handicap, Spina bifida,** *and p. 216 for* useful addresses

Hyperactivity

A term used to describe children who are particularly overactive. A child's level of activity varies according to the time of day, his age, health, emotional state, fatigue, amount of stimulation, and diet. Normal children are overactive sometimes, but hyperactive children are active for much of the time compared with their peers and have shorter attention spans.
Symptoms: Hyperactivity can often be traced back to the earliest months, when the baby was very alert and active. There may have been feeding problems and colic, and the baby probably slept far less than expected. An older child is fidgety, restless and can't sit still. He has a short attention span and finds it difficult to concentrate, to follow instructions or to learn from mistakes. He is easily frustrated and has a tendency to do things impulsively. Because of this behavioral pattern, hyperactive children often have learning disabilities although they may be

normally intelligent. Criticism and punishment from parents and teachers, together with possible unpopularity among other children, often lead to emotional problems and further behavioral difficulties. The child has low self-esteem and may become depressed.
What can be done: The family doctor or pediatrician are unlikely to discover any medical problems, though a very few hyperactive children have an overactive thyroid gland, some degree of lead poisoning, or some sort of mental retardation or psychiatric disorder. Some children seem to be hyperactive as a result of their diet, and it's worth trying a diet low in refined foods, foods containing additives, and foods particularly likely to cause allergy. Supervision by a dietitian is helpful if you decide to test for allergy. It's best to avoid overtiring or overstimulating a hyperactive child, and to give him a predictable daily routine and firm limits reinforced by rewards rather than punishment. Both parents and teachers may need extra support if they are to provide an encouraging, accepting background. Drug treatment may be necessary in some cases.
see also **Food allergy, Lead poisoning,** *and p. 216 for* useful addresses

Hypoglycemia – *see* Low blood sugar

Hypospadias

A condition present from birth in which a boy's urinary opening – normally at the tip of the penis – opens underneath the tip or further back along the underside of its shaft.
What can be done: An operation is necessary only if the opening is very displaced or if it allows too poor a stream of urine.

Hypothermia – *see* Emergencies and first aid p. 211

Hypothyroidism

Hypothyroidism, or lack of thyroid hormone, can lead to cretinism. It affects about 1 out of 3,500-4,000 white infants and about 1 out of 30,000 black infants, and can be difficult to diagnose early without a blood test. A lack of iodine in the pregnant mother's or baby's diet can also be the cause of hypothyroidism, though this is rare in the western world.
Symptoms: An untreated baby is sluggish, cold and cries little; is constipated; has thick yellow coarse skin, a large tongue and a distended tummy, perhaps with an umbilical hernia or a goiter; doesn't grow well; and has dry thin brittle hair and a hoarse deep cry. Eventually there is irreversible brain damage.
What can be done: Early treatment with thyroxine (thyroid extract) can improve the condition dramatically. All hospitals are now routinely testing for hypothyroidism using the blood taken for the Guthrie test.

Hypothyroidism from a lack of dietary iodine can be prevented by eating iodine-rich foods such as fish.
see also **Epilepsy, Goiter, Hernia**

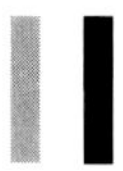

I

Impetigo

A highly contagious bacterial infection of the skin. Impetigo can complicate eczema, cold sores, urticaria, or scabies.
Symptoms: There are small red pimples which soon break down and weep, forming

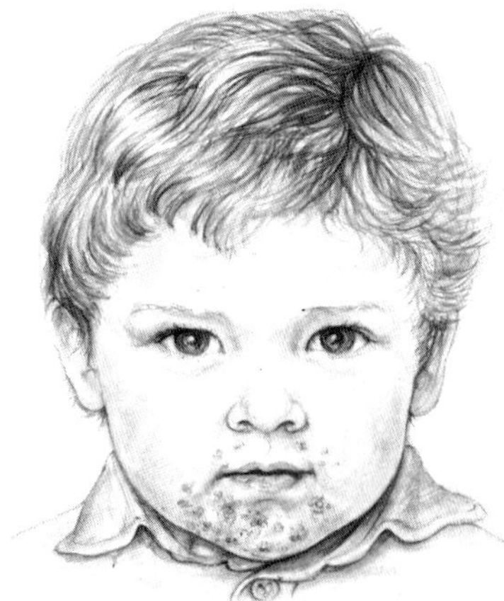

Impetigo rash can be distinguished by the yellow-brown crusts.

yellow-brown crusts. Healing is from the center, leaving rings of reddened skin.
What can be done: Your doctor will prescribe antibiotic ointment which cures impetigo quickly, but sometimes antibiotic medicine is needed too. Wash your hands well after touching your child's impetigo and discourage him from touching the infected skin.
see also **Cold sores, Eczema, Scabies, Urticaria**

Indigestion

Discomfort after overeating, eating too quickly, or eating foods which disagree can occur at any age. In babies, it is usually called colic and older children say they have a tummy ache. Any unexplained abdominal pain that doesn't get better within a few hours or which recurs should be reported to your doctor.
see also **Colic, Tummy ache**

Infectious mononucleosis

This viral illness is passed on in saliva. It rarely occurs in children under the age of 2 years.
Symptoms: These include a prolonged but low fever, tiredness and a general feeling of being ill, a sore throat, headache, swollen lymph nodes (glands) in the neck, and depression (which may last for months). Sometimes there is a slight rash, and mild hepatitis is common.
What can be done: The severity of this infection is very variable and there is no specific treatment. Your doctor may suggest that your child stays at home for some time and avoids undue exertion.
see also **Hepatitis,** *and p. 58 for* looking after an ill child

Influenza

A viral infection of the upper respiratory tract which tends to occur in epidemics.
Symptoms: The usual signs of a cold and a sore throat are followed by a fever, sweating, aches and pains in the limbs and back, painful eyes, and sometimes a cough, vomiting, diarrhea, croup or a nosebleed.
What can be done: There is no specific treatment, but secondary bacterial infections, such as middle ear infection, sinusitis, mastoiditis and pneumonia, call for antibiotics. Plenty of fluid is essential to replace that lost by sweating or with diarrhea and vomiting. Because flu viruses change so quickly and because there are so many types, immunity is short-lived.
see also **Croup, Mastoiditis, Otitis media, Pneumonia, Sinusitis,** *and p. 204 for* nosebleed

Inherited diseases and disorders – *see* Congenital malformations

Intestinal obstruction

A condition in which the intestine is unable to make its contents move along. There may be a physical obstruction, such as a twisted inguinal hernia or a volvulus, or the nerve supply to the intestine may be affected so it can't move properly, such as sometimes occurs in peritonitis.
Symptoms: The abdomen is swollen, but there may be little or no pain. Sometimes the child vomits a brown or green fluid.
What can be done: Tell your doctor at once if your child's tummy is swollen and he is ill.
see also **Hernia, Peritonitis, Volvulus**

Intoeing – *see* Pigeon toe

Irritability

Some children are naturally more touchy and quick to anger than others. Unusual irritability can have many causes, including coming down with an infection; recovering from an illness; tiredness; the normal physiological "down time" of the day; hunger; the sudden fall of blood sugar that occurs if the last meal was high in refined carbohydrate; unaccustomed excitement; teething; unhappiness and anxiety; and imitating the mood of someone close.
see also **Low blood sugar**

Itching

Itching is caused by many things: dry skin (from bathtime toiletries or sunburn); certain medications, household or other chemicals, cosmetics and plants; skin conditions such as eczema and urticaria; being too hot; fungal infections; some childhood infections; jaundice; kidney failure; diabetes; poor hygiene; pinworms; insect bites and stings; and tension and worry.
What can be done: The first thing to do is to discover the cause, with the help of your doctor if necessary, and if possible remove it. Itching can usually be successfully treated with skin applications or medicines recommended by your doctor.

see also **Allergy, Athlete's foot, Diabetes mellitus, Eczema, Jaundice, Kidney failure, Prickly heat, Ringworm, Scabies, Urticaria, Vaginal discharge, Worms,** *and p. 207 for* bites and stings

I J K

Jaundice

Jaundice may result from hepatitis or from taking certain drugs. In a baby, it may be caused by immaturity of the liver. Congenital abnormalities of the bile system, hypothyroidism, and internal bleeding can also lead to jaundice, as can almost any infection in a young baby.
Symptoms: Yellow staining of the skin and the whites of the eyes.
What can be done: Consult your doctor if you are worried about your baby's color.

see also **Hepatitis**

Jealousy

The emotions experienced with jealousy – envy, resentment, fear and suspicion – are uncomfortable and unpleasant, and tend also to be destructive of the previous relationship with the person they are directed towards. One of the main problems when it comes to jealousy of a child towards a new sibling is that the basis for the resentment is in fact very real; the child will never again have the same amount of attention from his parents. Another is the difficulty that most children have in learning that you can feel both love and hate towards the same person, and that the one doesn't shut out the other.
What can be done: Help your child not to think of himself as bad for having feelings of jealousy, which are after all quite normal. Let him know you understand and still love him.

Kidney failure

Shock, blood loss, burns, overwhelming infection and severe dehydration, as well as several kidney diseases, including glomerulonephritis, can lead to a reduction of the kidneys' filtering power serious enough to alter the body's chemical balance. This is known as kidney failure.
Symptoms: If the kidneys fail quickly, you will notice that your child is passing little or no urine, looks puffy, is drowsy and breathing fast, and may have convulsions. If the failure has developed slowly, the child may have headaches, stop eating, feel sick or actually vomit, and look pale. After a time, you may notice that he stops growing and has bone and joint pains, cramps, concentrates poorly and his skin becomes itchy and dry. At first, he drinks a lot and urinates frequently, but this changes until he is urinating very little.
What can be done: Apart from treating the underlying problem, your doctor will correct the chemical imbalance and put your child on a special diet. Your child may need drugs for high blood pressure as well. If the kidney failure continues, regular dialysis may be started and a kidney transplant considered.

see also p. 79 for dialysis, *and p. 216 for* useful addresses

Knock knees

The knees are close together, but the lower legs are splayed apart. Some children have just one affected knee. Some degree of knock knees is normal in young children, but most legs will have straightened out by about the age of 6. The commonest cause is obesity, and they may occur with rickets.
What can be done: It's best to seek a

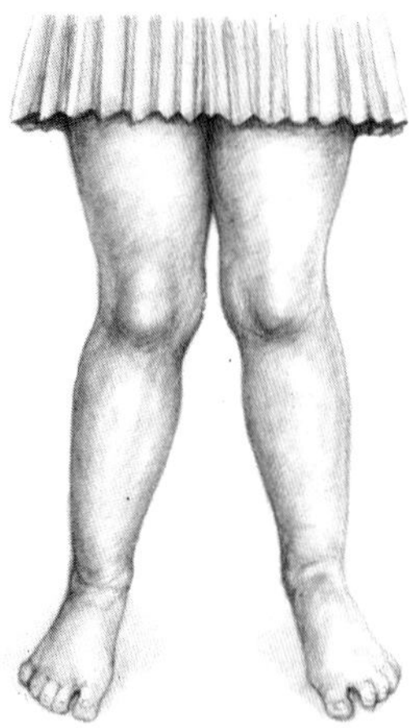

Knock knees often become obvious when a child is about 3 years old.

medical opinion, though the most likely outcome is that the child will be observed at regular intervals for signs of improvement.

see also **Obese child, Rickets**

L

Lactose intolerance – *see* Milk intolerance

Laryngitis

An inflammation of the larynx (voice box) usually caused by a viral infection and most common in winter. Laryngitis may be a complication of a cold, flu or various childhood infections. An infection of the trachea, lung or middle ear may follow laryngitis.

Symptoms: Hoarseness is the main problem; other symptoms can include a sore throat, fever, dry cough and croup.

What can be done: Humidification of the air (with a humidifier, or a kettle boiling safely in the room) is the most effective treatment for simple laryngitis, and antibiotics are prescribed only if there seems to be a bacterial infection. If your child has difficulty in breathing, get medical help at once.

see also **Croup**

Laziness

Laziness in children, as in adults, is most likely to be a simple lack of interest in doing what is required by others, or a wish for it to be done for them. However, it's worth remembering that tiredness, illness or coming down with an illness, poor eyesight or hearing, unhappiness or even actual depression can lead to a child being wrongly labeled "lazy." Pejorative labels such as this are rarely helpful to children, because a child tends to believe that they are permanent and so, however unconsciously, tries to live up to them.

What can be done: Encouragement, example and making attractive whatever it is you want your child to do are more likely to discourage laziness than nagging or threats.

Lead poisoning

A condition caused by the accumulation of excessive amounts of lead in the body, which can result from inhaling lead-containing gas fumes. Some types of putty, old paint and certain cosmetics are other sources of lead.

Symptoms: An affected child has tummy aches, occasional vomiting, anemia, a poor appetite and constipation, and may be irritable, hyperactive, aggressive or lethargic. Recently-gained skills may be lost if the poisoning is severe, and there may even be convulsions or a coma.

What can be done: Medical treatment includes removing the source of lead, treating anemia and prescribing drugs which make the lead pass out of the body.

see also **Anemia**

Left-handedness

About 1 in 10 boys and slightly fewer girls are left-handed. Babies tend to use both hands equally at first and gradually show a preference. Only a few change hands. Sometimes a delay in becoming definitely right- or left-handed is associated with learning problems later. Being left-handed can be a nuisance, but it shouldn't be a serious handicap. Writing can be difficult at first, as the letters formed tend to be hidden by the left hand. Never try to make your child use his right hand if he prefers his left one.

Leukemia

This is cancer of the white blood cells and is the most common childhood cancer. The causes are not yet clear, but both genetic and environmental factors play a part.
Symptoms: Early general symptoms include loss of appetite, irritability, lethargy and paleness. Other signs include easy bruising and bleeding, fever, and pains in the limbs and joints. The child may have had a viral respiratory infection or a rash a few weeks before, from which he has not fully recovered. Some children have swollen lymph nodes (glands), which can be felt in the neck, armpits and groin, and some have a headache and may vomit. The commonest form of leukemia, acute lymphocytic leukemia, occurs most often at 3 to 4 years old.
What can be done: The treatment of leukemia includes drugs, radiotherapy, blood transfusions and bone marrow transplants. The likelihood of prolonged remission or cure has improved greatly in recent years. Caring for a child who is receiving treatment (which may be unpleasant), or for a child who is dying or in whom a remission seems to be ending, is exhausting. Thankfully, we're now much more aware of the need for emotional support for both the parents and children.
see also **Cancer, Dying,** *and p. 216 for* useful addresses

Limping

A condition in which a child walks with an uneven step. Causes of limping include a foot injury, badly fitting shoes, a verruca, Perthes' disease, an infection of the hip joint, and congenital dislocation of the hip.
Symptoms: The affected leg takes the body weight for only a short time before the good hip takes over, giving the child's gait a dip towards the problem side.
What can be done: The treatment of a limp depends on the underlying condition, so, unless the cause is easy to correct, your child should be seen by your doctor.
see also **Hip dislocation, Perthes' disease, Warts,** *and p. 38 for* foot care

Lisping

The commonest sort of lisping is when "s" and "z" are pronounced as "th." Lisping may be a temporary developmental phenomenon, or may happen for a time after the front teeth have been lost and while the second teeth are growing down. Dental deformities, a cleft palate and deafness can also cause lisping.
What can be done: Speech therapy may be recommended for some children.
see also **Cleft palate, Deafness**

Low birth weight

A term used to describe a baby who weighs below 5.5 pounds (2.5 k) at birth. Seven per cent of newborns are of low birth weight, and of these 2 out of 3 are born before 37 weeks of pregnancy, so are premature (pre-term). Some babies are premature simply because their mothers normally have a short pregnancy. Other reasons for prematurity include pre-eclamptic toxemia (high blood pressure with swollen ankles and protein in the urine), diabetes or bleeding in the mother, or multiple pregnancy. Other low-birth-weight babies are lighter than expected for the length of the pregnancy, and may or may not be premature as well. They are referred to as "small-for-dates" or "dysmature." Smoking during pregnancy can make a baby small-for-dates, as can a placenta that isn't working well. A low-birth-weight baby may be born spontaneously, or – if the problem is recognized during pregnancy – the obstetrician may induce labor early or do a Caesarian section. Low-birth-weight babies are watched carefully; but in time, they tend to catch up with children of the same age who were of normal birth weight.
see also **Anemia, Jaundice**

Low blood sugar

This is a state in which there is too little glucose in the blood. It's relatively common in

newborn babies, particularly small-for-dates or pre-term ones. Causes include diabetes in the mother, malnutrition, severe illness, and some rare hormone and enzyme abnormalities. The commonest cause of low blood sugar (hypoglycemia) in older children is an inability to maintain blood sugar levels after illness, vomiting, not enough to eat, or a highly refined diet. Some children who eat a lot of refined carbohydrate have an abrupt swing of blood sugar to a peak (which makes them feel "high"), followed by a correspondingly abrupt swing down, when they experience symptoms of hypoglycemia. Episodes of low blood sugar, called "insulin reactions," occur in some diabetic children.
Symptoms: Low blood sugar can cause many symptoms and each child tends to have his own pattern. In school-age children, it commonly occurs in the morning. Often there is sweating, paleness, tiredness, yawning, hunger, a fast pulse, anxiety, shakiness, forgetfulness, weepiness and sensitivity to noise. There may be a headache, lack of concentration, confusion, and even convulsions and unusual behavior. A child used to a sugary refined diet may crave more sugar in the form of sweets, cookies, or sweet drinks, and refuse the unrefined carbohydrate he needs, so creating a vicious circle. Hypoglycemia can be difficult to identify in babies, but convulsions, poor feeding, lethargy, sleepiness, twitching, sweating and rolling of the eyes may be seen.
What can be done: Newborn babies in whom there is any suspicion of low blood sugar are carefully watched in the hospital. If you suspect your child is suffering from low blood sugar, discuss it with your doctor.
see also **Diabetes mellitus, Malnutrition,** *and p. 28 for* diet

Lying

Children lie for different reasons. It may be done to avoid displeasure from other people, to show off or boast, as a form of fantasy, or even to spare other people's feelings. Lying needs to be handled with tact and gentleness from the beginning, so a child realizes that speaking untruthfully with the intention to mislead or deceive is not the best way to behave. A lot of learning occurs by example, so if you are in the habit of telling white lies, your child will learn to do so too. If your child lies because he's done something wrong and is frightened of the punishment, consider whether your discipline is too strict. Loving guidance is the best way to discourage children from lying.

Lymphoma – *see* Cancer

Malabsorption

A condition in which the stomach and/or the small and large intestine don't adequately digest or absorb the nutrient content of food. The most common causes of malabsorption in the developed world are gastroenteritis, cystic fibrosis and celiac disease.
Symptoms: If many nutrients are being poorly absorbed, the child has a swollen tummy, large, pale and very smelly stool, muscle wasting, and poor weight gain and growth.
What can be done: The first thing is for your pediatrician to establish and treat the cause of the problem. The majority of children with mild malabsorption have had an episode of gastroenteritis from which the intestine hasn't recovered. In this case, sugar and protein (particularly milk protein) are liable to further damage the intestine lining and your doctor will advise you to cut these out of your child's diet for a while, while ensuring that he is adequately nourished with other foods.
see also **Celiac disease, Cystic fibrosis, Gastroenteritis,** *and p. 94 for* the digestive system

Malnutrition

A term meaning "bad nutrition" which is usually used when a child doesn't have enough food, or enough of the right kinds of food. However, having too much food or too much of certain foods can also be bad for the health. Malabsorption or maldigestion of food can also lead to malnutrition. Over the years there has been considerable controversy about what constitutes a "healthy" diet, but experts seem finally to have arrived at a consensus which makes life easier for parents and those who prepare food for children.

see also **Malabsorption,** *and p. 28 for* diet

Mastoiditis

An inflammation of the mastoid bone and the sinuses behind the ear, usually caused by chronic bacterial infection spread from long-standing middle ear infection (chronic otitis media). Mastoiditis is potentially dangerous because if untreated the infection could spread to involve the brain. It is much less common now that antibiotics are used when necessary to control otitis media.
Symptoms: As well as symptoms of acute otitis media, there is pain, tenderness, swelling and redness of the mastoid area behind the ear. The ear may be pushed forwards and down a little by the swelling.
What can be done: Your doctor will give penicillin injections and the ENT (ear, nose and throat) surgeon will drain the fluid from the middle ear. This is usually effective, but if not, surgery may be needed to clear the infection.

see also **Otitis media,** *and p. 84 for* the ear

Masturbation

Excitement of the genitals by handling them or rubbing them against something in order to cause sexual pleasure or even an orgasm. Young children often play with their genitals, and most soon discover that it feels pleasant. Boys seem to masturbate in childhood more than girls, but perhaps that is because the penis is so available and easy to play with. Girls masturbate too, but more secretly. Masturbation becomes more common at puberty in both sexes. Though some people feel uneasy about their children masturbating, it's quite natural and an almost universal phenomenon. Making an issue of stopping your child doing it may make him or her feel that there's something bad about touching the genitals.
What can be done: Simply and gently tell your young child not to handle the genitals in front of other people so he or she learns that masturbation is something that is done in private. If your child masturbates frequently, consider whether there is undue emotional stress around, and if so, try to give more loving support and security.

Measles

This is one of the most common infectious diseases in the world, although not very common in the US because of routine immunization. It is a viral infection and tends to occur in epidemics. The viruses are spread by droplet infection from an infected person coughing, sneezing, or speaking. The incubation period is from 10 to 12 days, but the child may be infectious to others within 7 days of contact.
Symptoms: There is a slightly raised temperature, conjunctivitis, dislike of the light, a dry cough, a cold, and perhaps Koplik's spots (small white spots) inside the mouth. A rash of small flat red spots appears on the third or fourth day, when the temperature rises sharply. The child stops eating, has a tummy ache, and swollen lymph nodes (glands) in his neck. There may be diarrhea and vomiting too. The rash is usually first seen on the face, neck and behind the ears, and spreads mainly over the upper half of the body. Complications include middle ear infection, bronchitis, pneumonia and – rarely – encephalitis.

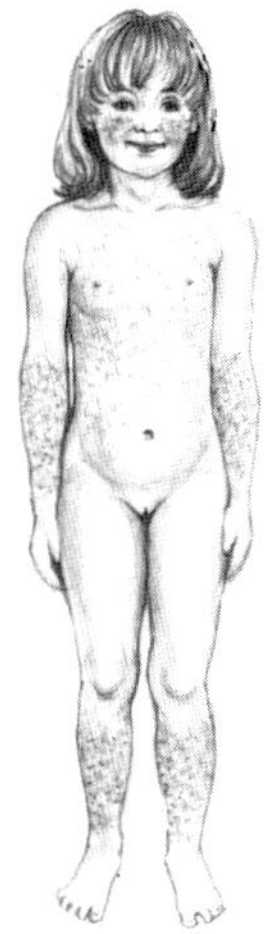

Measles spreads over 3 days. The rash is usually less intense on the hands and feet.

What can be done: Measles itself requires treatment only for the symptoms, because there is no specific cure. Acetaminophen will help bring down a high fever, and soothing cough medicine can be used to relieve a troublesome cough at night. Complications may call for treatment with antibiotics from your doctor. At the height of the illness, your child may feel more comfortable in bed. Let him eat and drink what he likes, but make sure he drinks plenty of fluid. Ideally, a child with measles should be kept away from non-immune people from 7 days after exposure to the disease until 10 days after the rash begins. Routine vaccination against measles is recommended for most children at 15 months of age, but shouldn't be given if the child is ill. Special precautions are needed if the child has had a nervous system problem (such as convulsions or meningitis), or is allergic to eggs (the vaccine is made with egg).

see also **Bronchitis, Conjunctivitis, Encephalitis, Otitis media, Pneumonia,** *p. 53 for* immunization, *and p. 177 for* infectious illnesses chart

Meningitis

An inflammation of the membranes covering the brain and spinal cord, usually caused by a viral or bacterial infection. Long-term effects of serious or untreated meningitis can include brain damage, blindness and deafness.

Symptoms: In a baby, these may include lying unusually still, extreme paleness, a bulging fontanelle (soft spot), as well as a cold or minor illness. In an older child, there may be a headache, tiredness, irritability, neck stiffness, vomiting, fever and sensitivity to light. Confused behavior and a rash are signs seen in certain sorts of meningitis.

What can be done: Meningitis is a potentially serious illness, and if you are at all worried about your child, consult your doctor. There is no specific treatment for viral meningitis, but bacterial meningitis is treated with antibiotics.

Mental retardation

A mentally retarded child is said to be handicapped if he is unlikely to cope with normal schooling. About 3-4 babies in every 1,000 are born with a severe handicap and more are mildly affected. Causes include those occurring before birth (genetic disorders, infection or malnourishment of the mother, placental problems, and certain drugs and poisons); at birth (lack of oxygen, head injury and jaundice); and after birth (infection, head injury, lack of thyroid hormone, and poisoning). Undue delay in any aspect of development may be the first sign of mental retardation.

What can be done: Take your child for his regular checkups so that he can be given the best possible help and any associated problems can be treated. Take advantage of practical support and special services offered in many communities.

see also p. 66 for looking after a handicapped child, *and p. 216 for* useful addresses

Mesenteric adenitis

A condition in which the lymph nodes (glands) around the intestine are swollen and tender. The cause is an infection elsewhere, usually in the respiratory tract. The lymph nodes trap bacteria or viruses from the blood or from the digestive system and swell while producing infection-fighting antibodies.

Symptoms: Tummy ache and a loss of appetite.

What can be done: Your doctor will make sure nothing else is wrong and will treat any infection. Let your child eat as he pleases and encourage him to drink plenty of fluids.

see also p. 104 for the endocrine system

Migraine

A recurrent headache to one side of the head, sometimes with nausea, vomiting and visual disturbances.

Symptoms: Classic migraine is preceded by an "aura," which may be a visual disturbance (floating or flashing lights or patterns, such as zigzags, in front of the eyes, and temporary patchy blindness), numbness, pins and needles in an arm or leg, and – rarely – complete temporary paralysis or inability to speak. Some experts think that food allergy is the commonest cause in children. Migraine is rarely a problem in young children, but

recurrent tummy ache is thought to be its equivalent – a sort of abdominal migraine.
What can be done: Quiet, rest, protection from bright light, and avoiding any foods known to precipitate migraine will help. Your doctor may prescribe drug treatment.
see also **Food allergy**

Milia

A rash on the face of a newborn baby, caused by blockage of the sebaceous glands.
Symptoms: Little pearly-white or yellow spots are seen usually on or around the nose.
What can be done: Leave the spots alone as they'll disappear in a few weeks.

Milk intolerance

Illness from drinking cows' milk or eating cows' milk products affects up to 7 percent of babies, as well as older children. The underlying cause may be allergy, non-allergic intolerance, protein sensitivity, or lactose (milk sugar) intolerance.
Symptoms: These are many and varied, and affect the digestive system (diarrhea, bleeding, constipation, tummy ache, gas and nausea); have general effects (failure to thrive, excessive weight gain, thirst, easy bruising, paleness, frequency of passing urine and leg cramps); can cause skin problems (eczema, urticaria and sweating); and affect the respiratory system (runny nose, wheezing, sneezing and cough) and the nervous system (restlessness, clumsiness, lethargy and epilepsy).
What can be done: If you suspect milk intolerance, eliminate all cows' milk products from your child's diet for 2 weeks to see if there is any improvement. Make sure, with help from your doctor, that your child gets the necessary nutrients from other sources. If your baby is bottlefed with a cows'-milk-based formula (which most bottlefed babies are), change to a non-cows' milk one, but check first with your doctor that the new milk is satisfactory for a baby. Most children with this condition can tolerate a reduced amount of cows' milk in their diet.
see also **Allergy, Eczema, Epilepsy, Sugar intolerance, Urticaria**

Moles

A mole is a birthmark which may not develop until after birth.
Symptoms: Moles can be all sorts of different sizes. They may be smooth flat marks or hairy ones.
What can be done: There is usually no problem, but if your child's mole ever bleeds, darkens, or becomes tender or itchy, consult your doctor as it can be removed surgically.

Molluscum contagiosum

A fairly common, mildly contagious, viral skin infection passed on by direct contact with an infected person or his clothing or bedding. The virus spreads from place to place on the skin if the spots are touched. Molluscum eventually disappears of its own accord, though this may take months or even years. The incubation period is between 2 and 8 weeks.
Symptoms: There are round pearly lumps on the face, eyelids and neck in particular. The lumps are about ¼ inch across and have a tiny central depression which contains a plug of cheesy-looking matter.
What can be done: It isn't essential to treat mulluscum in most children, but because it's

In molluscum contagiosum a dozen or so lumps can occur together. Warmth and moisture encourage the spread of the virus to other children.

mildly infectious, consult your doctor who may suggest hastening its departure by getting rid of the plugs. It is important to treat molluscum in children with atopic eczema or any sort of immunodeficiency, as the condition might otherwise spread rapidly.

Moniliasis

An infection of the mouth (thrush) or bowel (and less commonly the nails, vagina or skin) with the yeast fungus candida albicans. Children who have been on antibiotics are more likely to get thrush or bowel moniliasis, because the normal protective bacteria in the digestive tract are destroyed by the drugs. Vaginal moniliasis in a mother can infect her baby. If a breastfed baby has thrush, this can spread to the mother's nipples, and both mother and child must be treated. Unsterilized bottle nipples can lead to thrush or bowel infection.

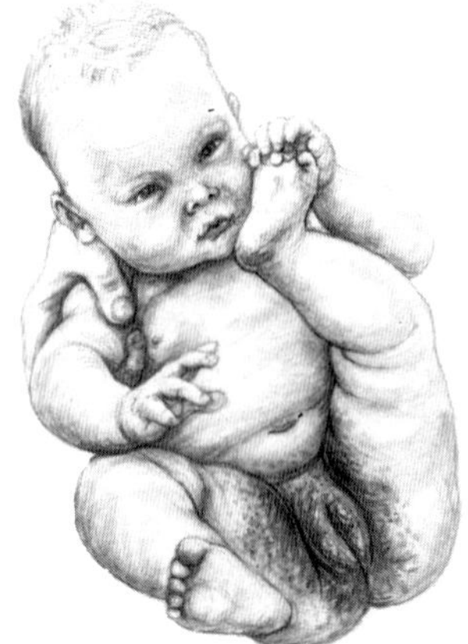

Moniliasis occurring after antibiotic treatment in older babies can be helped by giving live yogurt.

Symptoms: With thrush, there are white patches inside the mouth which can't be wiped off without causing bleeding, and the tongue may be white and furred. Monilial infection of the bowel leads to diaper rash or an itchy bottom.
What can be done: Thrush in the mouth can be treated by Nystatin suspension from your doctor. Use this to swab the patches in your child's mouth. Infections elsewhere need medical attention.
see also **Diaper rash**

Motion sickness

This is nausea and vomiting caused by the movement of a car, boat or plane.
Symptoms: Paleness, yawning, anxiety and sweating, as well as nausea and vomiting.
What can be done: If you give your child an antitravel sickness tablet, it is best taken half an hour before the journey. Give him a light non-fatty meal before traveling rather than no food or a large meal. Small snacks while traveling are also helpful. Distracting the child can be helpful, so encourage him to sing and play simple games like "I spy." Don't let him do anything which requires looking down, doing close work, or looking out of the side window. Take a paper bag lined with a plastic bag with you if your child is often travel sick.

Mouth ulcers

Mouth ulcers can be caused by moniliasis and herpes simplex infection, but the most common are aphthous ulcers which have no known cause.
Symptoms: Aphthous ulcers are small and painful, and monilial ulcers (thrush) usually have a white coating. Herpetic ulcers (including cold sores) are also seen on the lips, and the child feels unwell.
What can be done: The only specific treatment is for monilial ulcers. Aphthous ulcers tend to get better spontaneously.
see also **Herpes, Moniliasis**

Mumps

A viral infection with an incubation period of 2 to 3 weeks, spread by droplet infection from coughing, sneezing and talking.
Symptoms: Irritability and a feeling of being sick are followed by a fever, headache, muscle pains and swelling of one or more salivary glands, most often those in front of the ears. The mouth feels dry and hurts when eating or talking. Foods and drinks which stimulate saliva, such as lemon juice, cause pain in the swollen glands. The swellings last for 3 to 7 days.
What can be done: There is no specific treatment, but lots to drink, soft foods, frequent toothbrushing and mouth washes will make your child more comfortable and

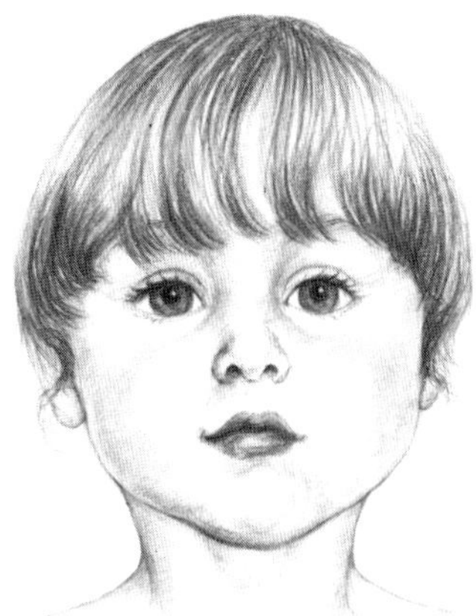

This viral infection of the salivary glands is commonest in children aged between 5 and 8. Typically the cheeks swell to fill in the normal valley under the ear lobes.

help prevent gingivitis. Mumps may be infectious from 24 hours or more before the salivary glands swell until 3 days after the swelling has gone down. In practice, your child can be considered non-infectious within 7 days as long as the swellings have gone down. Inflammation of the testes or ovaries is uncommon in young children and is not now thought to lead to sterility. Possible complications include meningitis, encephalitis and pancreatitis. Mumps vaccine is routinely given to all children aged 15 months.
see also **Encephalitis, Gingivitis, Meningitis,** *and p. 177 for* infectious illnesses chart

Muscular dystrophy

A disease causing progressive degeneration of the muscles, which may be inherited or result from a genetic mutation. Only boys are affected, though girls can be carriers of abnormal genetic material. Many boys with muscular dystrophy have a reduced lifespan.
Symptoms: Initially there is slowness at walking and running. The child may waddle and find it difficult to climb stairs or stand up. In the most common form of the disease the calf muscles swell.
What can be done: It's possible to detect whether a woman or a girl is a carrier of muscular dystrophy, and genetic counseling is available if necessary. Prenatal tests can detect whether an unborn baby is affected. There is no specific treatment, but both parents and child may benefit from advice and support from friends and professionals in the community.
see also p. 216 for useful addresses

N

Nail biting

This habit often begins with a child biting or chewing long or unkempt nails. It can also be triggered by insecurity or imitation. Some children simply like doing it.
What can be done: Because the nails look so unpleasant and the nail beds may become infected, and because it may be caused by an emotional problem, it's best to try to prevent the habit. It helps to make sure your child feels as secure and loved as possible, to praise or reward him when one or more nails aren't bitten, and to cut his nails regularly.

Nail infection – *see* Paronychia

Nearsightedness

This is a condition in which a child can see near objects clearly, but can't bring distant objects into focus. It is a common eye problem in young children and may often be inherited. In most cases, the eyeball is healthy, but it can be too long or the refractive power of the lens or cornea too great, thus preventing a clear image from being formed on the retina. The problem may not show up until the child's first year or two at school.
Symptoms: The child may tilt his head, screw up his eyes or look out of the corner of his eyes to try to see distant things clearly. He may want to sit close to the blackboard at school or hold his book close to his face when reading, and may not recognize familiar people or objects at a distance.

What can be done: Make an appointment with an optometrist or an ophthalmologist who will check his vision and prescribe glasses if necessary. Routine checkups at your doctor's office and at school include simple tests for nearsightedness and other visual problems.

see also p. 82 for the eye

Nephritis – *see* Glomerulonephritis, Urinary tract infections

Nervousness

Children who are anxious, fearful, sensitive, edgy, excitable or highly-strung are sometimes described as ''nervous.'' Your child's behavior and feelings are influenced by inherited personality factors and by his environment. Inherited characteristics can't be changed, but environmental ones often can.

What can be done: If you think your child is nervous as a result of anxiety or insecurity, try to discover the basic cause and attempt to improve matters. Habits, such as nail biting and head banging, and tics, such as blinking, tend to begin when a child is bored, lonely or frustrated.

see also **Habits**

Nightmares

Some children occasionally have an unpleasant dream, or nightmare, from which they wake frightened, and some children have night terrors during their sleep. Night terrors occur during deep dreamless sleep, and the child sees strange and frightening things which may not disappear at once on waking. He wakes terrified, screaming or crying out, and may not recognize you.

What can be done: If your child has a nightmare or night terrors, comfort him and stay with him for reassurance as long as he wants. An active imagination, heightened emotions and certain foods can be the cause of bad dreams. The older the child, the easier it is to discuss the dream to see if it throws any light on what is worrying him. Night terrors tend to be associated with anxiety, sleep walking and sleep talking.

Nits

Nits are the eggs of a head louse and are laid stuck to the hair, about half an inch from the scalp. Tiny, cigar-shaped and pearly-white, they darken before hatching into adult lice, which look like wingless mosquitoes.

Symptoms: Besides the nits and lice, you may see louse bites which cause itching, inflammation and sometimes infection and swollen lymph nodes (glands) in the neck. Lice are picked up by contact with, or by sharing the brushes and combs of, infected children. A louse can live for 24 hours off the head.

What can be done: Malathion lotion is the most effective treatment. Rub it into your child's hair at night and shampoo it out 12 hours later. Comb the wet hair with a fine-toothed comb, dipped into hot vinegar, to remove the stuck nits. Other members of the household should also use the lotion in case they have picked up nits too. Malathion acts on the hair for 5 to 6 weeks, so it's better not to swim in a chlorinated pool during this period because chlorine reduces the efficiency of the insecticide.

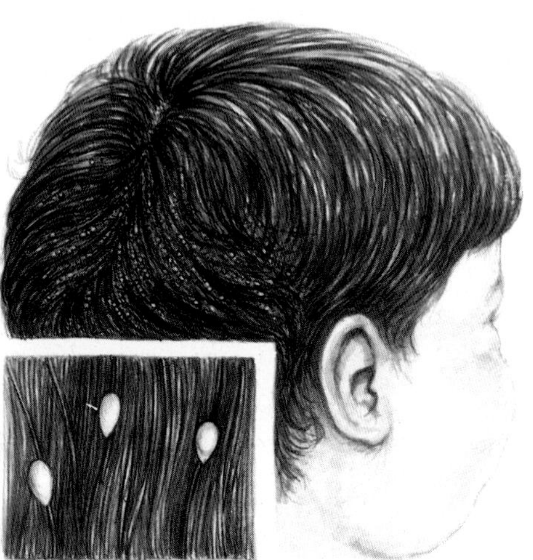

Nits are very common among school-age children and are not at all an indication of bad hygiene.

Nosebleed – *see* Emergencies and first aid p. 204

Nose picking

A socially unacceptable habit which, while usually harmless, can cause a nosebleed. A young child sometimes starts picking his nose if he's pushed a small object up there.

Nystagmus

A regular involuntary flicking of both the eyes from side to side. When nystagmus is present from birth it is often associated with poor vision.
What can be done: There are many possible causes of this condition and the doctor will almost certainly refer your child to a specialist.

O

Obese child

By medical standards a child is obese if he is 20 percent or more overweight compared with the ideal for his height, build and age. Both nature and nurture play a part. Undoubtedly some children are born with a tendency to put on weight easily, but poor nutrition – in the sense of too much food, and especially too much of certain foods – causes most children to put on weight. The rate at which a child burns up energy from food varies according to the amount of daily exercise. Exercise raises the metabolic rate (the rate at which the body burns up calories) for some hours afterwards, thereby continuing to use up extra calories. A child's emotional state can also influence the body's weight control system. Few obese children have anything wrong with their glands, but some have less brown fat (which converts excess calorific intake into heat instead of fat) in their bodies. Fat children are more prone to illness, as are fat adults, and can have social and practical problems too.
What can be done: If everyone in the family is encouraged to eat a healthy diet, then a child is much less likely to learn bad eating patterns. Regular exercise is important, and again it helps if it's considered important by the whole family. If your child is overweight, think in terms of keeping the weight steady rather than encouraging weight loss. Cut out foods high in refined carbohydrates and added sugar (for example, cookies and cakes), and limit the quantity of fatty foods.
see also p. 28 for diet

Osteomyelitis

A bacterial infection of the bone resulting from infection in a skin wound or in the blood.
Symptoms: Local symptoms include pain on movement, swelling and redness. There may be a fever and signs of acute illness, but in a surprising number of children these are absent. In babies particularly, the infection is likely to spread into a nearby joint, causing septic arthritis and a limitation of movement.
What can be done: Treatment includes antibiotics, immobilization and drainage of infected matter, and may need to be prolonged in order to avoid chronic infection, bone or joint deformity, or disturbed bone growth.
see also **Arthritis**

Otitis externa

This is an inflammation of the skin lining the ear canal caused by bacterial or fungal infection.
Symptoms: There is pain in the ear canal and this is made worse by movement. The canal lining is itchy and swollen, and the swelling may be bad enough to cause some deafness.
What can be done: Help prevent otitis externa by gently drying the outer part of the ear canal with a clean towel after swimming, bathing or shampooing. If your child develops it, keep his ears dry and try to stop him scratching. Your doctor will prescribe suitable treatment.

Otitis media

An infection of the middle ear usually following a cold, a sore throat, tonsilitis, influenza, measles, or whooping cough. Inflammation of the Eustachian tube blocks the normal drainage of fluid from the middle ear into the throat, causing a build-up of pressure.

Symptoms: Earache, a fever, loss of appetite and nausea are primary symptoms, with vomiting and deafness in an acute infection. If the eardrum perforates there is a discharge from the ear.
What can be done: Decongestant nose drops alone sometimes restore normal drainage down the Eustachian tube. If your child has increasing or severe pain, or vomiting, your doctor may prescribe antibiotics as well. Chronic middle ear infection can lead to a continuing discharge from a perforated drum, hearing loss from chronic effusion, or mastoiditis.
see also **Otitis Media with effusion,** *and p. 61 for* how to give nose drops

Otitis media with effusion

A condition in which there is sticky fluid in the middle ear as a result of blockage of the Eustachian tube. The blockage is caused by enlarged adenoids or by swelling of the tube's lining (from infection or allergy).
Symptoms: Because the fluid is a poor conductor of sound, the child is partially deaf on the affected side. Other problems associated with the condition can include earache, speech difficulties, a feeling of fullness in the ear and a sensation of clicking on swallowing or moving the jaw.
What can be done: Treatment may include antibiotics, decongestant medicines and nose drops, and antihistamines, though the value of these drugs is disputed. For recurrent or chronic attacks, an operation may be done in which the fluid is sucked out via a hole made in the ear drum, and a tiny plastic tube is inserted.
see also p. 84 for the ear

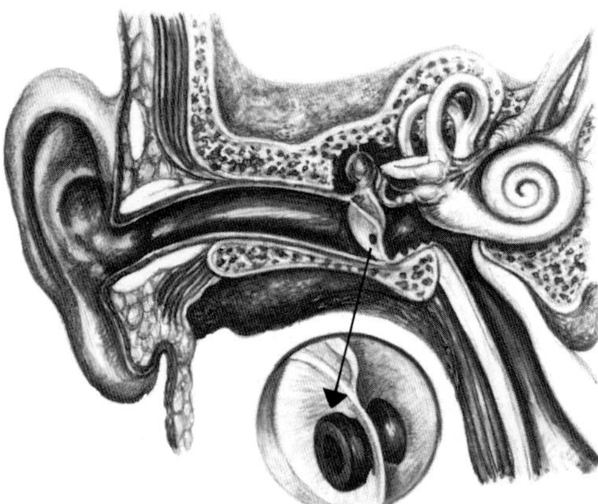

This illustrates where a plastic tube is inserted in the eardrum to drain the sticky fluid. The detail shows an enlargement of the plastic tube.

P

Pain

Because pain is the body's warning signal that something is wrong, it should never be ignored. The younger the child, the less likely it is that pain will be described accurately and it may not be reported at all. You may notice that your child is sick, irritable, not eating, pale and whiny. Most parents instinctively know when there is something wrong with their child.
What can be done: If you are worried, however minor the pain seems, consult your doctor.

Paralysis

A temporary or permanent loss of muscle power affecting one or more muscles, and caused by one of many conditions affecting the brain, spinal cord or nerves. Cerebral palsy and spina bifida are two of the most common problems causing paralysis today. The degree of disability depends on which muscles are involved and on whether the paralysis is complete or partial.
What can be done: Treatment depends on the cause, but physiotherapy and suitable aids are available to every child.
see also **Cerebral palsy, Spina bifida**

Paronychia

An infection of the skin around a nail is known as a paronychia or a whitlow, and is usually bacterial. An ingrown nail is the most likely cause, but bitten nails or hangnails often lead to infection too. If anyone in the house has a

monilial infection, broken skin around a nail can become infected with moniliasis.
Symptoms: Redness, swelling and tenderness around the nail.
What can be done: If a paronychia shows no sign of improving, your doctor will prescribe some antibiotic or antifungal cream, or oral antibiotics. Very occasionally minor surgery is needed.

see also **Moniliasis**

Peritonitis

An inflammation of the lining of the peritoneal cavity in which the abdominal organs lie. Peritonitis can follow appendicitis, or a twisting or perforation of the bowel. Very rarely, an infected naval causes peritonitis in a baby.
Symptoms: A child with this condition is obviously ill, with a fever, vomiting, a tense tender tummy and very pale skin.
What can be done: Contact your doctor urgently. Treatment usually involves surgery.

see also **Appendicitis**

Perthes' disease

This is a softening of the upper end of the thigh bone (femur) and happens more often in boys. The common age is between 3 and 10 years.
Symptoms: There is pain in the hip and a limp. Although the cause is unknown, some children who develop this condition have injured their hip before.
What can be done: Current treatment allows a child to continue to bear weight on the affected hip by wearing special casts or braces. Surgical procedures have also been developed.

Phenylketonuria

A rare condition affecting 1 in 14,000 newborn babies and caused by a deficiency of the enzyme converting the amino acid phenylalanine, present in food, to another amino acid, tyrosine.
Symptoms: Too much phenylalanine in the body leads to mental retardation and cataracts if not discovered early.
What can be done: Babies have a routine blood test (the Guthrie test) for this condition during the first 2 or 3 days after birth, before leaving the hospital. An affected baby is put on a diet low in phenylalanine which may preclude breastfeeding. In time, a child may be able to eat a normal diet.

see also **Cataracts**

Phimosis

A condition in which the foreskin is tight and can't be pulled back from the head of the penis.
What can be done: This is perfectly normal in young boys, and it's rarely necessary to do anything to a tight foreskin. Pull it back gently only as far as is comfortable when you wash your son's penis. In time most foreskins loosen and very few boys ever need surgery for this condition.

Phobias

Emotional disorders in which there is an abnormally intense dread of certain objects or situations. The most common phobias in children involve fears of animals, insects, the dark, noise and school. Phobias arise for different reasons in different children. In some they represent hidden anxiety, while in others they are an imitation of a parent's behavior.
What can be done: They tend to disappear rapidly if handled sensibly, but help is available from your doctor or child psychiatrist if necessary.

Physical handicap

A physical handicap can be inherited or can result from a disease or injury before or after birth. Cerebral palsy and spina bifida are the most common handicaps affecting the newborn. Accidents, infections and other rarer conditions can lead to disability in a previously normal child. Make sure the child has regular thorough medical checkups, so that other problems, such as deafness or a visual disorder, are not missed.
What can be done: Find out about all the practical help available, and remember that if you are caring for a handicapped child you

also need to look after yourself as well as finding support from your family, friends, community and professionals.

see also p. 66 for **looking after a handicapped child,** *and p. 216 for* **useful addresses**

Pigeon toe

A condition which can be caused by an inturning of the foot itself or by a twisting of the lower leg bone.

Symptoms: You'll probably first notice pigeon toes (intoeing) when your child starts walking. The toes are turned towards the midline and one leg may be "thrown" around the other in order to maintain balance while walking.

What can be done: The condition tends to improve spontaneously, so your doctor will probably advise you to be patient and bring the child for a further check.

Pimples – *see* Boils and pimples

Pink eye – *see* Conjunctivitis

Pleurisy

An inflammation of the pleural membranes with or without fluid or pus. Causes include pneumonia, cancer and, much less often, tuberculosis, rheumatoid arthritis or other conditions.

Symptoms: The main symptom is chest pain, made worse on breathing, coughing and straining. The pain is sometimes felt in the shoulder or the back instead of over the site of the inflammation. Fast or grunting breathing, fever and blueness are sometimes seen too.

What can be done: Your doctor will diagnose the underlying cause of the pleurisy. Make sure the recommended treatment is carried out and especially that antibiotics are given in the correct and complete dosage. Your child may need to go to the hospital.

see also p. 90 for **the chest and lungs**

Pneumonia

Inflammation of the lungs caused by infection, irritant fumes, a foreign body, vomit or allergy. Bronchiolitis is a type of pneumonia seen in children.

Symptoms: These include shallow, rapid breathing; a cough; fever; diarrhea; vomiting; and perhaps a stiff neck and tummy ache.

What can be done: Be guided by your doctor and be sure to give medications in the correct doses. Your child may breathe more easily if propped up when in bed. Hospitalization is usually only necessary for very young or very sick children.

see also **Bronchiolitis**

Polio

A viral infection mainly affecting the brain and spinal cord.

Symptoms: There is a fever, muscle tenderness, and pains in the back and limbs. A stiff neck, difficulty in passing urine and general weakness can complicate the picture, and then paralysis may occur, with the lower legs most often affected. The breathing muscles may become paralyzed, but this isn't usual. One in three children with polio suffers from paralysis, but this is usually temporary.

What can be done: Children with mild polio can be looked after at home, but if there is any degree of paralysis they are probably better off in the hospital, where care can be taken to watch for breathing difficulties and to prevent physical deformities from developing. However, prevention is the keynote. Routine immunization has virtually eradicated polio in the US.

see also p. 58 for **looking after an ill child,** *p. 53 for* **immunization,** *and p. 216 for* **useful addresses**

Prickly heat

Also known as heat rash, this is an itchy rash seen in hot weather.

Symptoms: Small raised pink spots are found on the neck and shoulders, and can spread to the face and chest. Each spot is centered on a blocked sweat pore, sometimes surrounded by a pink flare and may develop into a blister.

The prickly heat rash can be helped by giving vitamin C in the correct dose. It tends to be more pronounced where the skin is warmest.

What can be done: Help prevent the rash by dressing your baby or child in clothes which suit his level of activity as well as the weather, and keep the hair off the neck. Avoid man-made fibers and dress him only in cotton clothes in the heat. Frequent washing and careful drying to remove sweat can help soothe the rash. Cornstarch powder and calamine lotion may cake and irritate the skin more.

Prolapse of the rectum

In this condition, part of the rectum comes out of the anus. This can happen after severe straining to defecate and in children with cystic fibrosis.
Symptoms: You'll see part of the rectum lying in the crease of the bottom, and the child may complain that he can't wipe his bottom properly or that there's a lump there.
What can be done: Lay your child down on a bed with the foot of the bed raised about a foot high. Wrap some toilet paper around your finger, put your finger into the prolapsed rectum and push it gently back up the anus. Leave the paper there as you take your finger out (the paper will be expelled the next time your child goes to the bathroom. Tell your doctor what has happened, and prevent it happening again by putting your child on a high-fiber diet and giving him plenty to drink.
see also **Cystic fibrosis**

Psoriasis

A skin disorder which is more common in girls and tends to run in families. The cause is unknown, but one type may follow a streptococcal sore throat
Symptoms: Raised red spots join to form patches or "plaques" with sharp edges and thick silvery-white scales. The scalp, knees, elbows, belly button, genitals and face are most often affected. The nails are pitted and may come away from the nail beds.
What can be done: Your doctor will refer your child to a dermatologist if necessary. Medical treatment includes tar preparations that you can add to the bath or put on your child's skin, salicylic acid ointment to remove the scales, and steroid creams. Sunlight usually helps, but in a few children makes it worse.

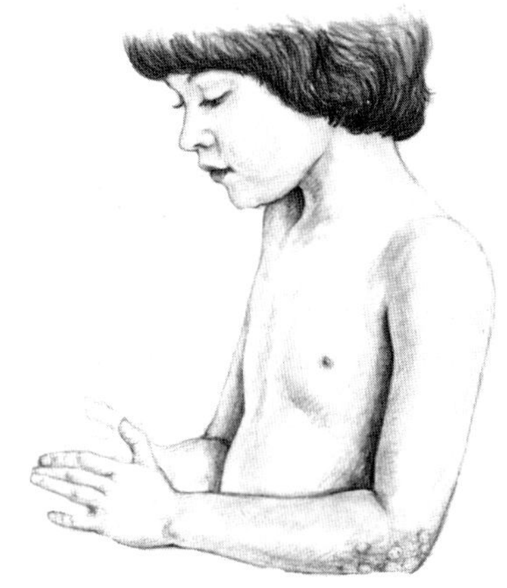

Sometimes the silvery scales of psoriasis clear, only to recur later.

Purpura

Bleeding into the skin causing purple patches, varying in size from pinpoints upwards. The causes include infection, inherited disorders, drug reactions and allergy.
Symptoms: Besides the tiny patches of blood in the skin, you may notice bleeding into the lips and gums, or nosebleeds. In one sort of purpura there is also arthritis, nephritis and bleeding into the stomach and intestine.
What can be done: Tell your doctor who will arrange for blood tests to help establish the underlying cause.

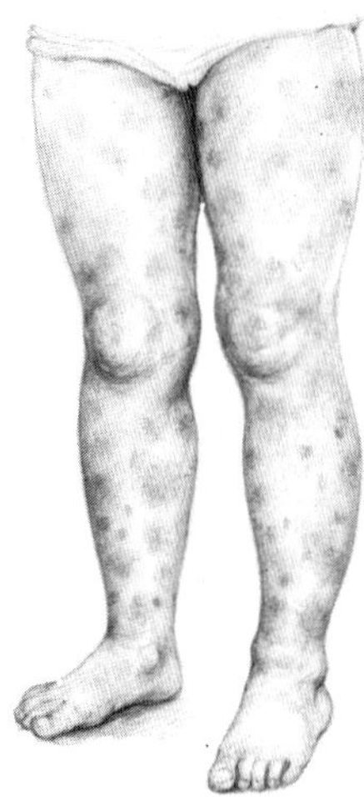

The tiny spots of purpura are quite different from the normal bruising seen in children who have hurt themselves while playing.

see also **Arthritis, Glomerulonephritis**

Pyelonephritis – *see* Urinary tract infections

Pyloric stenosis

A narrowing of the stomach's outlet (pylorus) into the small intestine. It is five times more common in boys than in girls. It is also more common in bottlefed babies.

Symptoms: Vomiting is the main problem and may begin soon after birth, though it doesn't develop its characteristic pattern until the baby is 2 to 3 weeks old. The baby usually vomits after a feeding and the vomit is sometimes propelled for some distance (projectile vomiting). Constipation and a slowing or stopping of weight gain may be seen, together with weakness and dehydration in badly affected babies.

What can be done: Take your baby to your doctor who may recommend seeing a specialist and taking barium X-rays to confirm the diagnosis. An operation to widen the stomach outlet or medicine to relax the tight muscle of the outlet may be advised. If your baby is thriving in spite of the vomiting, you may be advised to wait for the condition to get better by itself.

see also p. 94 for the digestive system.

Q

Quarreling

Finding fault with and picking on each other is something that all children do sometimes, and particularly when they are tired, upset or sick. Quarreling can be contagious too – the more that adults in the family do it, the more the children will.

What can be done: Help your children learn to settle their differences by showing them how to look at what has happened in a reasonable and fair way. Try not to take sides unless you know the whole story. Help them to see that life isn't always fair and that sometimes it's better to give in gracefully rather than to have to win.

R

Rabies

A dangerous viral infection caught from the bite of an infected animal, sometimes a dog. Rabies remains a problem in the US. It may take from 2 weeks to 2 years after being bitten for the infection to develop.

Symptoms: The child becomes feverish and has a sore throat, headache and aching muscles. Pain in the throat on trying to drink is followed by a fear of drinking at all. Hallucinations, paralysis and confusion follow.

What can be done: If your child is bitten, go to your doctor immediately for a vaccination and a dose of immune globulin. There is as yet no cure for rabies.

Rashes

A rash is any eruption on the skin, whether it's raised or flat; pink, red, white, yellow or purple; with blisters or pustules; itchy or painful; or smooth or flaky. There are many possible causes of a rash, including bites and stings, heat, local or general infection,

physical or chemical irritation and allergy.
What can be done: A rash is a warning sign that all is not well, so unless you are confident that you know what the rash is and can either treat it adequately at home or ignore it safely, consult your doctor.
see also **Allergy, Chickenpox, Detitis, Eczema, Fifth disease, German measles, Measles, Milia, Prickly heat, Rheumatic fever, Ringworm, Roseola infantum, scabies, Scarlet fever, Seborrheic dermatitis, Urticaria**

Recurrent abdominal pain syndrome

Children with the recurrent abdominal pain syndrome (also called the irritable bowel syndrome) have recurrent tummy aches, together with a fever and vomiting. Attacks tend to come and go suddenly, within a day or so. It's possible that it is caused in some children by particularly strong intestinal movements, while attacks in others may be triggered by emotional problems.
What can be done: If no obvious cause is found, make sure your child has plenty to drink to replace the fluid lost by vomiting, and keep him at home until the attack is over.

Reflux

This is the effortless bringing up of stomach contents, unlike vomiting in which there is retching and straining of the abdominal muscles. It is seen most often in babies who may bring up stomach contents at any time, though most often after a feeding. Often the regurgitation is accompanied by some wind.
What can be done: Most of these babies are perfectly well, but if your baby has any signs of illness, such as diarrhea, a fever, restlessness or lack of weight gain, consult your doctor. If the baby tends to regurgitate during sleep, lay him on his side so that he doesn't choke.

Reye's syndrome

An acute and potentially serious illness which is triggered in a susceptible child by a viral infection or by certain drugs and toxins. Taking aspirin has recently been noticed to precede the development of Reye's syndrome in some children.
Symptoms: Severe nausea and vomiting are followed within hours or sometimes days by hyperactive behavior which in turn leads to sleepiness, unresponsiveness and a coma.
What can be done: Don't give aspirin to any child under 18. Seek medical advice urgently.
see also p. 216 for useful addresses

Rheumatic fever

A rare complication of tonsilitis or middle ear infection, or any other infection with a certain strain of streptococcal bacteria.
Symptoms: The affected child develops a fever, headache, and pains in the knees, ankles, elbows or wrists which tend to move from joint to joint. There may be a rash and lumps under the skin. Complications involving damage to the heart or involvement of the brain are very rare nowadays.
What can be done: Consult your doctor who will prescribe penicillin to prevent further attacks.
see also **Otitis media, Tonsillitis**

Rickets

A disturbance of bone growth caused by a lack of vitamin D through sunshine and in the diet.
Symptoms: The child's ribcage and spine may be deformed, and knock knees and bow legs are common, as are constipation, weakness and irritability. The teeth appear late and decay easily. In a baby, the soft spot (fontanelle) in the skull closes late, and his head may be asymmetrical.
What can be done: The ultraviolet rays in sunlight make the skin manufacture vitamin D, so let your baby lie and kick in his carriage in the open air (under a sunshade if necessary), and encourage your older child to play outside when it's pleasant. A few hours' sunshine a day in the summer creates body stores of vitamin D for the winter. Dietary sources of vitamin D are less important, but include eggs, butter, margarine, cheese, liver, canned salmon, sardines, and fish oils. Breastfed babies obtain vitamin D from their mother's milk and bottlefed babies from their milk formula. If you are breastfeeding, get

plenty of sunshine and eat vitamin D-rich foods. A vitamin D supplement (drops or tablets) may be advisable for children who don't have enough sun or whose diet is poor.

Ringworm

A contagious fungal infection of the skin, hair or nails. The spores can be picked up from contact with an infected person or dog or cat, or from infected flakes of skin or hairs lying around.

Symptoms: On the skin, ringworm shows as circular flaky patches, usually in the groin, upper arms or face. On the scalp, it creates round or oval bald patches. In the nails, it causes white patches, thick distorted discolored nails, or infection beneath and at the sides of the nails. Between the toes, it causes athlete's foot.

What can be done: Ringworm can be treated locally with an antifungal ointment, and your doctor may also prescribe antibiotic tablets called griseofulvin to clear the infection. Keep the child's towel and washcloth apart from those of the rest of the family, and wash his bedsheets frequently. Throw away brushes or combs used while he was infected.

see also **Athlete's foot, Baldness,** *and p. 15 for* pet hygiene

Rocking – *see* Habits

Roseola infantum

A mild, probably viral infection, seen in children between 6 months and 2 years old, usually in the spring or autumn. The period of incubation lasts between 7 and 17 days.

Symptoms: There is a sudden high fever for 1 to 5 days, a cold and a sore throat. Just before the fever drops, there is a rash of flat spots or pimples on the chest and back which spreads to the neck, arms, face and legs, lasting for 24 hours. Some children have convulsions with the fever. Roseola may be confused with German measles. The main difference is the initial high fever with roseola.

What can be done: Keep your child comfortably cool and give him acetaminophen to ease the sore throat and bring down the fever. There is no need to isolate him.

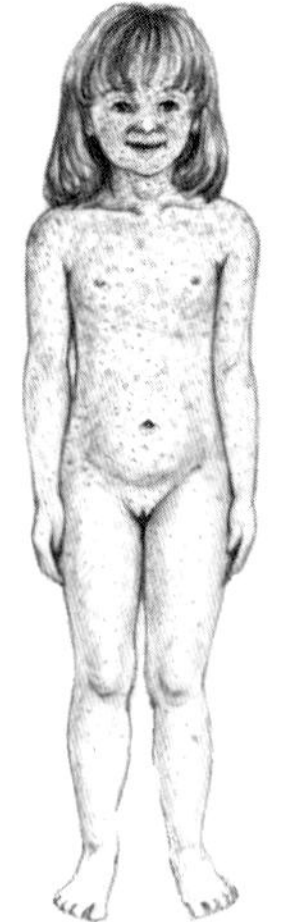
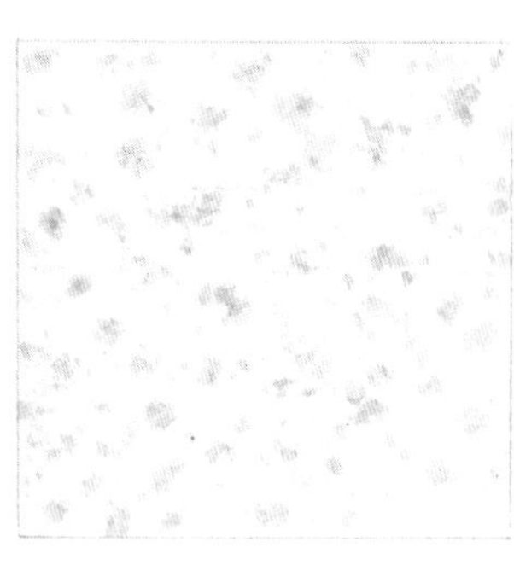

Roseola usually occurs between the ages of 6 months and 2 years.

see also **Convulsions,** *and p. 177 for* infectious illnesses chart

Roundworms – *see* Worms

Rupture – *see* Hernia

Rumination

This is when a baby brings food up from his stomach into his mouth and chews it. Rumination can easily become a habit which is encouraged by a lack of enough time to suck and by insufficient attention.

What can be done: Talk to your doctor about whether your baby needs more attention or more time to suck.

S

Scabies

A very itchy, contagious rash caused by the burrowing of tiny mites, caught from infested

people or animals. Allergy and bacterial infection may follow.
Symptoms: Blisters and fine zigzag lines are seen between a child's fingers and on his palms, wrists, elbows, armpits and waist.
What can be done: Your doctor will prescribe benzyl benzoate or another suitable solution which should be applied all over the skin (except round the eyes) after thorough washing or bathing in warm water. Let the solution dry, then apply a second coat. Next day, put on two more coats and wash bedding and clothing. Everyone in your family should be treated, and an infested pet treated by the vet.

see also **Allergy**

Scarlet fever

A mild infection caused by a particular strain of streptococcal bacteria. The incubation period is 1 to 7 days.
Symptoms: There is a sudden fever, a headache, swollen lymph nodes (glands) in the neck, a sore throat, vomiting, loss of appetite and perhaps a tummy ache. Within 24 hours a rash begins in the neck, armpits and groin. This rash spreads over the body during the next 24 hours, but spares the skin around the mouth. A week later the skin begins to flake. Middle ear infection (otitis media) is a common complication.

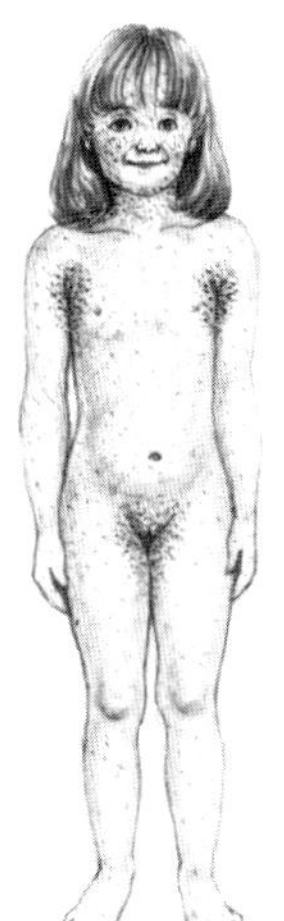

The scarlet fever rash looks like sunburn. It is much less common now with the use of antibiotics.

What can be done: Consult your doctor who will prescribe a course of antibiotics which will soon alleviate the symptoms.

see also **Otitis media,** *and p. 177 for* infectious illnesses chart

Scurf (Dandruff)

A layer of white flakes of shed skin on the scalp, together with skin oil (sebum) and sweat. A small amount is normal. An excess is called dandruff and is often associated with too much oil production.
What can be done: Consult your doctor or pharmacist about a suitable medicated shampoo.

Scurvy

A disease caused by a severe lack of vitamin C in the diet, and most often seen in babies.
Symptoms: There is tender swelling of the bones, painful joints, loosening of the teeth, swollen gums, poor healing of wounds, bruising, delayed growth, fever, tiredness and irritability.
What can be done: Prevent it by eating vitamin C-rich foods yourself if you are breastfeeding, or by giving special children's supplements to your baby if bottlefeeding. A weaned baby or young child needs a diet rich in vitamin C or else a supplement.

see also p. 28 for diet

Seborrheic dermatitis

A red, weepy, scaly rash which affects babies with an oily skin and often starts in the first few weeks of life. The cause is unknown, but affected babies may have a slightly higher risk of developing eczema.
Symptoms: The rash may be found on or behind the ears, on the forehead, nose, eyelids, eyebrows, in the folds of the thighs, the armpits, diaper area and scalp (often with cradle cap).
What can be done: Wash and dry your baby well, using a mild unperfumed soap. If you are worried or if you think the rash may be infected, consult your doctor.

see also **Cradle cap, Eczema**

Short child

A baby's length is determined by his genetic make-up, the duration of the pregnancy and whether it was single or multiple, and on the mother's nutrition and health during her pregnancy. A child's height is dependent on his diet, health, social circumstances and emotional state. Growth tends to be faster in the summer and slows down in the middle years of childhood.
What can be done: If you are concerned about your child's height, talk to your doctor. A record will have been kept at your doctor's of his rate of growth. If necessary, he will be referred to a specialist.
see also p.216 for useful addresses

Showing off

This is a form of attention seeking which may be temporary or may reflect a deeper need for love, security, praise and affirmation of the child as a lovable and worthwhile individual because of who he is, and not what he does or how he behaves.
What can be done: Look at the way you handle your child in social and emotional ways, and see if you can make him feel more important to you and thereby to himself, so that there is no need for him to crave a feeling of importance to others.

Shyness

Shyness is a normal form of behavior. Some children are naturally shyer than others and need the comfort of their parent's presence for longer than others. A change of environment or routine can cause temporary shyness. Some children are shy because they feel, or are, different from others. Shyness is a problem only if it hampers a child more than you feel it should for his personality, age and situation.
What can be done: Provide a safe base from which your young child can explore the world and to which he can return as soon as he wishes. Encourage independence, but don't force it. Help your child to make friends, for instance by having them to your house, but don't ever make him visit them if he doesn't want to.

Sickle-cell anemia

An inherited condition in which many of the blood cells are sickle-shaped instead of disc-shaped and are, as a result, destroyed too soon by the body. It is seen in some people of African, Indian and Mediterranean origin.
Symptoms: There is anemia and a variety of problems caused by blood clots in different parts of the body. Sufferers are more likely to get infections.
What can be done: There is no specific medical cure, but your child's symptoms can be treated as and when they occur.
see also **Anemia,** *and p. 216 for* useful addresses

Sinusitis

A viral or bacterial infection of the mucous membranes lining one or more of the sinuses in the face.
Symptoms: Your child has a cold which may continue, giving a yellowish-green discharge from the nose, tenderness and pain over the affected sinus, a fever and a sense of being ill.
What can be done: If necessary, give your child acetaminophen, together with decongestant nose drops to improve the drainage of the infected sinus into the nose. Your doctor may advise antibiotics or oral decongestants.
see also p. 61 for how to give nose drops

Sleep problems

Sleep "problems" arise from the fact that many parents expect children to go to sleep at a certain hour, for a set time, and not to wake up in between. But children tend to want to be with their parents, not alone, at night, and want to sleep when they feel like it, for as long as seems natural. If they wake in the night alone, it's normal to be frightened.
What can be done: If you want to impose a pattern on your baby or young child's sleeping habits, you and your partner should agree, first of all, on what sort of routine you want to achieve, then use loving, confident and consistent methods to help your child learn. Some parents are content to follow what their child seems to need, but for others a predictable routine is preferable. Behavioral

patterns alter in times of illness, change and anxiety, and then you'll need patience and sensitivity to meet your child's special needs.

Sleep talking

Talking while asleep can be normal, but is more common with a fever or at a time of worry or excitement. It may be part of dreaming sleep or a feature of a night terror.
What can be done: Go to the child and check that he's comfortable. If he wakes, see if he needs a drink, to go to the bathroom, or simply your presence and reassurance. Sometimes a specific worry is revealed by what the child is saying in his sleep.

see also **Nightmares**

Sleep walking

A sleep walking child usually has open eyes but isn't truly awake or aware of anyone. It looks as though he knows where he is going and when to go back to bed.
What can be done: Don't wake the child, but gently lead him back to bed and stay with him until you're sure he's asleep. Sleep walking is sometimes a sign of stress, so try to find out if your child is worried about anything.

Smallpox

A serious viral illness which has been declared eradicated by the World Health Organization, following extensive vaccination programs worldwide.

Smoking

Few young children actively smoke, but many are victims of passive smoking, during pregnancy or afterwards, simply by being with a smoker. A pregnant woman who smokes is more likely to produce a low birth weight baby unless she stopped smoking before the 20th week. Smokers have more complications in pregnancy and labor, and their babies are at greater risk of dying during labor and the first week of life. It's also possible that the breast milk supply may be affected. A slight but measurable negative effect of smoking during pregnancy has been found on physical growth and intellectual development up to the age of 11. Babies of parents who smoke have more chest infections, and children of such parents have more upper respiratory tract infections.
What can be done: Stop smoking when you are pregnant or, if you can't, decrease the amount that you smoke. It's really best to stop when you are trying to conceive. Smoke as little as possible in a confined space with your children. Because they may copy your smoking habits later, make sure they know of the risk of developing lung cancer, chronic bronchitis, emphysema and coronary heart disease.

see also **Low birth weight**

Sneezing

A baby's nasal passages are relatively so small that mucus or particles of dust are particularly likely to make him sneeze to get rid of them. This is why, with a cold, a baby is more likely to sneeze than an older child.

Soiling (Encopresis)

This is uncontrolled bowel movements in a previously trained child.
Symptoms: The child's pants may be slightly stained or heavily soiled. Some children have occasional accidents when they haven't long been trained. Soiling is most often caused by constipation. Soiling due to emotional problems can be harder to correct.
What can be done: Because soiling is often caused by liquid bowel movements leaking around hard, dry, constipated stool, treat any constipation. Never make your child think you don't love him because he has soiled. If anxiety or some other emotional disorder underlies the problem, try to resolve it with help from your doctor if necessary. If your child goes to school or daycare, send him with clean pants and baby wipes so that he isn't smelly all day.

see also **Constipation**

Sore bottom

A sore bottom in a child out of diapers can

result from diarrhea, certain spicy foods, inadequate washing, worms, a foreign object such as a toy in a girl's vulva or vagina, infection, masturbation or child sexual abuse. A split in the skin around the anus (an anal fissure) causes acute discomfort on going to the bathroom.
What can be done: Young children need to be taught how to wash and wipe their bottoms efficiently. Children can't always describe their symptoms accurately and may say they have a sore bottom when they actually have cystitis, which is often missed.
see also **Anal fissure, Diarrhea, Masturbation, Sugar intolerance, Urinary tract infections, Worms,** *and p. 33 for* keeping clean and dry

Sore throat

Four out of five sore throats are caused by viruses and the rest by bacteria. The tonsils are usually inflamed, and so is the back of the throat. Acute inflammation is known as tonsilitis. A sore throat can occur by itself or with a cold, infection of the ears or sinuses, glandular fever or, rarely, diphtheria.
Symptoms: Apart from soreness of the throat, there may be tummy ache and earache, a fever, irritability, loss of appetite, a cough, a runny nose and swollen lymph nodes (glands) in the neck. Mild sore throats usually only last for a few days and need no treatment.
What can be done: Keep your child at home while he feels ill, keep him cool if he has a fever, and let him eat and drink as he wants. Because some sore throats are due to bacterial infection, and because one sort of streptococcal bacterial infection can occasionally lead on to nephritis or rheumatic fever, some doctors like to give antibiotics every time, while others prefer to take a throat swab and only give antibiotics if necessary. A complication, such as an ear infection, sinusitis, or laryngitis, may need further medical treatment.
see also **Diphtheria, Glandular fever, Glomerulonephritis, Laryngitis, Rheumatic fever, Sinusitis, Tonsillitis**

Speech problems

The commonest "problem" is simply that a child is later than average at starting to talk, though he may still be within normal limits. There are many children who talk late because of a lack of opportunity to listen and therefore imitate. Other problems, such as lisping, stuttering, stammering and the muddling of consonants, usually clear up by themselves. Serious causes of language delay include mental retardation, deafness, dyslexia, autism and emotional problems.
What can be done: If you are worried, ask your pediatrician or family doctor for advice. They will refer your child to a specialist if necessary. It is worth considering whether your child gets enough listening experience and talking practice in a one-to-one situation.
see also **Autism, Deafness, Dyslexia, Lisping, Stammer and stutter.**

Spina bifida

A defect in one or more of the spinal bones varying from a simple absence of some bone, to a larger defect, often in the lower back, or to the complete exposure of part of the spinal cord. It is probably caused by a combination of inherited and environmental factors.
Symptoms: Severely affected children have paralyzed legs and incontinence of urine and bowel movements, and 90 percent have hydrocephalus. One in two is mentally retarded.
What can be done: Your child may need one or more operations, and, if seriously physically or mentally handicapped, will need continuous care for the rest of his life. A woman who has had a baby with spina bifida has an increased risk of bearing another affected baby, so may wish to have genetic counseling. Prenatal testing is also available.
see also **Hydrocephalus,** *p. 66 for* looking after a handicapped child, *and p. 216 for* useful addresses

Squint

A squint means that a child doesn't use both his eyes together. It is also known as a strabismus, a lazy eye, a cast or a crossed eye.

Symptoms: The eyes look in different directions for some or all of the time. Sometimes the squint alternates from eye to eye.
What can be done: Babies under three months naturally squint sometimes, but if you are worried, or if your older baby or child squints, consult your doctor to find out if your child needs to see a specialist. It's dangerous to ignore a squint because it can lead to blindness in one eye if not treated. Treatment of a squint may involve covering the good eye with a patch. Other treatments include correcting any visual defects and possibly one or more operations.
see also p. 82 for the eye

Stammer and stutter

A stammer is when the speech is interrupted or hesitant. With a stutter, the sounds are repeated several times.
What can be done: Both stammering and stuttering can be normal up to the age of about 6 and may happen because the child's brain is temporarily racing ahead of its ability to form the words. Don't ever comment on a stammer or stutter, and especially don't tease your child or become impatient. Most children grow out of the problem if no fuss is made, and very few need speech therapy.

Stealing

Children under 4 don't understand what's theirs and what isn't, and often like to take interesting things home with them. Slightly older children also like to borrow things, often without asking, even though they know they don't belong to them. If an older child deliberately takes something that belongs to someone else, it may be a sign of an underlying emotional problem.
What can be done: Overreaction and punishment are unhelpful – it's more constructive to try and find out what is troubling him. If you can't find out why your child is disturbed, ask for professional help from your doctor or a child psychologist.

Stomach ache – *see* Tummy ache

Stutter – *see* Stammer and stutter

Stye

A boil caused by an infection in the sebaceous (oil) gland at the base of an eyelash.
Symptoms: Part of the eyelid appears red, becomes swollen and painful, and eventually "points" to a head.
What can be done: To soothe the pain and encourage the stye to come to a head, soak a clean washcloth in hand-hot water, squeeze it out and hold it against the stye several times a day. Leave it there until cold. Boil any washcloths you have used to sterilize them and wash your hands after you have touched your child's stye, as the infection can be passed round the family. The stye may burst, or heal without discharging its pus. If a bad stye has come to a head, but won't burst, ask your doctor to pull out the offending eyelash with a pair of tweezers to give instant relief. Hold your child's head still while this is done to prevent any danger of the tweezers damaging the child's eye if he moves.

A stye takes about 5 days to become large enough to burst spontaneously. A diet low in refined foods can help prevent recurrent styes.

Sudden infant death syndrome – *see* Crib death

Sugar intolerance

Damage to the intestinal lining, such as with gastroenteritis or celiac disease, can prevent the absorption of one or more sugars into the

bloodstream by creating a shortage of the necessary enzymes. In rare cases, one of these enzymes is deficient at birth. Intolerance to lactose (milk sugar) becomes increasingly common from the age of 3, especially in black or oriental children, as a normal part of development. Lactose intolerance is one of the most likely sugar intolerances as a result of gastroenteritis.
Symptoms: Watery, frothy diarrhea, a swollen tummy, tummy rumbling and soreness of the skin round the anus occur after eating or drinking sugar. Mild lactose intolerance causes vague, crampy, central tummy ache with no obvious relation to drinking milk and no diarrhea. Continuing loose bowel movements and a sore bottom after gastroenteritis, especially if worse after sugary food and drink, suggest that temporary sugar intolerance may be the problem.
What can be done: If you suspect lactose intolerance, reduce the amount of milk in the diet and consult your doctor. It probably need not be cut out completely, but it's sensible for the child not to drink a lot at one time. Temporary sugar intolerance after gastroenteritis can be treated by cutting down you child's sugar intake for a while. Limit the amount of fruit juice you give him (perhaps by diluting it by half with water), reduce or cut out cows' milk, and reduce foods high in natural or added sugar. Make sure your child has an adequate diet by giving foods relatively low in sugar, but consult your doctor for advice if the child is young or if you are unsure what to do.
see also **Celiac disease, Gastroenteritis, Milk intolerance**

Sulking

Sulking is a way of expressing displeasure and anger, and some children find that it gives them considerable power to manipulate the adults around them. If you don't recognize it for what it is, it can prolong the bad feelings in your child instead of dealing with them. It can also make you feel angry or threatened yourself, and your response can then make the child feel worse.
What can be done: Show your child by your own example how to cope with feelings of anger, hurt and resentment in a healthier way. When your child does express his feelings more openly, help him to deal with them constructively. Most important is to set a good example and not to sulk yourself.

Swollen lymph nodes

Lymph nodes, or "glands," are antibody-production units found throughout the body. They enlarge when needed to fight infection and in certain blood disorders. The commonest cause of swollen nodes is a viral or bacterial infection.
Symptoms: The lymph nodes in the neck, armpits and groin can be felt when enlarged. Sometimes swollen lymph nodes are tender, and in mesenteric adenitis the nodes around the intestine give rise to tummy ache.
What can be done: Consult your doctor who will treat any infection. If he suspects that anything else may be wrong, he'll arrange for blood tests to help with the diagnosis.
see also **Mesenteric adenitis,** *and p. 102 for* the immune system

T

Tall child

The average girl is about half her future adult height at 18 months and the average boy half his future adult height at 2 years old. With improved health, nutrition and social circumstances, people are generally taller than their predecessors. Tall parents are more likely to have a tall child than are short parents, but there are often surprises. An excess of growth hormone is a rare condition that can make a child grow too tall.
What can be done: If you are really concerned about your child's height, check with your doctor that all is well medically. Bone X-rays can predict final height fairly accurately.

Teething

Teething can last from about 5 or 6 months to 2 years or more.

Symptoms: Many children drool a lot, have red patches on their faces, are restless or irritable, lose their appetite and sleep badly as each tooth comes through. The gums are itchy and sometimes inflamed, and the child often likes to chew on something hard.
What can be done: Freqent washing, careful drying and the use of a cream help a rash on the face. Don't make your child eat if he doesn't feel like it, because this is the way to start feeding problems. Try rubbing the gum with your fingertip and let your child chew on something like a teether. Giving him a hug and distracting his attention are time-consuming, but usually more helpful than anything else. If your child has bronchitis, diarrhea, a fever, keeps rubbing his ear or has a convulsion, don't put it all down to teething, consult your doctor.
see also **Bronchitis, Convulsions,** *and see also p. 86 for* the teeth and gums

Temper tantrums

A young child – usually between 2 and 4 years old – may have bursts of uncontrollabl anger or rage, most often because he can't do something, isn't allowed to do it, or is made to do it. Learning to accept that life doesn't always go as he wishes is a difficult lesson for a child. It may take him a while, and parents need patience to cope with the inevitable frustration in the meantime.
What can be done: Don't react to a tantrum by becoming angry yourself. These temper tantrums are simply the result of your child's wildly swinging emotions, and are frightening for him. Stay near your child and wait until it's over, then, without giving in over the issue, show the child that you still love him in spite of what has happened.

Tetanus

A bacterial infection causing muscle spasms. It's generally caught from infected dirt entering a cut.
Symptoms: Several months after the original cut or wound, there is a sore throat, followed by pain in the neck and muscles, then spasm of the jaw and mouth.
What can be done: Prevent tetanus by having your child routinely immunized against it in infancy, and by keeping up the immunity as necessary afterwards. If your child hasn't been immunized and has a deep wound or skin puncture, take him to your doctor or the hospital for an antitetanus injection.
see also p. 53 for immunization

Thalassemia

An inherited anemia found in people originating from the Mediterranean area, Asia and Africa.
Symptoms: A child has severe anemia and his growth may be impaired. Diabetes and heart conditions are longer-term problems.
What can be done: The child needs hospital treatment which includes blood transfusions. Sometimes the spleen has to be removed. If you know this condition runs in your family, you may wish to see a genetic counselor.
see also **Anemia,** *and p. 216 for* useful addresses

Thin child

Normal thinness is usually a result of a child's inherited body structure and appetite, together with his natural metabolic rate and the amount of exercise he gets. Some children are thinner than is good for them, and reasons may include both physical and emotional problems.
What can be done: Talk to your doctor who will help you identify the cause of your child's failure to gain enough weight.

Thirst

Thirst may be caused by reduced fluid intake, diarrhea, sweating, fever or vomiting. Because a baby or ill child can't get his own drinks, be sure to offer plenty of fluid if there's any chance he may be thirsty.

Thirst for no apparent reason, together with weight loss and passing lots of urine, could be a sign of diabetes, so ask your doctor to check your child's blood and urine.
see also **Diabetes mellitus**

Thrush – *see* Moniliasis

Thumb sucking

The sucking reflex is present from well before birth and the desire to suck continues for 2 to 3 years on average, though some children go on for much longer. Sucking is comforting and pleasurable, and is a relief from tiredness, boredom or feeling upset. Thumb sucking in a breastfed baby is often seen if the baby isn't allowed enough time at the breast.
What can be done: No medical problems arise from thumb sucking, but in some children the second teeth are pushed out of alignment and may need orthodontic care. If you want to encourage your older child to stop thumb sucking, remember to praise him when he is not doing it rather than nag when he is. Giving him extra attention and providing things to do when he is bored or tired may help too. Letting your baby stay at the breast for longer will help stop him thumb sucking and also increase your milk supply.

Thyroid disorders – *see* Goiter, Hypothyroidism

Tongue furring

Some furring of the tongue is normal, but an increase is found if a child suffers from dehydration or has a fever.
Symptoms: A thicker whitish or yellowish coating than usual. White sticky curdy patches may be caused by thrush (moniliasis).
What can be done: Treat thrush if it is present, but otherwise don't worry. As soon as your child's fluid balance is corrected or the fever gone, the furring will return to normal levels.

see also **Dehydration, Moniliasis**

Tongue tie

This is an extension of the normal amount of tissue tethering the tongue to the floor of the mouth.
What can be done: An operation is only done these days if medically necessary, for instance if it interferes with sucking.

Tonsillitis

Inflammation of the tonsils by viral or bacterial infection which usually shows that they are doing their job of fighting infection effectively.
Symptoms: The tonsils are enlarged and red, and may have spots of pus on them. Swallowing is painful and the child is irritable, not eating, has a cough, a fever and bad breath. Severe tonsillitis causes vomiting, swollen lymph nodes (glands) in the neck and a tummy ache. The younger the child, the less likely he is to complain of a sore throat. Tonsillitis usually clears up in a week or so. Complications can include ear infection and, rarely, nephritis or rheumatic fever.
What can be done: Give your child plenty to drink and let him eat what he wants. Acetaminophen helps relieve the soreness and bring down the fever. Your doctor may prescribe antibiotics if a throat culture is positive for a bacterial infection. Keep your child away from other children until he starts getting better, even if he is on antibiotics.

Tonsillectomy (removal of the tonsils) is not recommended unless the tonsils no longer work efficiently, they are so large that eating is difficult, infections are very frequent or the child is snoring at night. The operation will make the child feel better, eat more and lose his bad breath, but it won't reduce the number of ear or upper respiratory chest infections, or prevent laryngitis, sinusitis, hay fever or sore throats.

see also **Glomerulonephritis, Rheumatic fever,** *p. 88 for* **the upper respiratory tract,** *and p. 102 for* **the immune system**

Toothache

This comes from irritation of the dentine of a tooth. The commonest cause is dental decay.
Symptoms: Toothache is made worse by hot or cold foods, or by tapping the tooth. It seems worse at night.
What can be done: Acetaminophen in the correct dose and a covered hot water bottle (filled with warm, not boiling, water) against the face will help the pain until your child can see the dentist.

see also **Dental caries,** *and p. 86 for* **the teeth and gums**

Tooth discoloration

Lines across the teeth, opaque patches or pitting may have been caused by an illness or poor nutrition. White patches, severe brownish discoloration and pitting may be seen if a child had too much fluoride when young. Brownish-yellow staining and pitting of the enamel can also follow the use of certain medicines, such as tetracycline antibiotics.
What can be done: Check with your dentist that your child isn't getting too much fluoride. Ideally tetracycline should be avoided from the fourth month of pregnancy to 16 years to protect your child's teeth from staining. Superficial discoloration from plaque can be cleaned by thorough toothbrushing.

Torsion of the testis

Torsion, or twisting, of the testis on its spermatic cord happens mainly in older boys, though a modified form is sometimes found in newborns.
Symptoms: In the most common type of torsion, there is sudden pain in the scrotum, together with nausea, vomiting and a swollen tender testis. In a newborn, torsion of the testis shows up as a firm nontender mass in a discolored scrotum.
What can be done: An emergency operation is needed to fix the testis in place.

Toxocariasis – *see* Worms

Tuberculosis

A bacterial infection which has become much less common, thanks to better public health measures and drug treatment. Tuberculosis (TB) is usually spread by infected droplets from coughing, sneezing or speaking.
Symptoms: These are usually very few, even if the illness is progressing. Sometimes there is weight loss, a cough, tiredness and night sweating. The disease is most likely to affect the lungs, though other parts of the body can be involved.
What can be done: Skin tests for TB are routinely done at one year of age and frequently thereafter. Anyone working with children should have regular checks for TB, and people with active TB shouldn't work with children even if they are having anti-TB drug treatment.
see also p. 53 for immunization

Tummy ache

Both physical and emotional problems can cause tummy ache, and sometimes it's difficult to tell the difference. An infection anywhere in the body often gives rise to tummy ache. Measles and mumps can cause it, as can food allergy, a swallowed foreign body, obstruction of the bowel, asthma, sickle-cell anemia, worms, cystic fibrosis, diabetes, a tumor, lead poisoning, a reaction to a drug or medication, and emotional problems. Some children have pain before they defecate, while indigestion from the poor chewing of food, from eating quickly, or from eating certain foods is not uncommon.
Symptoms: The pain varies in its position, timing, severity and nature according to what is wrong. Look out for associated symptoms, such as pain, vomiting, a rash and signs of infection.
What can be done: The intensity of the pain may not be a reliable indicator of the severity of the condition, and it's always better to be cautious. Consult your doctor if your child's pain is bad enough to make him lie down; if it lasts more than 6 hours; if it's associated with vomiting for more than an hour or so; if it keeps recurring; or if you are worried. Always get medical advice if you are worried about your baby. If the problem seems to be emotional, try to find out what is leading to your child's fear or anxiety, perhaps with the help of your doctor or the child's teacher.
see also **Allergy, Asthma, Cystic fibrosis, Diabetes mellitus, Lead poisoning, Measles, Mumps, Sickle-cell anemia, Worms**

Umbilical hernia – *see* Hernia

Undescended testes

The testes are usually in their final position in the scrotum at birth, but in preterm babies their descent from the abdomen is delayed. In some babies, the testis on one or both sides fails to complete the journey to the scrotum and is said to be "undescended." In many boys, the testes are "retractile" – they disappear from the scrotum from time to time, especially when it is cold. This is normal and the testes return when warm again.
Symptoms: One or both sides of the scrotum feels and looks empty all the time.
What can be done: If you're at all worried, consult your doctor. If your son's testes are still not in the scrotum most of the time by the age of one year, an operation can tether them in place. It this isn't done, his fertility could be impaired.

see also p. 98 for the reproduction system

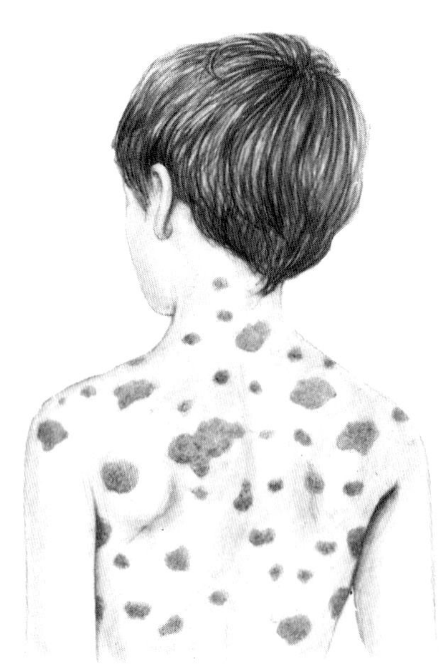

The skin lesions of urticaria tend to disappear in 48 hours, but new ones may continue to appear.

Urinary tract infections

Infections of the urinary tract are common in childhood and are usually caused by bacteria. When one or both kidneys are primarily involved, it is known as pyelonephritis. Inflammation of the bladder is called cystitis.
Symptoms: The child urinates frequently and it hurts him to do so. The urine may smell unpleasant. He also has day- or night-time wetting, with a fever, vomiting, tummy ache and a loss of appetite. Sometimes there are no symptoms and the infection is discovered during a routine urine examination.
What can be done: Your doctor will arrange for your child's urine to be tested for signs of infection. If antibiotics are prescribed, it is essential that the full course is taken to ensure that the infection does not recur.

see also p.96 for the urinary tract

Urticaria (Hives)

An allergic skin rash caused in susceptible children by certain drugs or foods, or by touching things to which the child is sensitive. It is also known as hives.
Symptoms: There are raised, red, itchy welts which can affect any part of the body. Urticaria involving the mouth, lips or genitals can cause considerable swelling. Sometimes it is associated with difficulty in breathing or swallowing, or with pains in the joints.
What can be done: Calamine lotion or even cold water help soothe the itching. If you can, find out which food, drug or contact item is the culprit and help your child to avoid it in future. If the symptoms aren't too bad, it makes sense to confirm your diagnosis by seeing if repeat exposure to the suspect substance causes urticaria again. Your doctor may prescribe antihistamine medicine or tablets which help within a short time. If there's trouble with breathing or swallowing, consult your doctor urgently.

Vaginal discharge

Some colorless or pale mucous discharge from the vagina is normal in a young girl, and in a newborn girl it can be quite profuse. An abnormal discharge can be caused by a urinary infection; pinworms; sensivity to chemicals; an object lodged in the vagina; bacterial, viral or fungal infection; lack of hygiene; or irritation from masturbation.
Symptoms: A foul-smelling or copious discharge, perhaps with itching and tenderness.

What can be done: Look for pinworms, check on your child's cleanliness and, with an older child, ask whether she's pushed something into her vagina. Consider whether she could have been sexually molested, and gently give her the opportunity to tell you. If you can't find the problem, consult your doctor who may check for infection by sending a swab of the discharge and a sample of urine to a laboratory for analysis.

see also **Masturbation, Worms**

Verruca – *see* Warts

Volvulus

A twisting of the small intestine causing obstruction.
Symptoms: Signs of intestinal obstruction including frequent persistent vomiting, abdominal swelling and a lack of bowel movements.
What can be done: Seek medical attention urgently.

Vomiting

The forcible ejection of stomach contents through the mouth. It doesn't strictly speaking include regurgitation or rumination.

There are many possible causes of vomiting in children, including food intolerance, pyloric stenosis, gastroenteritis, infection, migraine, poisoning, appendicitis, jaundice, injury, certain drugs, a foreign body, motion sickness, shock and anxiety.
What can be done: Consult your doctor urgently if there is red or black blood in your child's vomit, if he has a severe tummy ache, or if he becomes irritable or lethargic. Unless you are confident that your child's vomiting is nothing to worry about, ask for his advice anyway. Dehydration can be avoided by giving frequent small drinks. If the child can't drink or can't keep fluids down, hospitalization may be essential.

see also **Appendicitis, Food intolerance, Gastroenteritis, Jaundice, Migraine, Motion sickness, Pyloric stenosis**

W

Warts (Verrucae)

Growths in the skin caused by a particular viral infection. A wart on the sole of the foot is a plantar wart.
Symptoms: The commonest wart is a rough yellowish lump usually found on the hands. Flat, brown "plane" warts are seen on the face, neck and hands. A plantar wart is painful and, because it is embedded in hard skin, it can be difficult to spot when it is still small enough to treat easily.
What can be done: Eight out of ten warts, including plantar warts, disappear spontaneously in time, but as you can't tell which ones won't go, it's worth treating all of them. If your child has a plantar wart, make sure that the foot is covered with a special sock from the pharmacist before he goes swimming in a public pool. He shouldn't share a bath mat or walk barefoot at home. Various chemical applications can be bought over the counter to get rid of warts. Sometimes specialist treatment is needed from the podiatrist, surgeon, dermatologist or your pediatrician, in the form of liquid nitrogen, stronger chemical treatment or surgery.

Water on the brain – *see* Hydrocephalus

Wax

Wax is made by the lining of the ear canal to remove dirt and dust from the canal. Some children make more wax than others and some make harder wax. Normal wax produces no problems, but a build-up of hard wax can cause partial deafness.
What can be done: If you are worried that there is more wax than normal, ask your doctor to examine your child's ear. Hard wax causing deafness may need to be softened and then syringed. Don't poke anything down your child's ear when cleaning out wax. Simply remove what you can easily see.

Wheezing

A high-pitched whistling sound made by air flowing through a narrowed air passage, usually worse on breathing out. An infection, such as bronchiolitis or pneumonia, or an allergic response, such as asthma, are the commonest causes. An inhaled foreign body can also cause wheezing.
Symptoms: Apart from the wheezing, there may be difficulty in breathing, or a fever.
What can be done: Unless your child frequently has asthma and you are confident that you can cope with it, consult your doctor. If a bacterial infection is suspected, he'll prescribe antibiotics. Medicine to enlarge the diameter of the air passages may also be helpful. Give your child plenty to drink and try to keep the air moist (with a humidifier, or a kettle boiling safely in the room). Wheezing can be frightening for a child, so don't leave him alone.
see also **Asthma, Bronchiolitis, Pneumonia**

Whipworms – *see* Worms

Whooping cough (Pertussis)

A bacterial infection which is very contagious and potentially serious. It is spread by coughing, sneezing and talking. The incubation period is 8 to 14 days.
Symptoms: The child has a cold, then starts to cough. The typical "whooping" cough isn't always present, especially in young babies. When present, it consists of a series of short coughs followed by a "whoop" as air is breathed in. A child often vomits with the cough and this can lead to weight loss. A few children are so short of oxygen during a coughing bout that they go blue and may even have a convulsion. The cough may, at worst, last for many months. Complications include ear infections and lung disease.
What can be done: The child is infectious for 4 days before the illness begins and should be isolated from non-immune people for 21 days from the onset of the cough, unless your doctor prescribes an antibiotic (erythromycin) in which case isolate the child for 7 days. Cough medicines don't stop the cough. Putting an affected baby to the breast sometimes stops a bout of coughing. Routine immunization is available and can be very useful. Some children should not be immunized. Discuss this with your doctor.
see also **Convulsions,** *p. 53 for* **immunization,** *and p. 177 for* **infectious illnesses chart**

Worms

Several worms can live in the body. The commonest in children in this country are pinworms, but roundworms, whipworms, hookworms and tapeworms can also be a problem. Toxocariasis is an infestation with the larvae of the cat or dog roundworm.
Symptoms: With pinworms, there is itching round the anus and sometimes an inflammation of a girl's vagina and urinary passage, and vague tummy aches. With roundworms, there is tummy ache, fever, wheezing, and sometimes blood is coughed up. Whipworms cause diarrhea, and hookworms cause itching where the worm larvae entered the skin, tummy ache, diarrhea and anemia. A tapeworm can cause tummy ache. Toxocariasis can cause damage to the liver, lungs, brain and eyes following an initial fever, cough and wheezing.
What can be done: Your doctor will make the diagnosis and prescribe worm-killing drugs.

For pinworms, the whole family should take the medicine. Strip the affected child's bed and, after allowing the dust to settle, vacuum the floor and wipe all surfaces thoroughly with a damp cloth, because the worm eggs can live for 2 to 3 weeks outside the body. Then wash the bedclothes and bedding, cut your child's fingernails and scrub them (in case he has scratched his bottom). Tell his teacher or daycare provider that your child has caught worms, so the other mothers can check whether their children are infested, and teach your child to wash his hands really thoroughly after using the bathroom anywhere, but especially away from home.

Roundworms and whipworms are seen only in areas where there is poor sanitation or where human sewage is used as a fertilizer. Good hygiene prevents worm eggs entering the body from anything that might have been contaminated with eggs from the bowel movements of an infested person.

Hookworms are most common in warm climates (including the southeast part of the US), and it's sensible not to go barefoot in a hot country if there's any danger of the ground or water being contaminated with sewage.

Toxocariasis can be prevented by making sure children don't put their hands to their mouths after playing where dogs or cats have defecated.

see also p.15 for pet hygiene

Common Infectious Illnesses

Illness	Symptoms	Infectious period
Chickenpox *Incubation:* *13-17 days*	*At first:* A headache, swollen lymph nodes, fever, and a transient blotchy rash. *1-2 days later:* Classic rash of little pimples which appear over 3-4 days, are most profuse on the trunk, and develop in a few hours into blisters which dry and scab unless infected. These fall off in about 10 days.	Most infectious 1-2 days before classic rash. Unlikely to be infectious when scabs have dried.
Fifth disease *Incubation:* *7-28 days* *(average 16)*	A "slapped cheek" rash plus a blotchy rash on the forearms and lower legs and slightly on the trunk. The rash is itchy and is worse when the child is hot or upset. As it fades it has a lacy appearance. The child is usually well and the rash lasts from 2-39 days, with an average of 11 days.	No isolation is necessary as this is such a mild illness.
German measles *Incubation:* *14-21 days*	*At first:* A runny nose, sore throat, conjunctivitis, a slightly raised temperature, loss of appetite, tiredness, and swollen lymph nodes behind the ears and at the back of the neck. *24 hours later:* A rash of flat or slightly raised pink spots (which may join up, especially on the face) appears behind the ears and on the forehead and spreads to the rest of the body, sparing the feet, ankles, and around the mouth. The rash may itch. It usually goes in 3 days.	Possibly from 7 days before the rash to up to 8 days after it has gone. Isolate especially from women who may be in early pregnancy.
Measles *Incubation:* *10-12 days*	*At first:* A slightly raised temperature, conjunctivitis with dislike of light, a dry cough, a cold, and white Koplik's spots under the cheeks opposite the molar teeth. *3-4 days later:* A sudden high fever, loss of appetite, tummy ache, swollen lymph nodes in the neck, diarrhea, vomiting, and a rash of flat red spots which begins at the hairline and spreads to the face (where the spots may merge) and the rest of the body in 24 hours.	Possibly from 7 days after exposure to up to 10 days after the rash begins. In practice it is likely to be noninfectious within 3 days of the rash beginning.
Mumps *Incubation:* *14-21 days*	*At first:* A fever, headache, and aching muscles. *1-2 days later:* Swelling of one or more salivary glands (usually the parotids just below the earlobes) lasting 3-7 days. Dry mouth which hurts on eating, talking or when saliva is stimulated by sour food or drink.	May be infectious from 6 days before swelling to 3 days after swelling has subsided.
Roseola *Incubation:* *7-17 days* *(average 10)*	*At first:* A sudden high fever and perhaps a slight cold, sore throat and headache. *1-5 days later:* The fever goes and a rash appears. Flat spots or pimples spread from the chest and back to the neck and arms, face and legs.	Thought to be no need for isolation as the illness is so mild.
Scarlet fever *Incubation:* *1-7 days*	*At first:* A sudden fever, headache, swollen lymph nodes in the neck, vomiting, loss of appetite and tummy ache. *24 hours later:* A fine rash of small red spots which may feel like sandpaper spreads from the neck, armpits and groin to the rest of the body except around the mouth. It lasts for about a week and is followed by flaking.	Infectious until 1-2 days after beginning of antibiotic treatment and 24 hours with no fever.
Whooping cough *Incubation:* *8-14 days*	A cold followed by a cough which may be a classic "whooping cough." There may be vomiting and blueness with the cough. The child may lose weight.	From 4 days before the cough begins to 21 days after.

Part Four
SAFETY

One of the most important things that we as parents do for our children is to protect them and keep them safe from danger. Obviously it is impossible to prevent all accidents, but if enough attention is paid to prevention, then we will feel that we have done our very best to make our children's environment as safe as is reasonably possible.

Young children under five have nearly all their accidents at home, with the kitchen providing the most potential hazards, followed by the living room and the yard. As children grow older, they have increasing numbers of accidents and dangerous experiences outside the home, particularly on the roads. Your child learns by observing and imitating you, so the way that you deal with safety will obviously influence her. If you are always careful when using equipment and scrupulous about car and road safety, then your child will become aware as she grows up that safety is important.

As she becomes more capable of looking after herself, you have to find the balance between trying to provide protection for her and letting her discover, learn and take increasing responsibility for her own safety, at first under supervision and later alone. When deciding whether something is safe for your child to do, be guided by her ability and experience rather than by her age. Allowing her to be dependent for as long as she needs is the key to giving your child her independence.

THE DEVELOPING CHILD

Children grow, develop and acquire new skills rapidly, but not always as you might expect. This is why it pays to be familiar with the stages of development that your baby and young child will go through. If you know which new skills and abilities are likely to come next you can anticipate necessary safety precautions. Your child develops faster in the first two years than at any other time of her life and every few weeks, or even days, she'll learn something new. The baby who at first can't move from place to place very soon becomes able to roll over. Soon she'll learn to sit, grasp things, crawl, pull herself up to stand, walk around furniture and then walk alone. Whatever her stage of development, a healthy child is curious about herself and her surroundings, constantly wanting to find out more and put everything to the test.

Patient repetition

The younger the child, the less aware she is of danger and she is therefore particularly dependent on you to protect her. Older children gradually learn only to take reasonable risks, but babies and toddlers don't learn from a single bad experience. This isn't their fault and it certainly doesn't mean they're naughty – it's just the way babies are. It will be some years before your child learns by her mistakes or pays attention to you the first time that you warn her about something.

The early months

Young babies soon learn to suck their fingers or whatever else finds its way into their mouths, such as bedding or clothing. Gradually they learn to lift up their heads and some babies will roll over before they are three months old. Accidents can happen even to such young children, but they are less likely with a little forethought.

Remember that older brothers and sisters may be jealous and show their feelings towards the baby in ways that are frankly dangerous. If you sense this is a problem, don't leave the baby with the older child. Remember that even well-intentioned and loving things done by an older child can backfire and be dangerous for a baby.

Equipment and toys

Always check that any equipment you use for your baby is sturdily constructed, with no sharp edges or places where fingers and limbs could get stuck. Make sure that crib and playpen bars are spaced so that a baby's head cannot get caught. Federal regulations now require that crib slats be spaced 2⅜ inches apart. There are strict safety standards for the manufacture of most items of equipment, so check that what you have chosen conforms to government regulations.

Choose toys that can't easily break or come apart. Don't give your baby anything sharp or pointed. Check that soft toys' eyes and any small parts are firmly fixed; remove any ribbons.

IMPORTANT

- Make sure a cat can't get into the crib or carriage and lie on your baby's face.
- Never give your young baby a pillow as she might suffocate.
- Never leave your baby lying unprotected from the sun, and remember that the sunlight will move.
- Never put your baby's infant seat or bouncing cradle on a raised surface – it only takes a little movement to make it fall off.
- Never leave plastic bags or wrappings near your baby.
- Never leave your baby alone with a bottle or food in her mouth.
- Never let a baby go to sleep in a bib or clothes with ribbons that tie at the neck.
- Never put a necklace or pacifier on a ribbon or cord around your baby's neck.

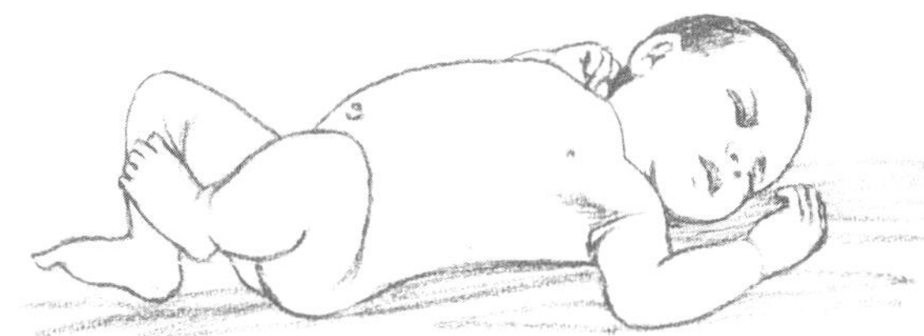

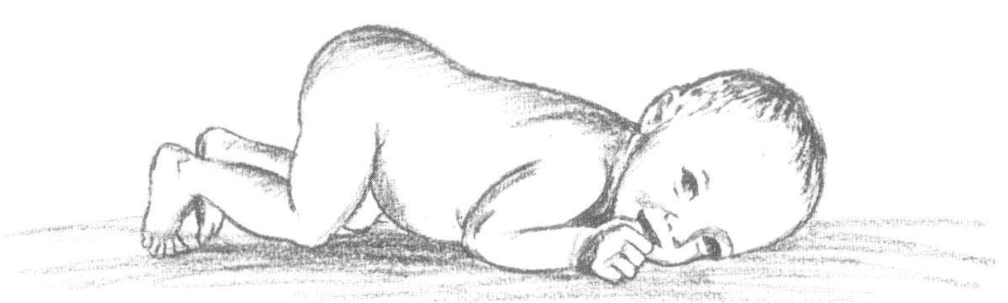

Rolling and reaching

Babies start trying to roll over any time from the end of the third month and by five months most have managed to turn themselves over. They usually roll from their tummy to their back first and it's not long before they become very good at it. If you're changing your baby's diaper on a raised surface, make sure that you have everything you require at hand, so that you don't need to turn away or leave her, even for a moment. Better still, change her on a changing mat on the floor.

Although some equipment is sold with an integral harness, buy a separate safety harness and make sure that your baby is harnessed with this whenever she is in her stroller or high chair. Ensure that the anchor straps are short enough to prevent her slipping down or, later standing up.

Grabbing and grasping

Babies start reaching for things at four or five months and there'll come a time when your baby reaches for something and actually grasps hold of it. She may not know what to do with it at first, but eventually her clenched hands will find their way to her mouth and she'll start sucking or gnawing it. Once successful at picking something up, a baby's curiosity knows no bounds and anything within reach is grabbed and examined in her mouth. Check that toys and other accessible objects are not small enough for her to swallow and choke on. Keep small, hard items of food, such as nuts and popcorn, well out of her reach.

Learning to sit

Your baby will soon learn to sit up by herself – most babies can sit without support some time between five and eight months – but while she's learning there'll be many a time when she topples over. Don't leave her sitting alone supported by cushions, because she might fall over, bury her head in a cushion and not be able to move away.

IMPORTANT

- Never leave a baby sitting alone on a sofa, chair or the floor.
- Never leave a young baby sitting with her head unsupported.
- Never leave a baby alone with a dog or cat.
- Never carry a hot drink while holding a baby.
- Never let a baby play on the floor near a door that could open.
- Never leave a baby unattended near water.
- Secure any seat cushions which could come off if she grabbed hold of them.

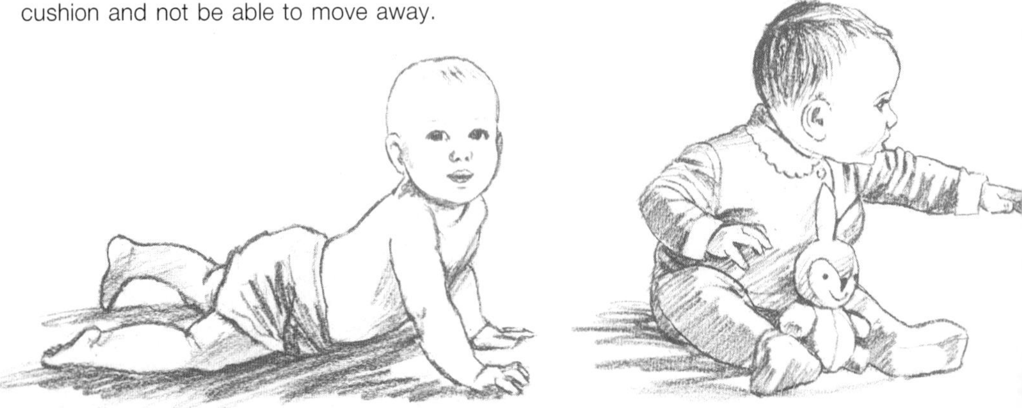

Crawling and walking

Once your baby can crawl, your life with her will never be the same again because she'll be able to get virtually anywhere and will be into everything. Most babies can crawl by ten months, though some babies become so good at shifting themselves along on their bottoms that they have no desire to crawl and may go straight from bottom-shuffling to walking.

Becoming more mobile

When your baby can stand, it won't be long before she starts walking or cruising around the furniture, or from person to person as they're sitting down, and then it's only a short step to walking. However a baby gets around, it's essential to clear anything from the room that might be dangerous for her to hold or get near, and remember that a baby who can stand or walk can reach things at a higher level than a crawler. Babies of this age have no notion of danger at all. You have to give them all the protection you can. Fire and water are particularly fascinating and it's essential to have any fire adequately guarded and never to leave your baby or young child unattended near water – indoors or out.

Make your home safe

If you haven't already done so, this is the time to go through your home and yard (see pages 186-91) to make them as "child-proof" as possible. Take time to think through possible hazards room by room. Any unstable furniture needs to be put away in case it topples over when your baby tries to pull herself up on it. Put a safety gate at the bottom of the stairs if you are downstairs, or at the top if you are upstairs. Make sure any medicines, nail polish remover, hair spray and other cosmetics, cleaning equipment or other poisonous items are safely locked away. Make sure that cupboards containing dishes or glasses are fitted with safety catches.

SAFETY EQUIPMENT

- A guard for the stove top or hobs.
- A fireguard to fit around any open or unguarded fire.
- Safety catches to secure drawers and cupboard doors.
- A safety gate to prevent access to stairs or any other part of the home.
- Safety glass to replace any ordinary glass fitted in doors and windows or covering table tops.
- Safety covers for all unused electric sockets.

Climbing and running

A child who can climb and run can easily find herself in a lot of danger. Some young children seem to have a good idea of their capabilities, but others are without fear and climb into positions from which they can't get down. A children's playground is a good place to see how different children behave at this stage. Whatever precautions you take at this age, your child is bound to fall over and hurt herself occasionally. It would be wrong to stop a child from enjoying herself, but there are some simple precautions you can take to ensure she is as safe as possible.

Slipping and sliding

Secure slippery rugs, especially at the foot of the stairs. Replace glass in your home with tempered glass, laminated glass, plexiglass or lexan. Remember that a glass door or window near the foot of the stairs is particularly dangerous. If your child has lace-up shoes, tie the laces with a secure knot so they won't come undone easily and trip her up. Don't let a child run around on slippery floor with socks or slippers with slippery soles. Teach her not to run with pointed objects in her hands or with anything in her mouth.

IMPORTANT

- Never allow your child to run unattended near a road.
- Never call to your child from across the road.
- Never let her climb on the banisters.
- Never leave a young child in a room with open windows that she could climb out of, and make sure upstairs windows are secured.
- Never let your child tease pets or leave her alone with a strange dog or cat.

Growing independence

Whatever her age, a child's progress in exploring the wider world isn't always straightforward. Illness, changing school or any other anxiety can make a child take a temporary step backwards in her growing independence.

Unless a child is ready and willing to venture forth from you, it's best to let her be as clingy as she wishes. This applies in many areas, whether it's learning to ride a bicycle or jump into the swimming pool. If a child is uneasy about doing something, then she probably won't enjoy it and may even endanger herself if she's physically or emotionally tense.

Safety outside the home

When your child ventures outside the home on her own, try always to remind her of particular points of danger she may meet and what to do about them. An older child may tease you about being too careful, but she knows deep down that you are doing it because you love her.

Teaching your child to "keep safe"

Most parents teach their children that they shouldn't accept sweets from strangers, but it's important also to tell your child never to accept a lift in a car from a stranger, or go with a stranger, whatever story is given to persuade her.

The more time your child spends out of your care, the more you may find yourself worrying about her being approached by a stranger, particularly with so much publicity being given to cases of abduction and sexual assault. In fact, the awful truth is that the majority of sexual assaults on children are by people they know already, so warning your child darkly about "strangers" is not necessarily enough. You can, to some extent, protect your child by talking to her about potential risks. Teach her that she has the right to say "no" when she feels uneasy in a situation or if anyone touches her in a sensitive area or in a way that she doesn't like. Try always to be sensitive to your child's feelings. Encourage her not to keep secrets and never dismiss what she says as a fanciful story.

Try to make sure that your child knows how to keep safe in any situation. Remind her that she can always ask a teacher or policeman for help or go into a store. Help her to learn her address and telephone number and, once she is old enough, how to make an emergency telephone call.

There are now many books available to help you teach your child to be confident about dealing with potentially threatening situations. In addition, in some areas the police will come into schools to give talks and show films on safety. There are also home videos, such as "Strong Kids, Safe Kids" and "Home Alone," aimed at teaching "good sense defense."

IMPORTANT

- Never ignore your child if she's struggling to tell you something that she thinks is important.
- Teach her not to get close to a stranger who approaches her and not to be afraid to shout or scream to draw attention to herself.
- Never leave your child unattended or under the supervision of another child.
- Never leave a child under twelve in a room alone with an unguarded fire.
- Never allow your child near a road alone until she is responsible about road safety (see page 192).

SAFETY AT HOME

Children are likely to spend most of the first few years at home and it's here that they have most of their accidents. Some safety precautions benefit both adults and children, but others are specifically geared towards children.

Preventing burns and scalds

The commonest household accidents involving children are burns and scalds. Homes are full of potential sources of burning, including open fires, electric, kerosene or gas fires, the stove, the electric coffee pot and other kitchen appliances, electric gadgets and lighting throughout the house, the hot water supply, cigarettes, matches and candles.

Open fires must always be guarded with a fireguard safely secured in place. Children are fascinated by flames, yet don't understand their danger. Never let them poke a fire or throw things on to it. Never hang washing to dry or air over a fireguard. If you use a kerosene heater, put it where it can't be touched by small children or knocked over and never move it when it's lighted.

Young children find stoves intriguing, especially when they can smell something cooking and want to see what's inside the pan or to stir the contents themselves. Install a hob or stove guard so that pans can't be pulled off and turn pan handles inwards so a child can't readily knock them or catch hold of them. Keep your child out of the way when you're handling hot pans or dishes and when the oven door is open.

Install smoke alarms and buy a fire extinguisher. The extinguisher should be kept somewhere central and easily accessible, such as on a wall in the hall. The kitchen isn't a good place to keep it because fires often start there and you may not be able to reach it in an emergency. When they are old enough to understand, it's a good idea to discuss with your children what you would do if there were a fire in your home. The most important rule is to get everyone out of the house and to a safe place. Then you should call the fire department. When you are responsible for children, your first job is to look after them.

Your hot water supply is best heated to a temperature no higher than 120°F so that it will not scald a child if she turns on the faucet. When running a bath, always run the cold water first and take care that your child never jumps into the bath before you've checked that the water isn't too hot.

Most children love to play with matches and lighters, so keep them well out of sight and reach. If you smoke, make sure your cigarette butts are always put out, and empty ashtrays after use. Outside, don't let young children play near a bonfire and make sure that any barbeque is put out at night.

Making electricity safe

Electricity is potentially dangerous and a shock from an outlet could kill a child. Teach your child never to poke anything into sockets or switch on appliances. Fill empty sockets with safety socket covers and turn off switches on appliances when they aren't in use.

Use only safety listed electrical appliances, bearing the UL label. Don't overload the circuit by running too many appliances off the same socket – have more outlets installed. All appliances need regular servicing and should be fixed or replaced if faulty. Check that your cords aren't frayed and don't run them under carpets or rugs. Don't let an electric coffee pot cord or any other cord dangle from the countertop because it is tempting for a toddler to pull on it.

Your child may be tempted to play with the electric iron because she sees you using it. The best policy is to keep the iron and its cord entirely out of the reach of children at all times. The weight of a falling iron, combined with its heat and electrical connection, pose a major safety threat to children.

Electric toys with cords that plug directly into outlets are best reserved for children old enough to have respect for electricity. Remember that batteries can be very dangerous to young children, particularly the tiny ones used in watches and calculators – a child could easily put one into her mouth and swallow it or push one up her nose.

Use electric blankets in accordance with the manufacturer's instructions. Electric blankets aren't safe for children who might wet the bed or spill drinks. Avoid kerosene heaters with exposed elements that a child or her clothing could come in contact with. Keep young children away from space heaters – especially when they are wearing nightgowns which could be sucked in by a draft created by the heater and ignited. If you are using an approved, UL labeled space heater or heating stove in your child's bedroom, be sure to turn it off or turn it low before going to bed.

IMPORTANT

- Never overestimate what your child can do.
- Don't believe that because you've told your child not to do something, she'll necessarily remember it.
- Never take risks yourself; she will learn from the example you set.
- Don't be complacent, particularly where water, fire, gas, electricity, glass or roads are concerned.
- Don't judge what your child is capable of by what another child can do.
- Don't leave your child anywhere without thinking about the possible dangers and taking necessary precautions.

Doors, balconies and windows

If your front or back door opens on to a road, fit some sort of bolt or lock that a young child can't undo. Clear glass doors are a real hazard and the glass should be replaced with laminated or tempered glass, plexiglass or lexan. In the meantime, at least put stickers on the glass so your child knows it's there.

If your home has a balcony, make sure that your child can't climb on to anything and lean over the railings, and check that she can't climb over the railings or barrier itself. Fit safety locks or special catches to all windows, so that when they are opened the gap is too small for a child to fall through.

Safety in the house

The bathroom

Lock medicines away safely. They should be in well-labeled, child-resistant containers. Remember that child-resistant doesn't mean child-proof. You should always check what you are giving and all old medicines should be flushed down the toilet. Be careful about medicines which may be in houses that you are visiting.

Nonslip flooring is a sensible precaution, as is a nonslip mat in the bath for young children. Never use an electrical appliance in the bathroom, unless it is equipped with a ground fault circuit interrupter (GFCI), which automatically shuts off an appliance when it comes in contact with water. Scissors, razors, tweezers and manicure equipment should be locked away or kept out of reach.

The kitchen

The kitchen is a potentially hazardous place for a child. Apart from making it as safe as you can, teach her as she grows older to be wary of kitchen appliances and never to turn on or play with electrical gadgets. Safety catches will keep toddlers out of low cupboards and drawers. Sharp knives and plastic bags should be kept out of reach. If you use a tablecloth, buy special securing clips for it if you have a very young child who could pull it off the table. Keep hot drinks and teapots out of reach. It's easy to fall on highly polished or wet floors, so either don't polish floors or use a nonslip polish if you have a child running around, and mop up spills at once. The kitchen is a convenient place to keep your first aid kit as long as it's out of your child's reach and not anywhere that is steamy.

The hall, stairs and landing

It's easiest to have two safety gates, one at the top and one at the bottom of the stairs, though one will do if you move it to whichever floor you and your crawling baby or young toddler are on. A child needs to learn how to cope with stairs, but she needs you with her as she crawls up and slides down backwards on her tummy and later tries walking up one step at a time. Check that the stair carpet is securely fixed and not frayed and that a mat or rug at the bottom of the stairs has a non-slip backing if it's on a smooth floor. Don't carry a child up or down stairs if you are carrying anything else, if you're in socks or panty hose because you could so easily slip, or if you're wearing a long nightgown you could trip over. Never leave things lying on the stairs, and try to make sure stairs and landings are well lit.

The living room

Check that free-standing furniture can't be pulled or pushed over, and don't make the common mistake of positioning a mirror over the fireplace because clothes can so easily catch fire when someone is looking in a mirror. Try and get into the habit of checking the living room every time your baby or toddler is in there. When a room is in constant use, small dangerous objects may be brought in there without your knowledge. Plastic record sleeves are a potential cause of suffocation, and needles, pins and scissors in your sewing kit make fascinating but hazardous playthings, so put them out of reach. If you have trailing house plants, put them on a shelf high enough that a toddler can't pull the whole pot down on her head. Make sure heavy ornaments are well out of reach.

IMPORTANT

- Never leave a child alone in the bath, however little water there is.
- Never leave a young child alone with an unguarded fire.
- Never assume that your child will be safe in someone else's home. Have a good look around to make sure.
- Never put household chemicals in old or unmarked bottles or in food containers.
- Make sure cleaning equipment and household chemicals are always out of reach of children, including when they are in use.
- Never let a child play with a pet's bowl, bedding or litter tray. Children can catch worms from dogs and cats.

Safety outdoors

For those who live in suburban or rural areas, it is very important to make sure that the places where your child plays outdoors are safe.

Never leave any electrical equipment such as a lawnmower or a hedge trimmer running or unattended with children around. If you're mowing the lawn, check the grass for stones because they could be hurled in the air by the mower. Don't leave weedkillers or pesticides lying around as some of these chemicals are very poisonous. Garden tools can be dangerous in young hands, so take care not to have more out than you need and don't let your child play with them. If a child is playing near you as you dig or use a fork, remember she may move quickly, so don't turn rapidly or swing the tool backwards or sideways without looking. Never leave a rake with its prongs upwards or someone could step on it and be seriously hurt by the prongs or by the handle hitting them in the face.

A septic tank must be safely covered, as must a well or cistern. A pond or swimming pool should be surrounded by a high fence, and many municipalities now require this. However shallow the water, it's a real danger because a young child can drown in just a few inches. Always supervise young children in the wading pool and always empty it if your child is playing in the yard without you.

Lawn ornaments such as cement birdbaths can all too easily be pulled over, so cement them in place. Make sure stone or paved steps and paths are level and safe.

Sheds and garages

Garden sheds contain many sharp, heavy and poisonous things, so should be kept locked. Hang garden tools safely on the wall where they can't be reached or pulled down. Keep chemicals locked away and never put them into unlabeled bottles. Keep children away when you're doing any do-it-yourself projects. In one third of do-it-yourself accidents, it's the watching child who is hurt.

The same principles apply to the garage. Keep gasoline, oil and other chemicals, such as those you use to clean the car, out of reach and don't let children play with car maintenance tools. Never let a child come near a jacked-up car and don't prop a car up on bricks. Always remember to check that your child is well clear when you drive away. It's very easy not to notice a small child when you're in a hurry. Take special care that your child is nowhere near the car door as you shut it. Children move quickly and car doors can readily crush fingers or deliver a nasty blow. Be particularly cautious if you're feeling unwell or are anxious or angry. That's just the time when accidents are most likely to happen.

POISONOUS PLANTS

- Never let your child eat any garden plants. These are particularly dangerous: aconite; arum lily; broom (seeds and pods); bryony (berries); cotoneaster (berries); daffodil and narcissus (bulbs); daphne (berries); deadly nightshade (berries); foxglove; hemlock (young leaves and unripe fruits); holly (berries); honeysuckle (berries); ivy (berries); laburnum (seeds and pods); laurel (leaves and berries); lupin (seeds and pods); mountain ash or rowan (berries); potato (fruits and green tubers); pyracantha (berries); rhododendron (leaves); rhubarb (leaves); or yew (berries).
- Teach her not to pick or eat any mushrooms or toadstools.
- Avoid these poisonous indoor plants: dumb cane (sap); oleander; poinsettia (sap); or solanum or Christmas cherry (berries).

If your child does eat any of these, get medical help and be ready to show or describe what she's eaten.

Recreational safety

Swings and jungle gyms can rust, lose their bolts or break, so overhaul all outdoor play equipment at least once a year. Teach children to keep well clear when a swing is being used, as either the seat or a child's foot can deliver a very hard blow. Bicycles should also be regularly overhauled with particular attention being paid to the brakes. A child can easily be thrown over the handlebars if she tries to stop at speed when her back brakes aren't working.

If you take your child to a public playground, choose one in which the swings and slides are well maintained and set on grass or on a special, shock-absorbent surface. Ordinary blacktop or concrete is more dangerous if children fall on it. Supervise your child when she is climbing until she gains confidence, and try to encourage her to climb only as far as she knows that she safely can.

It's sensible to teach children how to use their common sense when playing. Lessons such as not pointing guns and bows and arrows at each other's faces have to be repeated time after time before they sink in. Make sure your child knows that she should never put a plastic bag over her head.

Buy the right safety equipment for sports and make sure that children are properly supervised. When it comes to the fourth of July, don't let children light fireworks or investigate those which have been lit, but haven't gone off. Keep them well away from the area where fireworks are lit.

Older children who may play away from home must be warned never to play on railway embankments, on building sites, by canals or rivers, and on landfills. Discarded refrigerators, ovens and car trunks can easily form airtight traps which are impossible for a child to escape from.

Water safety

Never let young children play in or near water unsupervised, however shallow it is. Many children have drowned in just a few inches of water before anyone realized what was happening. Teaching your children to swim is sensible, but never let children swim without some supervision, however able they are. Rivers, canals and flooded quarries can be dangerous as they may be deep, weedy, or have fast currents. When you're by the sea, make sure you can always see your child when she is swimming without you. Inflatable toys, rafts and boats can easily be swept out to sea, so keep them on a line or go into the water with them. If your child likes fishing, teach her always to fish somewhere within sight of other people.

If you take your child in a boat, make sure there is a suitable life jacket for her. Small children may be safest if tied to part of the boat with a fine rope.

VACATION SAFETY

- If traveling outside the U.S. or Canada, check what immunizations will be needed and get any necessary ones done well in advance.
- Check that any children's equipment provided is safe.
- Guard against sunburn and heatstroke (see page 210).
- If you are going abroad, check whether the local water is safe to drink.

ROAD SAFETY

Roads wouldn't be safe places for children even if every vehicle were driven within the speed limit by a driver who was alert and concentrating on the task in hand. Many accidents involve children in carriages or strollers, or who are pedestrians, cyclists or passengers in cars. Children need to know that the road is as dangerous as a cliff edge. Our job is to protect our children by helping them to learn to respect traffic and cope with it as safely as possible. Most children have to travel near or on the roads, so traffic awareness is one of the most important skills they can have.

Never push a carriage or stroller out into the road until it is absolutely safe to cross. Don't use the carriage or stroller as a signal to a motorist that you are there because he may not see it. Make sure your child is always safely harnessed into her carriage or stroller. It's easy to be distracted when crossing the road with a crying, talkative or whining child so be especially vigilant then. If your toddler is walking by your side, don't rely

on her holding on to the carriage – she might run off to look at something interesting. She should wear a safety harness or, failing that, you should hold her tightly by the hand.

Never take the chances you might be tempted to take on your own. When you are with children you can't move fast enough to get out of trouble. Always behave in traffic as you would wish your child to behave when you're not there.

Children shouldn't be allowed to cross a road by themselves until you are confident they know how dangerous it is. They should know how to choose where to cross and how to cross. If you want your child to walk to school alone, walk with her, letting her make decisions, until she seems able to do it safely. Plan the route so she can cross at a traffic light, pedestrian crossing or attendant-controlled crossing. Don't let a younger child go on the sidewalk alone, even just next door.

It's sensible to forbid your child to bicycle on the road until she has passed a bicycling proficiency test such as the police organize in many areas. She should wear a bicycle safety helmet and, if she must ride at dusk, she needs well-maintained lights as well as reflective strips on her clothing (which should be light-colored).

SAFETY IN THE CAR

Babies should travel in Federal Motor Vehicle safety-approved infant car seats until they weigh 17-20 lb and measure about 26 in. All infant safety seats must face the rear of the car, anchored to the vehicle's safety belt.

Children who weigh more than 17-20 lb and can sit up by themselves need a forward-facing safety seat. For children between ages 4 and 8 a car booster seat with harness or shoulder belt gives excellent protection. A car lap belt that fits securely under the abdomen is the next best choice.

When choosing a car seat, look for one that has been "dynamically tested," that is, tested in a crash situation.

Most car doors have child safety locks, so use these if you carry young children. Never let children lean out of the window or put their heads through the sunroof.

If you are anxious or distracted by a child or by anything else, take extra special care.

ROAD SAFETY CODE

Before you cross the road:

- **STOP**
- **LOOK**
- **LISTEN**

If traffic is coming, WAIT.
If not, cross, looking and listening as you go.

Part Five

EMERGENCIES AND FIRST AID

However sensible we are about providing a reasonably safe and secure environment for them, our children will inevitably have accidents as their natural curiosity and desire to learn about, explore and experience their world leads them into potentially dangerous situations. And not all emergencies are caused by accidents or dangerous situations. Some children have chronic illnesses or conditions which flare up from time to time and need first aid for the acute crisis.

Taking the time to learn about first aid and emergency treatment is like having an insurance policy – it pays off in times of trouble. It helps a great deal to attend a course on first aid and to learn vital techniques such as cardiopulmonary resuscitation (CPR). Accidents often seem to happen at the worst possible time and this is when you need to be clear-headed and confident about first aid. Find out who runs first aid courses locally: the American Red Cross, the American Heart Association (see Useful Addresses, p. 216); the rescue and first aid squads and the hospitals in your town may also offer programs.

First aid is just what it says – the very first care given to an injured child or in any medical emergency. First aid is partly common sense and as such can save lives, but knowledgeable first aid combined with common sense is even more valuable. No one expects you to be as capable of coping as a doctor, but if you know the right way to go about coping with an accident or other crisis, you could not only relieve unnecessary suffering but might one day save your child's life.

Medi-Kit

Being prepared

In addition to taking a basic first aid course with an emphasis on accident prevention, you should learn how to do **mouth-to-mouth resuscitation** (rescue breathing) to restart breathing, and **cardiac compression** (manual chest compression) to get the heart beating if it has stopped. If there's no heartbeat, breathing will have stopped too and mouth-to-mouth resuscitation and cardiac compression must be done together. This is known as cardiopulmonary resuscitation (CPR). Its purpose is to keep the body's cells supplied with oxygen until breathing is restored or until advanced medical help arrives. Brain cells begin to die after four to six minutes without oxygen. That is why your ability to perform CPR at the time of an accident or sudden illness could be vital. No one, however, should attempt to perform CPR without proper training from certified instructors.

Here are some other steps you should take in order to be prepared:

- Try to imagine yourself faced with an emergency, and work out how you would like to react. Knowing what you ought to do is quite different from actually doing it, but if you have thought through a situation, it can give you confidence when facing a real emergency.
- Have an emergency fire escape plan that includes at least two possible ways to get outdoors from every room in the house. Discuss and practice this plan with each family member. Remember, the two most important things to do in case of a fire are: first, get everyone out of the house; then, call the fire department.

How to get help

Ensure that you and anyone looking after your child knows how to get help.

- Dial 911 for an ambulance:

for a life-threatening emergency;
if the child is too badly hurt for you to transport him safely to the hospital;
or if he needs trained care on the way.

- State clearly:

your full address and phone number, any helpful landmarks for finding your house and details of the emergency.

- Electrocution is a common cause of injury in the home. An electric shock can knock a child down, cause unconsciousness and may stop his breathing and heartbeat. Learn where the main house electrical switch is in case of **electric shock** (see page 201), so that you can turn off the supply before touching the child.
- Always have a list of emergency phone numbers at hand. Post the following phone numbers and information near your telephone:

pediatrician or family doctor
hospital emergency room
poison control center
burn center
life support unit
fire department
police
nearest neighbor.

- If there isn't a telephone in the house, make sure that you know where the nearest available one is.
- Make sure that you know where the nearest hospital is and when it is open.
- If your child is cared for by someone else on a regular basis, either in your home or the caregiver's, or at a day care center, be sure that you give them a written consent form indicating that, in the event of an emergency, you give them permission to take your child to the nearest hospital for emergency medical treatment. This form must be signed by you and should include on it the name of your insurance company and your policy number. It is extremely important that you do this because most hospitals will refuse to treat a child without their parents' or a close relative's consent, and your sitter may be unable to reach you quickly.
- Assemble a first aid kit and have it ready in your home before an accident occurs (see page 215). Make sure that anyone caring for your child knows where it is located. Check regularly that it is well stocked and keep it out of the reach of children. However, don't lock it away as you may need it in a hurry. It's a good idea to practice bandaging techniques on your child. In the event that they should really have to be used, you will be more confident in applying them, and your child will be familiar with them and, hopefully, more cooperative and less anxious.

Emergency procedure

One of the most important points to remember in an emergency is to keep calm and do your best. One of your main roles will be to reassure the child.

- Remember:

Under no circumstances should you move an injured child unless you really have to or unless she can easily move herself.

Don't give her anything to eat or drink if there is the remotest chance that she will need a general anesthetic for an operation.

Consider your own safety. Don't cause more problems by endangering yourself through thoughtless actions:

Once you have checked that no further danger threatens, check if the child is breathing.

How to tell if breathing has stopped

- Look. Is her chest moving up and down?
- Listen. Can you hear any breaths?

- Feel. Put your cheek against the child's mouth. If you can't feel anything, purse her lips and feel again.
- If you have a small mirror, put it to her mouth to see if it steams up.

If breathing has stopped

1. Keep calm.
2. If you are alone, start **mouth-to-mouth resuscitation** immediately (see page 198), no matter how long it may be since the child last breathed.
3. If someone is with you, send them to phone for an ambulance unless they are better able to give first aid than you.
4. Check every three minutes whether the child's heart is beating (see page 199). If the heart has stopped, start **cardiac compression.** You can do mouth-to-mouth resuscitation and cardiac compression by yourself, or if there is someone else trained in CPR techniques with you, they can do cardiac compression while you do mouth-to-mouth resuscitation or vice versa.
5. If the child doesn't start breathing by herself, carry on. It's particularly important to continue for a long time after **drowning** (see page 211) or **electric shock** (see page 201).
6. Continue until the child starts breathing again or until someone else takes over.

If the child is breathing, but unconscious

If the child is unconscious or very drowsy, but breathing without any difficulty, turn her head to the side so that she doesn't choke on her tongue or vomit.

Mouth-to-mouth resuscitation

Mouth-to-mouth resuscitation is the best method of artificial respiration. You blow air from your body into the child's lungs to give her oxygen. You don't have to get rid of the air from her lungs: they naturally push it out when you stop inflating them.

● Don't waste time; do the first two inflations as soon as possible.

How to do it

1 Lay the child on her back. Turning her head to one side, open her mouth and remove any vomit, blood or obstruction.

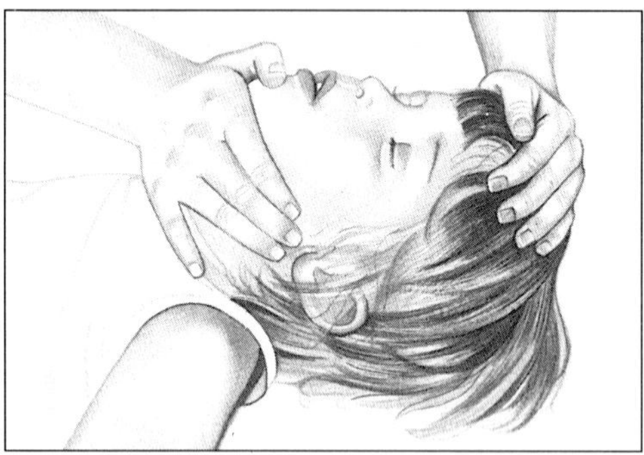

2 Cup her chin in one hand and with your other hand on her forehead, tilt her head back to raise the chin. Now there is little danger of the tongue obstructing the airway. Sometimes this maneuver starts her breathing again.

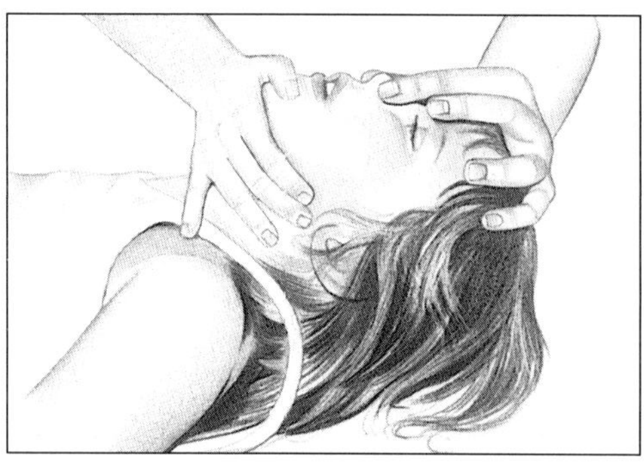

3 Leave the heel of your hand on her forehead to keep the head tilted back and use your fingers to pinch her nostrils shut.

4 Take a breath, put your mouth over her mouth to make a tight seal and blow gently into her mouth twice. Watch to see if her chest rises.

FOR A BABY, put your mouth over his mouth and nose. Make sure his mouth stays open. Only blow in the air you can hold in your cheeks, otherwise you might blow in too much and damage his lungs.

5 Blow in two quick breaths and then check if the heart is beating. If it is, continue to blow in one breath every five seconds.

6 If the heart is *not* beating, give cardiac compression with mouth-to-mouth resuscitation.

7 When the child starts to breathe by herself, turn her head to the side, summon help and stay with her.

Cardiac compression

If your child's heart has stopped beating, cardiac compression may start it working again and save his life. This has to be done at the same time as **mouth-to-mouth resuscitation** because a child whose heart has stopped beating will soon stop breathing.

How to tell if the heart has stopped

- Feel the child's pulse. The easiest pulse to feel is in the neck, below the jaw and in line with the earlobe. Practice feeling your own until you become used to finding it.
- Look at the child's pupils: they will be larger than usual.
- Look at the skin: it will be pale or greyish.
- Put your ear to the chest, on the left of the breastbone, and listen for the heart.
- Feel in the same place for the heart. If you're already doing mouth-to-mouth resuscitation, but the child's color is getting worse and if you don't think you can feel a pulse or feel or hear the heartbeat, start doing cardiac compression.

What is cardiac compression?

When you do cardiac compression, you compress the heart between the breastbone and spine. Unitl it starts beating by itself, this does the heart's job of pumping the blood round.

How to do it

1 Lay the child on his back on a hard, flat surface.

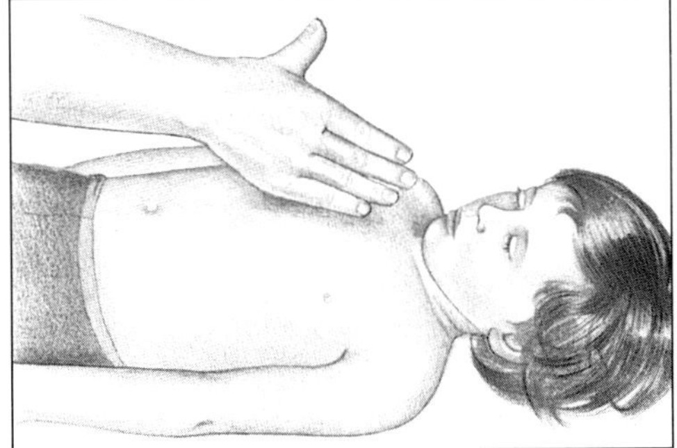

2 Find the center of the breastbone (the bone which runs down the center of the chest).

3 Place the heel of your hand on the center of the breastbone and press firmly at a rate of

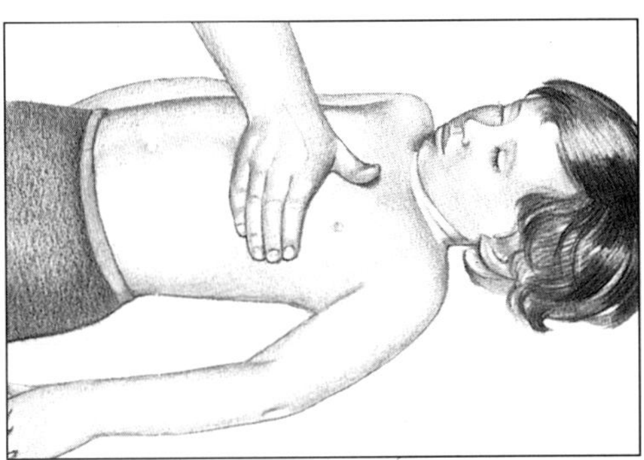

about 80 compressions per minute, to a depth of about 1-1½ inches. Make the compressions smooth and regular, not jerky and stabbing.

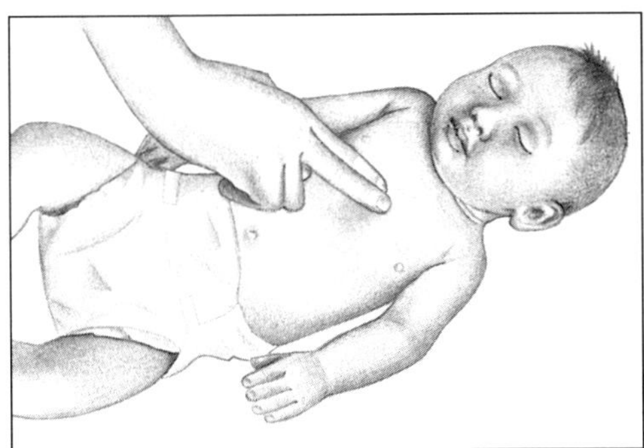

FOR A CHILD UNDER ONE, press with two fingers on the middle of the breastbone about 100 times a minute, to a depth of about ½-1 inch.

4 After five compressions, do one breath.

5 Continue cardiac compression and mouth-to-mouth resuscitation blowing in one breath for every five heart compressions.

6 Check the pulse every three minutes or so. When the heart starts beating, stop doing cardiac compressions.

Don't press on the child's ribs because you might easily break them.

Never do cardiac compression if the heart is beating.

Unconsciousness

An unconscious child is unaware of his surroundings. Fainting is a temporary loss of consciousness due to a brief reduction in the blood flow to the brain. Concussion is temporary unconsciousness caused by a fall or a head injury. Some other forms of unconsciousness last longer and need prompt care.

A coma is unconsciousness from which a child cannot be roused. A semiconscious child can be roused briefly and may talk before lapsing into a stupor or becoming delirious.

What you can do

1 ***Most important*** is to check whether the child is breathing. If not, make sure that his airway isn't obstructed by his tongue and do **mouth-to-mouth resuscitation.** Keep checking his breathing because it may become irregular or stop if the coma deepens.
Also check whether the heart is beating. If not, start cardiac compression.
2 Check for **bleeding** (see page 204) and **fractures** (see page 212) and take measures to prevent **shock** (see opposite page).
3 Check whether a Medic-alert medallion is worn or carried. This may assist you and other helpers in knowing what to do.
4 If the child is breathing turn his head to the side unless there is any possibility of a broken neck, pelvis or back.
5 Call an ambulance.
6 ***Don't*** give anything to drink or eat.
7 Stay with the child.

Fainting

A child who is about to faint feels shaky, short of breath, sick, sweaty and light-headed. He looks pale and has a weak, slow pulse.

What you can do

IF HE FEELS FAINT, sit him down with his head between his knees, open a window to let in fresh air and give him small sips of water and something to eat when he recovers.

IF HE HAS FAINTED, lay him on his back with his legs raised above the level of his head and loosen any tight clothing at his neck, chest and waist. Turn his head to the side if he doesn't come round quickly.

Seizures/convulsions

A seizure may be accompanied by jerking movements, a cry, frothing at the mouth and wetting the pants. After a seizure a child may be confused, sleepy and headachy. For more about seizures/convulsions, see page 128.

What you can do

1 Protect the child from hurting himself as he falls and during the convulsion.
2 Put something soft under his head.
3 ***Don't*** restrain his movements or put anything into his mouth.
4 Turn his head to the side when the jerking has stopped.
5 Contact your pediatrician. Phone for an ambulance if the child has several seizures, if he is injured or if he takes longer than fifteen minutes to regain consciousness.

Head injury

Falls and bangs on the head are common in childhood and usually trivial, but it is possible for even a minor injury to cause bleeding inside the child's skull which can lead to compression of the brain either at once, or even hours or days later.

If you are worried, your child should be taken to the hospital for observation and given a skull X-ray if necessary.

What you can do

1 If your child seems all right or feels a bit sick and has a slight headache, watch him carefully and report any worsening or new symptoms to your doctor.
2 You should wake him once during his first few hours of sleep to check that he can be roused.

YOUR CHILD SHOULD BE SEEN URGENTLY BY A DOCTOR IF: he has lost consciousness; he is increasingly drowsy; his breathing is noisy; he has a continuing, severe or worsening headache; he continues to feel sick and vomit; he is dizzy or seeing double; there is a clear or bloody discharge from his ear or nose; he has any bruising in or around the eye; he has pupils of unequal size; he has any trouble speaking or moving; he behaves strangely; he has a seizure; or there is a depression or a soft area in his scalp.

Shock

Physical shock (as opposed to emotional shock) can lead to circulatory failure and can be fatal if not treated. Watch out for shock after serious external or internal bleeding, bad bruising, severe burns or other blistering, prolonged diarrhea and vomiting, severe infection or allergy and after anything that has stopped the heart beating.

What to look for

The child may be pale, cold, sweaty, yawning or gasping, breathing rapidly and shallowly, feel weak, faint or giddy and have a rapid pulse. He may also appear restless and anxious, feel thirsty or nauseated, vomit or become unconscious.

What you can do

1 Call an ambulance immediately.
2 Check whether the child is breathing and has a heartbeat. If not, CPR must be performed.
3 Control **bleeding** (see page 204) or any other cause you can detect.
4 Don't move the child unnecessarily. If he is breathing without difficulty, turn his head to the side.
5 Dress wounds and treat injuries.
6 Loosen tight clothing.
7 Cover him lightly to prevent chilling, but don't overheat.
8 Don't give him anything to eat or drink.
9 Keep checking breathing and heartbeat.
10 Comfort him.

Anaphylactic shock

This is caused by a massive allergic reaction and can develop within minutes of, for instance, a drug injection, an insect sting or – rarely – an ingested allergen such as penicillin or shellfish.

What to look for

The child may be shocked, nauseated, or vomiting, sneezing, faint or wheezing or gasping for air. He may have swelling of the face and especially the eyes, a rapid pulse and increasing confusion which may lead to unconsciousness.

What you can do

1 Treat for **shock** (see left).
2 Phone for an ambulance.

Electric shock

What you can do

1 ***Don't*** touch the child as the shock can be transmitted to you.

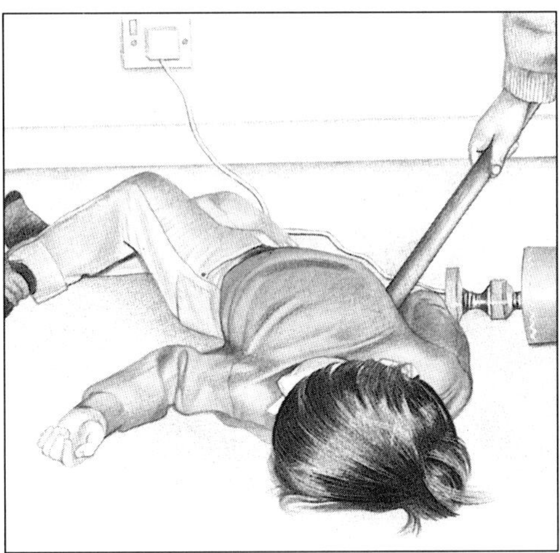

2 Switch off the main electric switch or outlet, *or* push the child away from the source of the current with an insulating object such as a wooden broom handle or chair. Remember that water is an effective conductor of electricity, so keep away from anything wet.
3 Check his breathing and do **mouth-to-mouth resuscitation** if necessary. If there is no heartbeat, do **cardiac compression.**
4 Persevere with resuscitation because sometimes an electrocuted child revives after a lengthy interval.
5 Turn his head to the side if he is unconscious, but breathing.
6 Treat for **burns** (see page 202) and **shock** (see left).
7 Call an ambulance immediately.

● If a child has suffered a high voltage shock, for instance from a fallen power cable or a railroad power line, call the rescue squad or ambulance and ***keep away.*** Electricity can jump a considerable distance, so don't approach the child until you are certain that the power has been cut off.

MOUTH-TO-MOUTH RESUSCITATION p. 198 CARDIAC COMPRESSION p. 199

Burns and scalds

Burns can be caused by fire, electricity or chemicals or by coming into contact with a hot object. Scalds are caused by steam or hot liquid. The dangers of a bad burn or scald are that the child will lose a lot of fluid from the burnt skin, leading to shock, and that the skin will become infected.

What you can do

1 Remove the source of the burning or remove the child from the source.

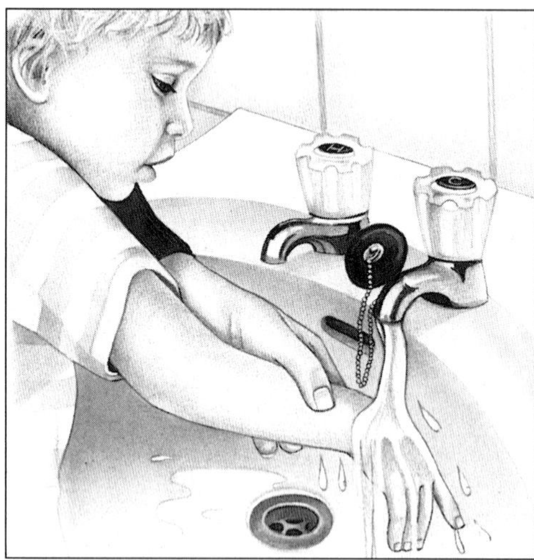

2 Cool the burnt area immediately under cold running water for ten minutes or by repeatedly pouring cold water over the skin.
Don't use ice water or a shower.
3 Carefully remove tight clothing or jewelry before swelling makes this impossible.
4 ***Don't*** pull away charred clothing sticking to the skin, but gently remove any other clothing around the burn. If it is a chemical burn, be careful not to burn yourself or him further.
5 If the burn is superficial, covers a small area and is not on the face, genital area, palm, fingers, sole or a joint, treat the child at home.
6 Otherwise, take the child to the hospital emergency room for treatment or call an ambulance.
7 While waiting for the ambulance, look for and treat signs of **shock** (see page 201).

How to treat burnt skin at home

1 Cleanse the wound with a mild soap and rinse with sterile saline.
2 Leave the blisters alone. If they have ruptured, trim away the loose skin.
3 After cleansing, apply silvadene cream lightly over the burn area.
4 Twice a day, wash with warm water and apply silvadene cream.
5 If the burn is on the child's face or neck, do not apply a dressing.
6 For burns to the hands or feet, apply a nonadherent petrolatum gauze over the silvadene cream and cover with a gauze dressing and roller gauze.
7 Give acetaminophen to relieve the pain, if necessary.

What to do if a child's clothes are on fire

1 If you are near a tap or other water supply, douse the clothes with lots of water.

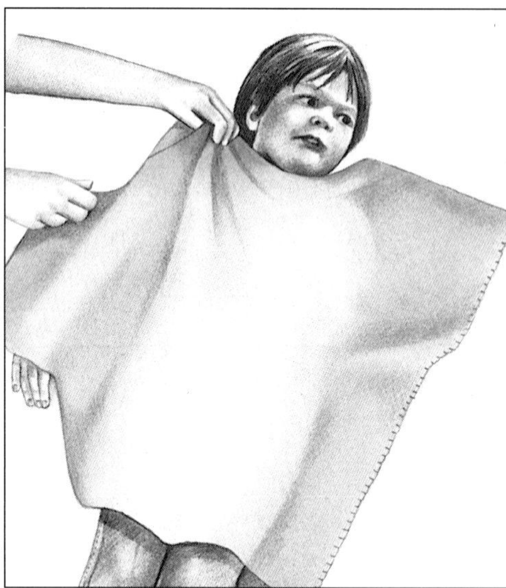

2 If not, cover the child in a rug, blanket, coat or curtain. Don't use anything made of synthetic material as this could make the flames worse.
3 If there is nothing at hand, lie on the child and smother the flames with your own body. Fire needs oxygen to burn, so the idea is to cover the flames and prevent more air from getting to them.
Don't roll the child along the ground as this could increase the area burnt.

Asphyxia

This includes anything that prevents a child from getting air, such as choking on a foreign body (see below), smothering, poisoning, being shut in a small airtight space, having a seizure and swelling of the airway lining from infection, a sting or a scald.

What you can do

1 Remove any obstruction, provide fresh air, and get a doctor if necessary.
2 If breathing has stopped, do **mouth-to-mouth resuscitation.**

Choking

Choking is common and distressing as well as potentially life threatening. Usually there is enough room for air to be breathed in round the object on which the child is choking, so the child can cough and dislodge it. If the wind pipe is completely blocked, he can't breathe, cough or speak and may panic and go blue.

What you can do

1 Quickly open his mouth to see if there is an obstruction you can hook out. Be very careful not to push it further down.

2 Lay him over your knee with his head down and slap his back four times between the shoulder blades. This may dislodge the object.

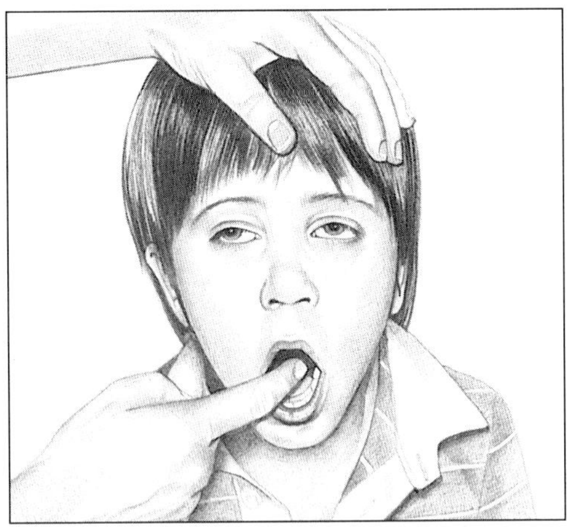

3 Remove the object from his mouth if it hasn't been spat out. Use your crooked finger to hook it out quickly.

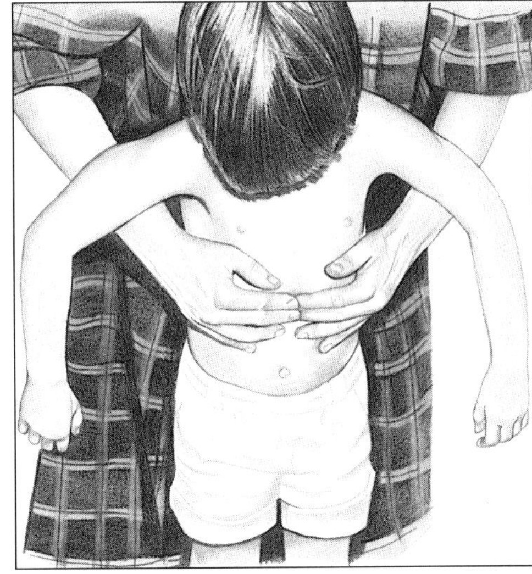

4 If this fails, perform the Heimlich maneuver. Stand the child in front of you, facing away. Put your arms round his waist and put two fingers of one hand over his stomach between his navel and his ribcage. Put two fingers of the other hand on top and press firmly back towards you, making four sharp thrusts. This sharp pressure should drive the air out of the lungs and take the offending object with it. If not, repeat three times. Call for help if that fails.
5 If breathing stops, get someone to call an ambulance while you do **mouth-to-mouth.**

MOUTH-TO-MOUTH RESUSCITATION p. 198 CARDIAC COMPRESSION p. 199

Heavy bleeding

This must be controlled quickly.

What you can do

1 Ask someone to call an ambulance. If alone, control the bleeding first.

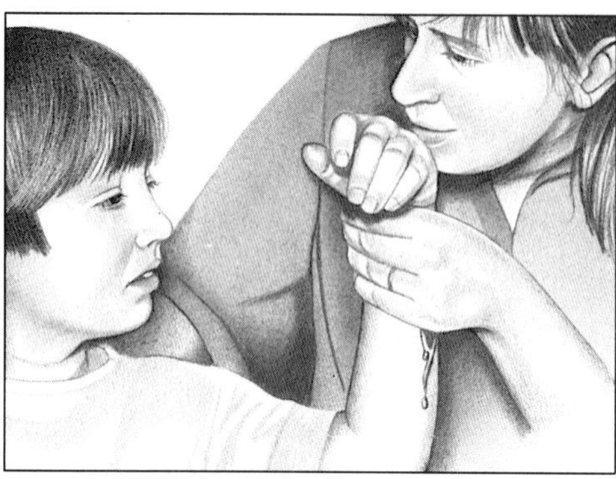

2 Raise the bleeding part to reduce blood flow *unless* you suspect a **fracture** (see page 212).
3 If you have a sterile dressing (see page 214), cover the wound with it. Otherwise use a clean nonfluffy material.

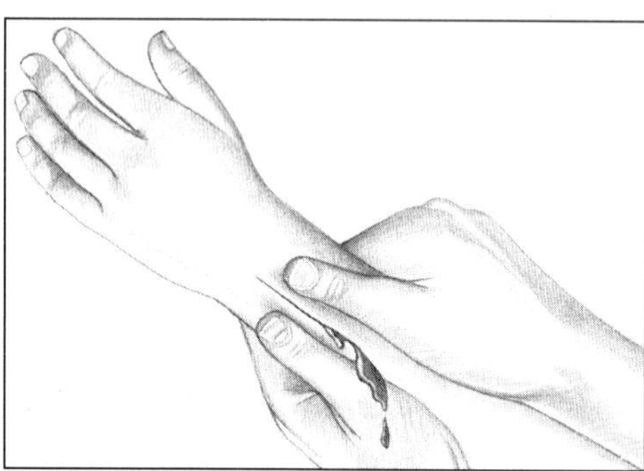

4 Close the edges of the wound firmly together with your fingers *unless* a broken bone or foreign body is protruding. If so, press around the bone or object, not over it.
5 ***Don't*** remove any object sticking out of the wound as it may be controlling the bleeding.
6 If closing the wound isn't enough, press firmly over the dressing with a large pad of clean material. Add more pads if the blood soaks through and bandage firmly but not too tightly in place, or secure with adhesive tape.
7 Watch out for and treat **shock** (see page 201) if necessary.
8 Call an ambulance as soon as you have controlled the bleeding.
Don't use a torniquet or pressure points unless you have been trained and know exactly what you're doing.
9 Keep calm and reassure the child.

Minor bleeding

Light bleeding usually stops in a few minutes as the blood clots.

If it doesn't stop

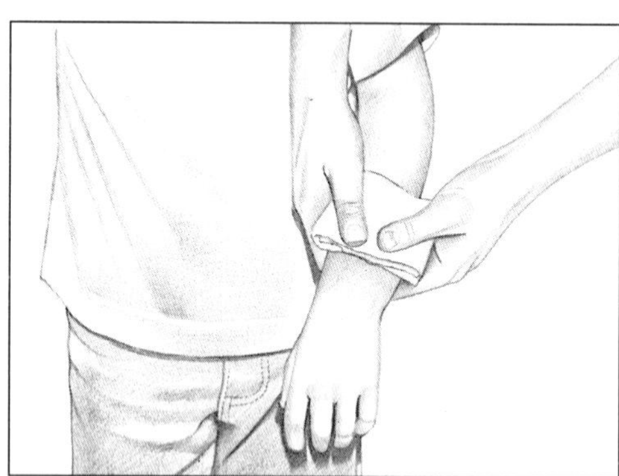

1 Press firmly with a pad of clean (preferably sterile) material over the wound for five to ten minutes.
2 If it stops, put on an adhesive bandage or a sterile dressing.
3 If it doesn't, press for another ten minutes. If that fails, take the child to the hospital emergency room.

Nosebleed

What you can do

1 Sit the child with his head upright.
2 Pinch the soft part of his nose (above the nostrils) firmly for ten minutes.
3 Try to prevent him blowing his nose or sniffing.
4 Inform your doctor if your child has repeated nosebleeds or if you cannot stop a nosebleed.

- Get urgent medical attention if a nosebleed follows a **head injury** (see page 200).

Puncture wound

Take this apparently minor wound seriously as it could cause a deep infection.

What you can do
1 Check that your child's tetanus protection is up to date.
2 Take him to the doctor if the wound throbs or becomes inflamed, or there is a discharge.

Bruising

What you can do
1 Apply a cold compress (a pad of material soaked in cold water or a plastic bag of ice cubes).
● Severe bruising needs medical attention as it may indicate serious internal bleeding which can cause **shock** (see page 201).

Crushed finger

What you can do
1 Hold finger under cold water to ease pain.
2 Take your child to the hospital emergency room if the injury is severe.
3 If part of a finger has been severed, put it in a clean plastic bag and wrap this well in some material. Put it in a container of ice and take it with you to the hospital.

Cuts and scrapes

What you can do
1 Clean gently with lots of warm water and mild soap, or, if very dirty, with an antiseptic solution.
2 Remove foreign bodies such as grit unless deeply embedded, in which case take the child to the hospital emergency room.
3 Dry the cut and apply an antibacterial cream or ointment to promote healing.
4 Cover a scrape with a sterile dressing to stop it getting dirty.
5 Put several thin strips of adhesive bandages, or butterfly closures, across a large or gaping cut, pulling the edges together as you put them on. For a very large cut, use a sterile dressing and attach it with a rolled gauze bandage. A small cut or scrape is best left uncovered.
6 Take the child to the emergency room if there is a very large or gaping cut, or if the cut needs stitching or better cleaning.
7 Check his tetanus protection is up to date.

Splinters

Tiny splinters under the skin usually work their way out on their own.

For a protruding or large splinter

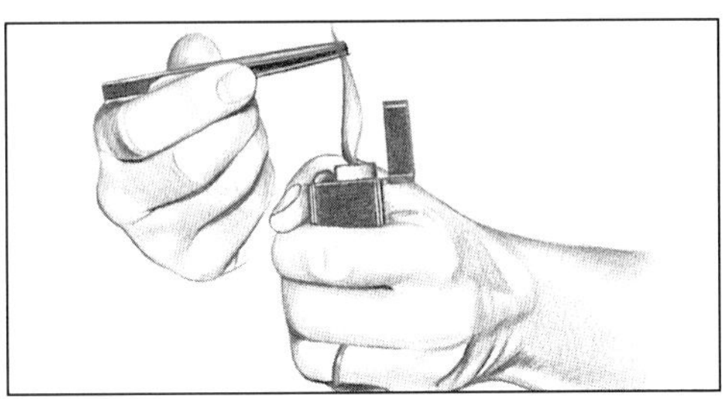

1 If possible, pull it out smoothly with tweezers or clean fingernails. Sterilize tweezers by holding in a flame until red-hot and let them cool before using them.

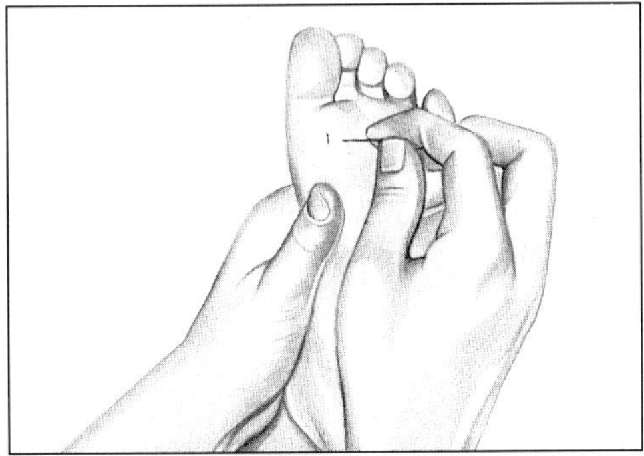

2 If you can't quite grasp the splinter, sterilize a needle in the same way as above, then work the splinter gently out until you can grip it with tweezers.
3 Wash and dry the area and apply an antibacterial cream or ointment.
4 Let a doctor remove a splinter under the nail; a large splinter that has broken off or isn't protruding; or a glass or metal splinter.
5 Check that your child's tetanus protection is up to date.

Poisoning

Young children sometimes swallow poisons out of curiosity or because they mistake them for something else. ***Always*** take poisoning seriously, however much or little you think your child has swallowed. If he is conscious and old enough to understand, try to find out what and how much he has swallowed.

What to look for

Signs of poisoning will vary depending on what has been swallowed. The child may vomit, be delirious and have convulsions (see pages 128 and 200), have burns around his mouth or become unconscious. Vomiting might indicate food poisoning (see page 137).

What you can do

1 Call a Poison Control Center or your pediatrician immediately. If told to make the child vomit, give ipecac syrup and then several ounces of fluid. If instructed to get the child to the hospital try and take a sample of the poison or the empty container with you.

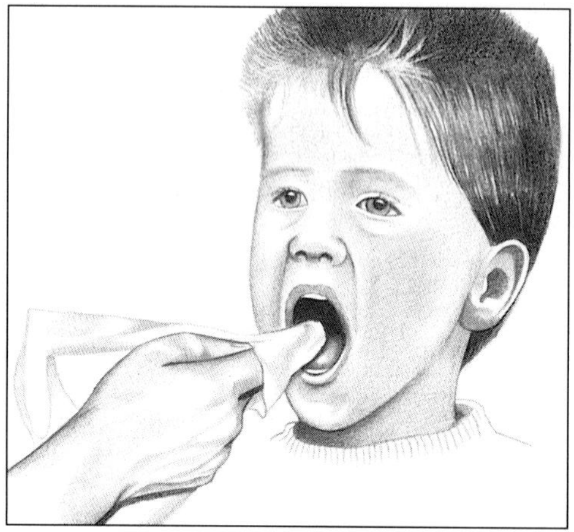

2 While waiting for medical help, wipe any remaining poison from the child's mouth.

IF THE CHILD IS CONSCIOUS AND VOMITS NATURALLY, bend him forwards so he can't choke.

IF THE CHILD IS CONSCIOUS AND HAS SWALLOWED A CORROSIVE POISON (possibly indicated by burns around the mouth), give him milk to drink to dilute the poison and protect the stomach. Remove any clothing soaked in corrosive fluid.

IF THE CHILD IS UNCONSCIOUS BUT BREATHING WITHOUT DIFFICULTY, turn his head to the side. Watch his breathing and heartbeat, and perform mouth-to-mouth resuscitation and cardiac compression if necessary (see pages 198-99).

Don't attempt to give him anything to drink.

POTENTIAL POISONS

There are many substances around the house that may seem harmless to you because you know how to use them correctly. Never forget that your child doesn't possess this knowledge, and make sure that everything that could be poisonous to him is safely put away out of his reach. Watch out in particular for:

Bites and stings

Get medical help at once if an insect bite or sting involves the mouth or throat, or if the child has a serious allergic reaction. Treat for **shock** (see page 201) if necessary, and give the child an ice cube to suck to minimize swelling.

Bee stings

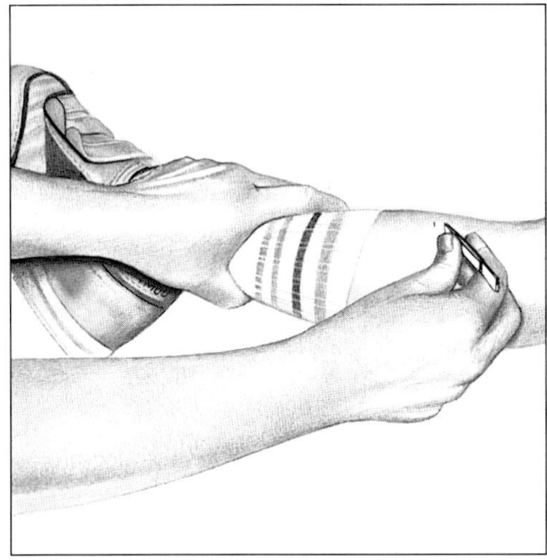

1 Remove the sting with your fingernails or tweezers, or push it out with a needle held flat against the skin. Don't try to remove the sting if it's in deep.
2 Grasp the sting very close to the skin to avoid breaking the poison sac.
3 Apply a cold compress, calamine lotion or a paste made of mixture of bicarbonate of soda and water, or hold the affected area under a cold tap.

Wasp stings

1 Don't bother to look for a sting because a wasp doesn't leave one in the skin.
2 Put some lemon juice or vinegar on the affected area.
3 Apply a cold compress or ice.

Other insect stings

1 Put some calamine lotion on the skin.
2 Antihistamine, taken by mouth as liquid or tablets, or over-the-counter sting relief creams may help relieve severe itching.

Snake bites

1 Immobilize the bitten part and keep it below the level of the heart. Keep the child as still as possible.
2 Wash area thoroughly with soap and water.
3 Try to remember the appearance of the snake, as this may help medical staff to identify the poison.
4 Take the child to the hospital immediately or phone for an ambulance.
Don't suck the venom out or cut the bite.
Don't put on a tourniquet or apply any medication.

Animal bites and scratches

1 Wash the wound thoroughly with soapy water, then dry it.
2 Wash it well with antiseptic solution.
3 Apply a dressing if necessary.
4 Check that your child's tetanus protection is up to date.
NB Any animal bite carries a great risk of infection, especially rabies. See your doctor immediately about necessary precautions.

Jellyfish stings

1 Cover your hands with sand and pick off any pieces of jellyfish immediately.
2 Apply a soothing lotion, such as calamine lotion.
3 If your child shows symptoms other than local itching, consult a doctor.

Foreign body in the eye

Most foreign bodies are found on the inside of an eyelid and can easily be removed.
Never use anything sharp to remove a foreign body from the eye.
Never remove anything on the colored part of the eye or stuck to the eye. Cover the eye and take the child to the hospital.

What you can do

Don't let your child rub his eye. Make him blink several times and blow his nose. If this fails to dislodge the object:
1 Sit him in a good light with his head tilted up and stand behind him.

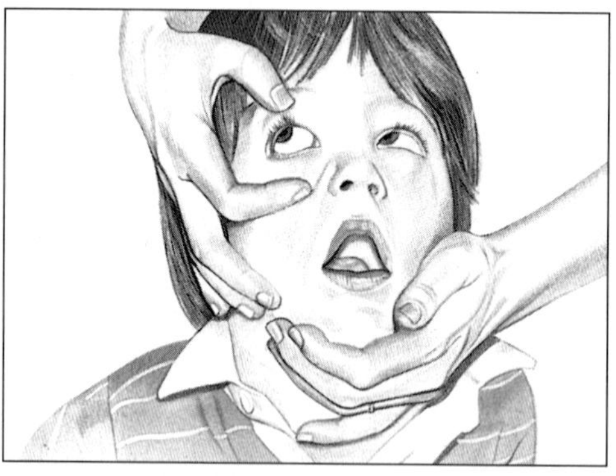

2 Separate the lids with your thumb and index finger, and look for the object as he looks up and down and round.
3 If you can see it, try to flush it out with cold water.

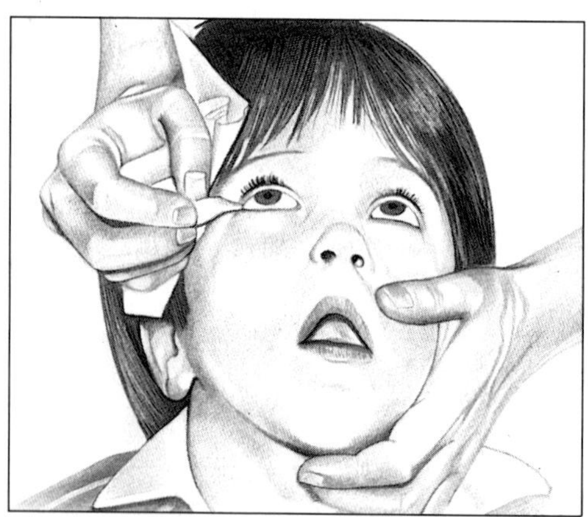

4 If this fails and the object is *not* stuck, carefully remove it with the damp corner of a clean handkerchief.

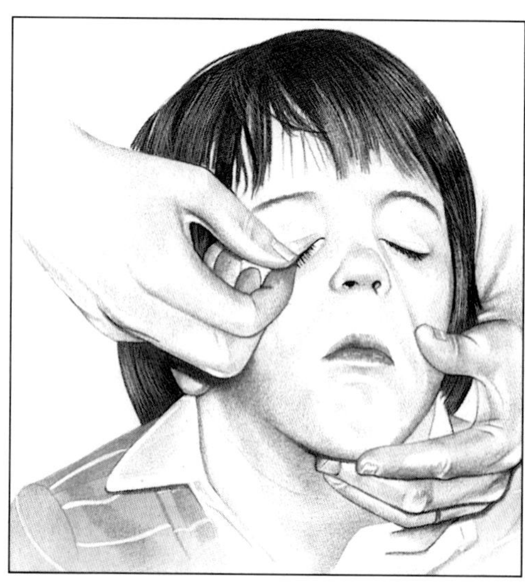

IF THE OBJECT IS UNDER THE UPPER LID, make the child look down and pull the lid by its lashes over the lower lid. The lashes of the lower lid may brush the object off.
IF THE OBJECT IS UNDER THE LOWER LID, dislodge it with the damp corner of a handkerchief while pulling the lid down.

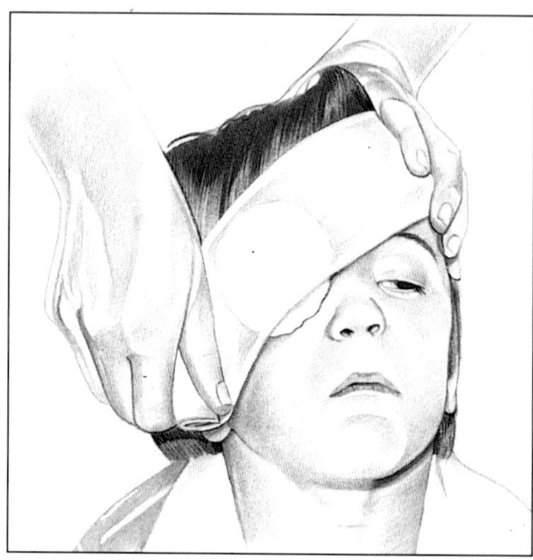

5 If you are unsuccessful, cover the eye and take the child to the hospital.

Corrosive fluid in the eye

What you can do

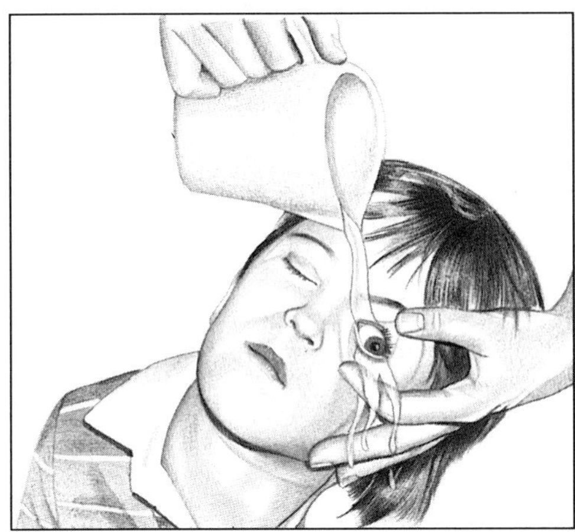

1 Wash the eye at once under a gently running cold tap, or with clean water from a jug.
2 Take care that the water doesn't flow into the good eye.
3 Seek medical help immediately.

Foreign body in the ear

What you can do
Never poke anything into the ear because you may damage the eardrum.

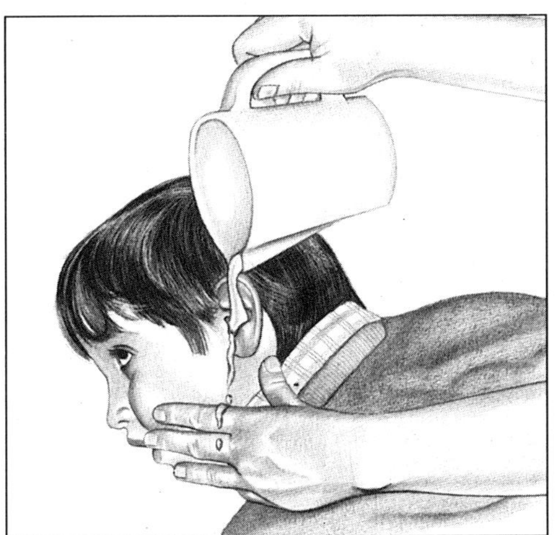

1 If you know it is an insect, lay the child on his side with the affected ear uppermost and pour tepid water into the ear. The water should flush the insect out.
2 If this fails or if it isn't an insect, take the child to your doctor or to the hospital.

Foreign body in the nose

What you can do
Never poke anything up the nose.
1 Close the clear nostril and ask your child to blow gently through the other one.
2 If this fails to dislodge the object, tell your child to breathe through his mouth and take him to your doctor or to the hospital.

Swallowed foreign body

What you can do
1 If the object is stuck in your child's throat, treat as for **choking** (see page 203).
2 If you are worried that the swallowed object is too large or awkward a shape to pass through the digestive system safely, or if it might be poisonous, take your child to the hospital emergency room.

Dislodged tooth

Apart from losing his first teeth, sometimes a child's tooth may be dislodged or knocked out.

What you can do
1 Push a dislodged tooth back into position.
2 Primary teeth should not be re-implanted. If a secondary tooth comes out, wash it and, if the child is old enough to hold it in place, put the tooth back in its socket. Otherwise, place it under your own or the child's tongue, or in a container of milk.
3 Phone the dentist or the hospital emergency dental clinic for an urgent appointment (within 30 minutes) and take the tooth with you.

● If, when a first tooth comes out, the socket continues to bleed for a long time:
1 Don't rinse the mouth as you may stop a clot from forming.
2 Put a thick pad of sterile gauze *across* the socket (not in it) and ask the child to bite hard on it for ten minutes.
3 Call your dentist if the bleeding continues.

Heatstroke

This happens when the body can't get rid of excess heat. Babies and young children are especially vulnerable, so never leave them in full sun without adequate protection. Heatstroke develops fast, can be serious and needs urgent treatment.

What you can do

The child looks flushed and his skin feels hot and dry. He has a rapid pulse and a high temperature. Other symptoms are vomiting, irritability, restlessness, a headache and dizziness. He may finally lose consciousness.

What you can do

1 Move the child to a cooler place.
2 Cool him down slowly by taking off his clothes and fanning him.
3 Sponge him with cool or tepid water and give him sips of cool liquids.
4 Once his temperature comes down, cover him with a dry sheet and keep him in a cool room.
5 If he becomes unconscious, turn his head to the side.
6 Phone the doctor.

Heat exhaustion

This usually happens after heavy exercise in a hot moist environment and is caused by losing too much salt and water in the sweat. It comes on more slowly than heatstroke. You can help prevent it by giving extra liquids and a little more salt.

What to look for

The child may have a slightly raised temperature and his skin is pale, cold and moist. He has a rapid, weak pulse and his breathing is fast and shallow. He feels lethargic, restless and dizzy, has a headache and may faint. He may feel sick or vomit and he may have muscular cramps in his stomach and his legs.

What you can do

1 Make him rest.
2 Give him plenty of sips of cool liquids.
3 Phone your doctor for advice. Your child may need added salt.

Sunburn

Too much sun can cause redness, itching, swelling, hotness and blistering. It is most important to protect your child from the sun (see below). Always apply sunscreen ½ an hour before he goes outside.

What you can do

1 Tepid-sponge the child with cold water.

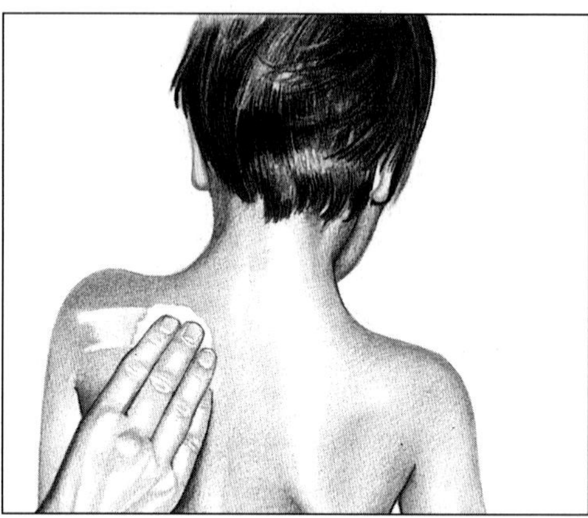

2 Gently put on a cooling application, such as calamine lotion.
3 Give plenty of sips of cold water.
4 Keep out of the sun until the skin inflammation has subsided.
5 Get medical help urgently for severe blistering. ***Don't*** break the blisters.

HOW TO PREVENT SUNBURN

- **Let your child get used to unaccustomed sunshine gradually. Start by allowing him to spend a short time (15-30 minutes) in the sun and increase it a little each day.**
- **Avoid strong midday sun.**
- **Use a high protection factor sunscreen on your child and reapply it at regular intervals during the day as well as after swimming.**
- **Remember that salt water or sweat, being by the sea and high altititude all increase the burning effects of the sun.**
- **Make your child wear a T-shirt even when he's swimming.**
- **Make your child wear a hat all the time.**
- **Use a carriage canopy or stroller umbrella.**

Drowning

Drowning prevents air getting to the lungs because of the water inside them or because of spasm of the throat.

If the child is having great difficulty in breathing or isn't breathing, ***don't*** waste time trying to empty water out of his lungs, but ***do*** get air into his lungs immediately.

What you can do

1 Swim to the child and start **mouth-to-mouth resuscitation**. Give him occasional breaths as you swim ashore or to shallower water.
2 Get to the shore if you can do so quickly or if the water is very cold.

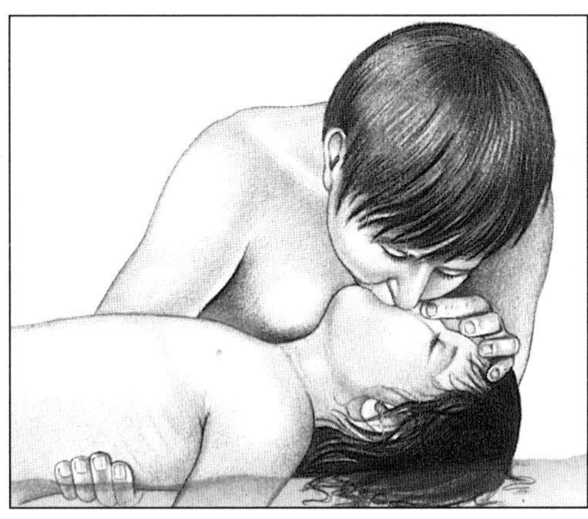

3 If not, once in your depth, support the child with one arm and seal his nose with the other hand while you do mouth-to-mouth resuscitation.

What to do when on dry land

1 Check whether he is breathing. If he isn't, continue mouth-to-mouth resuscitation. Don't stop for at least an hour: children can still be revived after long periods of not breathing.
2 Check the heartbeat and do **cardiac compression** if necessary.
3 When breathing restarts, turn his head to the side if he is unconscious. He may vomit the water he has swallowed.
4 Remove wet clothing and get him dry, then cover him to prevent further chilling. Treat for **hypothermia** (see right) if necessary.
5 Call an ambulance or take the child to the hospital.

Hypothermia

Hypothermia – when the body temperature drops below 95.9°F (35.5°C) – can follow any sort of prolonged or severe chilling. Babies are especially vulnerable.

What to look for

Initially the child may shiver uncontrollably. His skin is cold, pale and dry, and he may be drowsy, confused or even unconscious. His heartbeat and breathing become very slow. A baby may look pink and well, but refuse food and be very quiet.

What you can do

- Rewarm at the speed at which the cooling took place, i.e. quickly after falling into cold water and slowly if hypothermia has developed overnight.

1 If possible, put the child in a hand-hot bath after rapid cooling or a lukewarm one after slow cooling.
2 If not, remove any wet clothing and replace it with dry.
3 Put a covered hot water bottle under the left armpit or over the breastbone.
4 Add more clothing or covers.
5 Check his breathing and heartbeat regularly if the child is unconscious.
6 If he's fully conscious, give hot sweet drinks.

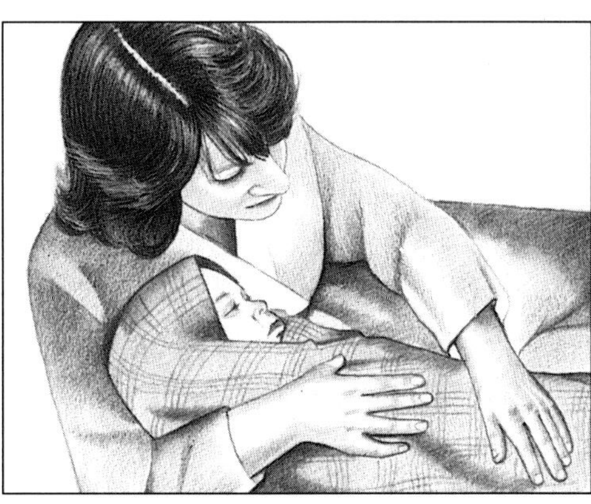

7 If outside, put the child on a rug and lie down by him or cuddle him on your lap, close to your body, and wrap coats or blankets around both of you.
8 Get medical help urgently for a baby or if you are worried about an older child.

MOUTH-TO-MOUTH RESUSCITATION p. 198 CARDIAC COMPRESSION p. 199

Fractures

A fracture is a partial or complete break of a bone. If the bone is cracked on one side and buckled on the other, it's known as a "greenstick" fracture. These are common in children's limb bones and usually heal quickly. For more information about fractures, see page 107.

What to look for

A fracture is obvious if the bone is floppy or if it's poking through a wound in the skin, when it's known as an "open" fracture.

Suspect a fracture if the injury is painful, tender, swollen or bruised, if the child can't move the part at all, if movement is restricted or if the pain is worse when the child moves. Sometimes, however, a child with a fractured bone only has slight discomfort.

What you can do

Don't move the child, if it can be avoided, particularly if there is any possibility of a fractured back, neck or pelvis.

- If you suspect a fractured skull and there is a discharge from the ear, turn the child so that side is down.
- If you suspect *any* fracture:

1 Check whether the child is breathing, has a heartbeat, is bleeding or is shocked, and treat accordingly.
2 Telephone for an ambulance.
3 Don't give the child anything to eat or drink as she may need an anesthetic.
4 Keep the injured part as still as possible to avoid damage from the broken ends of bone.
5 If you have to move the child, first immobilize the joints above and below the injured part. If you don't have bandages and slings you can improvise with scarves, panty hose, ties and torn fabric. Anything used to cover an open wound must be clean and preferably sterile.

FOR A FRACTURED ELBOW: if bent, treat like a broken arm; if straight, put soft padding between the arm and trunk, and bandage the whole arm to the body taking care not to bandage over the break.

FOR BROKEN RIBS: support the arm on the injured side in a sling.

FOR A BROKEN ANKLE OR FOOT: support the leg in a raised position to reduce swelling.

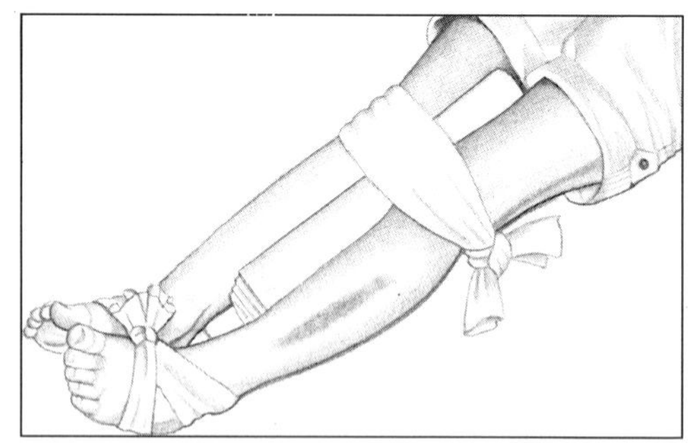

FOR A FRACTURED LEG: put soft padding between the legs, then bandage the injured leg to the good one, avoiding binding over the break.

FOR A BROKEN ARM: place soft padding between the arm and chest, and support the arm in a sling. Secure the arm comfortably to the chest with a broad bandage across the sling.

Strains

Muscle strain occurs when a muscle has been overstretched and causes pain, swelling, bruising and limitation of movement.

What you can do

1 Rest and elevate the affected part.
2 Apply a cold water compress or bag of crushed ice to reduce immediate pain and swelling.
3 A firm elastic bandage may make the child more comfortable.

Sprains

A sprain is a violent wrench that stretches and tears one or more ligaments and other tissues around a joint. Sprained wrists and ankles are very common.

What to look for

There is rapid swelling caused by inflammation of the ligament and other injured tissues. The area becomes hot and painful, especially on moving the joint, and movement is limited. A bruise often appears later.

What you can do

1 If there's any possibility of a **fracture,** treat as though it is one until you have seen a doctor.
2 Rest and elevate the sprained part.
3 Apply cold, wet packs or place crushed ice wrapped in a thin towel on the affected area.

Bandaging a sprained ankle

(this can be adapted for a wrist)
1 Support the ankle with one hand and put the foot on your knee.
2 Working from the inside to the outside, wrap an elastic bandage round the middle of the child's foot.

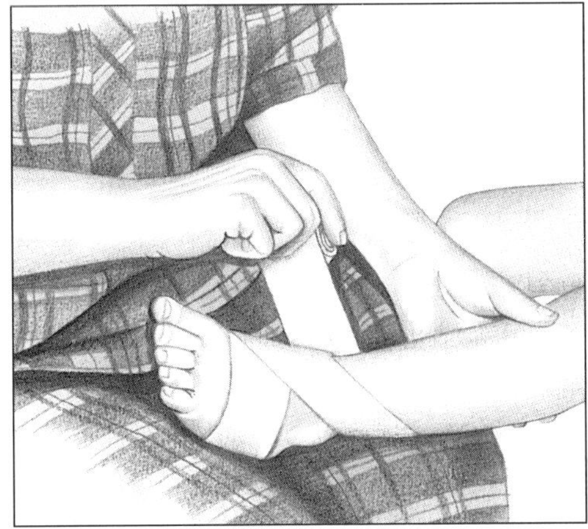

3 Take the bandage across the top of the foot, around the back of the ankle and back underneath the foot. Overlap two thirds of the previous turn each time. Repeat this figure eight until the ankle is bandaged from the top of the toes to just above the ankle.

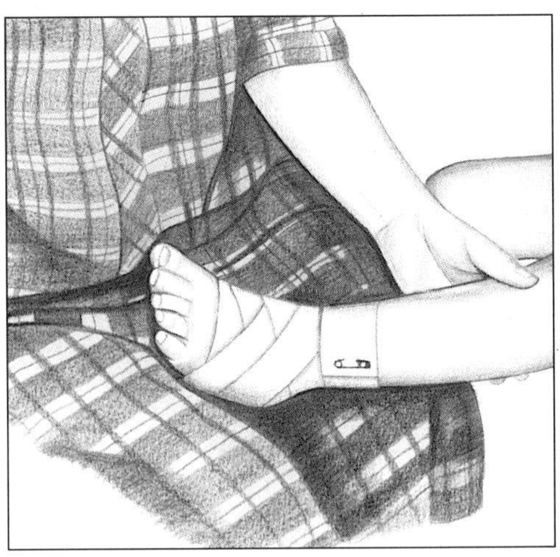

4 Finish off with a turn above the ankle and secure with a safety-pin or tape.

Bandaging a sprained knee

(this can be adapted for an elbow)
1 Starting below the knee, put one turn of an elastic bandage around the leg just below the kneecap.
2 Do a figure eight with one turn alternately above and below the knee until the whole area is covered, overlapping two-thirds of the previous turn each time.
3 Finish off with a turn around the leg and secure with a safety-pin or tape.

Dislocations

A dislocation is when a sprain is bad enough to wrench a bone from its socket in the joint. The bone may return at once or it may stay out and need to be replaced into its correct position. Ligaments may be sprained at the same time and there may be a fracture too.

What to look for

It may be difficult to know whether a joint is dislocated unless there is some obvious deformity of the joint. There may be some pain and limitation of movement.

What you can do

1 ***Don't*** try to replace a dislocated joint.
2 Treat as a **fracture** (see opposite page).
3 Take the child to the hospital or call an ambulance.

Dressings

Dressings are protective coverings used to help stop bleeding, soak up blood and discharge, and prevent infection. Ideally, keep some packs of sterile dressings at home as well as an assortment of adhesive bandages. If you haven't a suitable dressing, improvise with a clean handkerchief, towel or other piece of linen, or a pile of tissues or pieces of paper towel.

When dressing a wound

Keep the wound clean: wash your hands well before applying a dressing; avoid touching the wound; don't talk or cough over the wound or dressing; and if a dressing slips off, replace it with a new one.

- If blood comes through the dressing, add another dressing before bandaging.
- Always use a large enough dressing.

Adhesive bandages

The best bandages have a water-repellent covering which allows moisture to evaporate from the skin. If you use a waterproof one, only leave it on for a few hours, otherwise the wound will become waterlogged and won't heal so well. Make sure the skin around the wound is clean and dry before you put the bandage on, otherwise it won't stick. As you remove the bandage, make sure you don't open the wound up again. Butterfly closures are useful for closing wounds.

Sterile dressings

These are bought pre-packed and are made of layers of gauze over a pad of absorbent cotton. They are useful for wounds too large for an adhesive bandage. Non-adhesive sterile dressings are good dressings for burns.

Bandages

These are pieces of material used to keep dressings in place, prevent swelling, apply pressure over a dressing to stop bleeding or support a limb or joint.

You can buy several sorts of bandage: triangular cotton ones (for slings, for folding into broad or narrow strips or for bandaging the head, hand or foot), rolled gauze or other ones of various widths, and tubular gauze ones with a special applicator. Improvise by tearing up an old pillowcase, sheet, clothing or other clean material, or by using ties, scarves or panty hose.

When bandaging

1 Support the injured part in the position in which you want it to stay.
2 Use soft padding before bandaging to fill natural hollows, protect the bones and give some potential space for further swelling.
3 Keep checking during and afterwards that you haven't restricted the circulation.
4 Tie all knots on the uninjured side of the child's body.

When using a rolled bandage

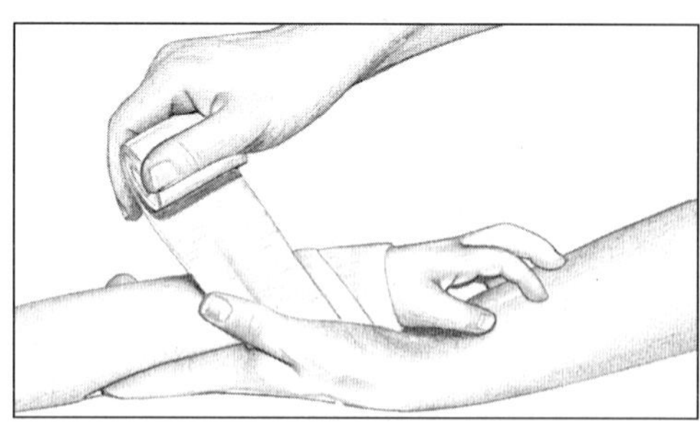

1 Hold the bandage with its "head" uppermost and unroll a little at a time.
2 Work from the inside of the limb outwards and from below the injury upwards.

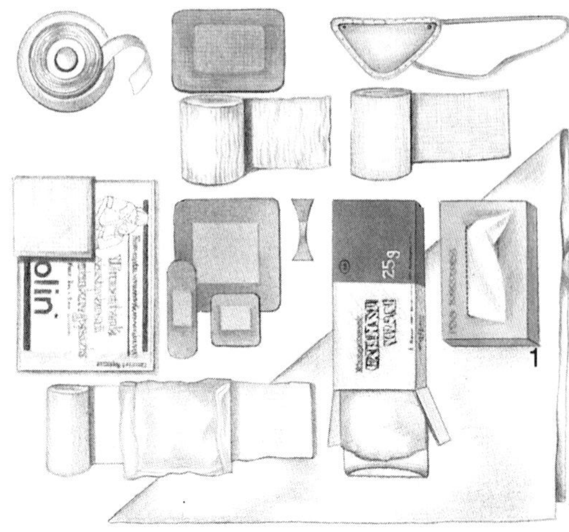

1

First aid kit

It's sensible to collect together the things you might need in a hurry if your child has an accident, and to put them in an airtight tin or a wooden or plastic box large enough for you to easily see where everything is. Mark your first aid kit clearly on the outside and put it somewhere easily accessible to you but out of reach of small children. Don't lock it up because you might not be able to find the key quickly in an emergency. Remember to tell anyone looking after your child where you keep the box. On the inside of the lid, tape a piece of paper with the name, address and phone number of your family doctor, and the address and phone number of the nearest hospital. You could add the names, addresses and phone numbers of two neighbors in case you should need extra help while waiting for an ambulance or for looking after other children while you go to the hospital with an injured child.

The dressings and bandages suggested are the most convenient to use. You can improvise bandages with whatever household material you have to hand, but dressings should ideally be prepacked and sterile.

WHENEVER USING AN ELASTIC BANDAGE
If the part beyond the bandaged area goes pale, blue, numb or tingles, reapply less tightly to avoid impeding the circulation.

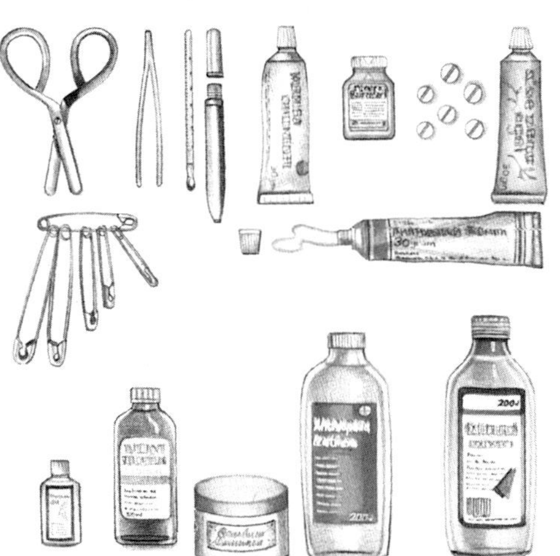

What to include

- Small packs of white paper tissues
- Scissors
- Blunt-ended tweezers
- Large safety-pins
- Thermometer
- Adhesive bandages in assorted sizes, some waterproof, including butterfly closures
- Prepacked sterile dressings in various sizes including large ones
- Nonadhesive sterile dressings (for burns)
- Roll of absorbent cotton (for cleaning cuts or scrapes; for making a compress for a sprain; for applying on top of a dressing and under a bandage to soak up blood; for cushioning an injured arm when putting it in a sling; and for filling in hollows and protecting bones when splinting an arm to the body or an injured leg to the other leg)
- A rolled elastic bandage (for a sprain)
- A rolled gauze bandage (to keep a burns dressing or an eye pad in place)
- Adhesive tape (to secure dressings or bandages)
- A sterile eye pad (with an eye mask to keep it in place)
- Large linen or cotton triangular bandages (for a sling and for making folded bandages to immobilize an injured arm against the body or an injured leg against the other leg)
- Calamine lotion (soothing for bites, stings and sunburn, but not to be used if the skin is weeping)
- Antiseptic lotion or spray (for cleaning dirty cuts and scrapes)
- Antibacterial cream (for splinters or infected wounds)
- Acetaminophen (pain-relieving medicine or tablets, depending on the age of your child)

USEFUL ADDRESSES

When writing for information please enclose a self-addressed stamped envelope.

SPECIFIC ILLNESSES AND HANDICAPS

Asthma and Allergy Foundation of America
1717 Massachusetts Ave.
Suite 305
Washington, D.C. 20036
202-265-0265
800-7-ASTHMA (toll-free)

American Juvenile Arthritis Organization
1314 Spring St. N.W.
Atlanta, GA 30309
404-872-7100

National AIDS Hotline
Centers For Disease Control
1600 Clifton Road N.E.
Atlanta, GA 30333
800-342-AIDS (24-hour toll-free hotline for answers to general questions and referrals)

Association For Retarded Citizens of the United States
PO Box 6109
Arlington, TX 76005
817-640-0204
Provides services and infomation for children with mental retardation and their families; referrals to local and state chapters.

Human Growth Foundation
4720 Montgomery Lane
Bethesda, MD 20814
301-656-7540
Provides information for families of children with short stature.

American Speech-Language-Hearing Association
10801 Rockville Pike
Rockville, MD 20852
301-897-8682
800-638-8255 (toll-free, voice and TDD)
Information on communicative disorders in children.

National Center for Stuttering
200 E. 33rd St.
New York, NY 10016
212-532-1460
800-221-2483 (toll-free outside NY)

Spina Bifida Association of America
1700 Rockville Pike
Suite 540
Rockville, MD 20852
301-770-7222
800-621-3141 (toll-free outside NY)

American Society for Deaf Children
814 Thayer Ave.
Silver Spring, MD 20910
301-585-5400
301-585-5401 (TDD)

American Diabetes Association
Information Service Center
1660 Duke Street
Alexandria, VA 22314
703-549-1500
800-ADA-DISC (toll-free outside VA and metro Washington, D.C.)

Juvenile Diabetes Foundation International
432 Park Ave. S.
New York, NY 10016
212-889-7575
800-223-1138 (toll-free)

Orton Dyslexia Society
724 York Road
Baltimore, MD 21204
301-296-0232
800-ABCD-123 (toll-free)

Epilepsy Foundation of America
4351 Garden City Drive
Landover, MD 20785
301-459-3700
800-332-1000 (toll-free)

Association for Children and Adults with Learning Disabilities, Inc.
4156 Library Road
Pittsburgh, PA 15234
412-341-1515

National Kidney Foundation
30 E. 33 St.
New York, NY 10016
212-889-2210
800-622-9010 (toll-free)

American Kidney Fund
6110 Executive Blvd.
Suite 1010
Rockville, MD 20852
800-492-8361 (for MD only)
800-638-8299
Provides direct financial assistance to needy kidney disease victims.

Osteogenesis Imperfecta Foundation, Inc.
PO Box 14807
Clearwater, FL 34629-4807
813-855-7077
Information about this hereditary bone disorder.

National Leukemia Association, Inc.
585 Stewart Ave.
Suite 536
Garden City, NY 11530
516-222-1944
Information and referrals; provides financial aid to leukemia patients and their families.

American Cancer Society
Tower Place
3340
Peachtree Rd. N.E.
Atlanta, GA 30026
404-320-3333
800-227-2345 (toll-free)

American Cleft Palate Craniofacial Association
National Office
1218 Grandview Ave.
Pittsburgh, PA 15211
412-481-1376
800-242-5338 (toll-free outside PA)
800-232-5338 (toll-free in PA)
Provides information, referrals to support groups and medical cleft palate teams.

American Celiac Society
45 Gifford Ave.
Jersey City, NJ 07304
201-432-2986

National Down Syndrome Congress
1800 Dempster St.
Park Ridge, IL 60068-1146
312-823-7550 (IL only)
800-232-NDSC (toll-free outside IL)

National Hemophilia Foundation
110 Green St., Rm 406
New York, NY 10012
212-219-8180

Children's Liver Foundation
76 S. Orange Ave.
Suite 202
South Orange, NJ 07079
201-761-1111

National Mental Health Association
1021 Prince St.
Alexandria, VA 22314
703-684-7722

Autism Society of America
1234 Massachusetts Ave. N.W.
Suite 1017
Washington, D.C. 20005
202-783-0125

American Council of the Blind
1010 Vermont Ave. N.W.
Suite 1100
Washington, D.C. 20005
202-393-3666
800-424-8666 (toll-free)

Muscular Dystrophy Association
810 Seventh Ave.
New York, NY 10019
212-586-0808
Check your phone directory for local chapter.

Association of Birth Defect Children
3526 Emorywood Lane
Orlando, FL 32812
407-859-2821
Information on birth defects and prosthetics.

National Reye's Syndrome Foundation
PO Box 829
Bryan, OH 43506
419-636-2679
800-231-7393 (toll-free Ohio only)
800-233-7393 (toll-free outside Ohio)

National Association for Sickle Cell Disease, Inc.
4221 Wilshire Blvd.
Suite 360
Los Angeles, CA 90010-3503
213-936-7205 (for CA residents)
800-421-8453 (toll-free for all states except CA)

Cystic Fibrosis Foundation
6931 Arlington Road.
Bethesda, MD 20814
301-951-4422
800-FIGHT-CF (toll-free)

United Cerebral Palsy Association
66 E. 34th St.
New York, NY 10016
212-481-6300
800-872-1827 (toll-free for all states except NY)

National Spinal Cord Injury Association
600 W. Cummings Park
Suite 2000
Woburn, MA 01801
617-935-2722
800-962-9629 (toll-free)

PKU Parents
c/o Dale Hilliard
Eight Myrtle Lane
San Anselmo, CA 94960
415-457-4632
Information and support for parents of children with phenylketonuria (PKU).

Cooley's Anemia Foundation
(Thalessemia)
105 E. 22nd St.
Suite 911
New York, NY 10010
212-598-0911
800-221-3571 (toll-free outside NY)
800-522-7222 (toll-free in NY only)

SUPPORT FOR FAMILIES

Al-Anon Family Group Headquarters, Inc.
PO Box 862
Midtown Station
New York, NY
10018-0862
212-302-7240
800-356-9996
Support for relatives and friends of persons with an alcohol problem.

Children in Hospitals
31 Wilshire Park
Needham, MA 02192
508-369-4467
Offers help and advice on negotiating with hospital staff in order to minimize the trauma of hospitalization.

Compassionate Friends
PO Box 3696
Oak Brook, IL 60522
312-990-0010
Support for families over the death of a child.

Adoption Services Information Agency
7720 Alaska Ave. N.W.
Washington, D.C. 20012
202-726-7193
Information and referrals on adoption.

American Association For Marriage and Family Therapy
1717 K St. N.W.
Suite 407
Washington, D.C. 20006
202-429-1825
Provides lists of division presidents in your area.

Childhelp USA
PO Box 630
Hollywood, CA 90028
800-4-A-CHILD (24-hour hotline for victims of child abuse, parents who think they might abuse their children, and anyone reporting suspected child abuse.)

La Leche League International
9616 Minneapolis Ave.
Franklin Park, IL 60131
312-455-7730
Breastfeeding information and support. (Check phone directory for local chapter or write to the above address.)

National Committee for Prevention of Child Abuse
332 S. Michigan Ave.
Suite 950
Chicago, IL 60604
312-663-3520
Publishes material about child abuse and parenting.

March of Dimes Birth Defects Foundation
1275 Mamaroneck Ave.
White Plains, NY 10605
914-428-7100
800-626-2410 (toll-free)
Organizes support groups for families of children with birth defects.

National Sudden Infant Death Syndrome Foundation
822 Professional Place,
Suite 104
Landover, MD 20785
301-459-3388
800-221-SIDS (toll-free)
Referrals to local chapters.

Parents Anonymous
6733 South Sepulveda Blvd.
Suite 270
Los Angeles, CA 90045
Counseling for parents who have or who are tempted to abuse their children. (Check phone directory for local chapter or write to the above address.)

Parents Without Partners
8807 Colesville Road
Silver Spring, MD 20910
301-588-9354
800-637-7974 (toll-free)
Mutual support group for single parents and their children.

Stepfamily Association of America, Inc.
602 East Joppa Road
Baltimore, MD 21204
301-823-7570
Clearinghouse for all educational materials dealing with stepfamilies.

National Organization of Mothers of Twins Clubs Inc.
12404 Princess Jeanne N.E.
Albuquerque, NM 87122-4640
505-275-0955

Parent Care
101½ S. Union St.
Alexandria, VA 22314
703-836-4678
Information and support for parents of premature and high-risk infants.

Center for Study of Multiple Births
333 E. Superior St.
Suite 476
Chicago, IL 60611
312-266-9093
Provides information on caring for twins and multiple birth children.

Postpartum Support International
c/o Jane Honikman
927 N. Kellogg Ave.
Santa Barbara, CA 93111
805-967-7636
Self-help mutual aid group to support mothers with postpartum emotional syndrome.

National SHARE Office
c/o St. Elizabeth's Hospital
211 S. Third St.
Belleville, IL 62769
217-544-6464
Support for parents who have lost a newborn through miscarriage, stillbirth, or early infant death.

United Way of America
701 N. Fairfax
Alexandria, VA 22314
703-836-7100
Several thousand United Way offices throughout the country provide information and referrals to health and human care services.

INFORMATION ON HEALTH, FIRST AID, SAFETY, AND EDUCATION

American Academy of Pediatrics
141 Northwest Point Blvd.
P.O. Box 927
Elk Grove Village, IL 60007
312-228-5005
800-421-0589 (toll-free IL only)
800-433-9016 (toll-free)
Information and referrals.

American Dental Association
211 East Chicago Ave.
Chicago, IL 60611
312-440-2500
Pamphlets and information about care of children's teeth.

American Heart Association
National Headquarters
7320 Greenville Ave.
Dallas, TX 75231
214-750-5300
Check phone directory for local chapter.

American Red Cross
National Headquarters
17th and D Sts N.W.
Washington, D.C. 20006
202-737-8300

National Fire Protection Association
Batterymarch Park
Quincy, MA 02269-9101
617-770-3000
Conducts fire safety education programs.

National Center for Education in Maternal and Child Health
38th and R Sts. N.W.
Washington, D.C. 20057
202-625-8400
Information on genetics, chronic illness/disability, pregnancy, and nutrition.

National Information Center for Handicapped Children and Youth
Box 1492
Washington, D.C. 20013
703-893-6061
800-999-5399 (toll-free)
Provides information concerning educational rights to parents of children with physical, mental, and emotional handicaps.

National Highway Traffic Safety Administration
U.S. Department of Transportation
400 7th St. N.W.
Washington, D.C. 20590
202-366-0123
800-424-9393 (toll-free outside Washington, D.C. for information about car seats and automotive safety)
For local information, contact your state's Office of Highway Safety.

National Safety Council
444 N. Michigan Ave.
Chicago, IL 60611
312-527-4800
800-621-7619 (toll-free) or 800-421-9585 (toll-free)
Publishes material on safe toys and furniture, safety restraints, etc.

US Consumer Product Safety Commission
1750 K St. N.W.
Washington, D.C. 20207
800-638-2772 (toll-free for complaints about faulty items and information on safe ones)

National Center for Educational Statistics
US Dept. of Education
1200 19th St. N.W.
Washington, D.C. 20208
800-424-1616

INDEX

A

B

C

T

U

V

W

ACKNOWLEDGMENTS

Author's acknowledgments
I would like to thank my husband Andrew for his loving encouragement and support; my children Susie, Amy and Ben for all I have learned from them; the many women who have shared with me their experiences of living with their children in health and in sickness; and Jane O'Shea, Emma Russell, Ann Burnham, Nicki Seymour and Prue Bucknall at Conran Octopus for their warmth, courtesy and attention to detail which have made working with them such a pleasure.

Conran Octopus wish to thank the following for their help in the preparation of this book –

Donna Sammaritano, M.D. (Philadelphia) a mother and a pediatrician, for her valuable contribution on current concepts of pediatric practice, and Emily van Ness, for her conscientious editorial work on the American edition.

For illustrations: Kathy James, Meridian Design Associates, David Smee and Linda Worrall

For design help: Ann Cannings and Jane Warring

For taking part in the photography: Richard and David Bates, Jack Burnham, Thomas Harvey, Jessica and Charlotte Heal, Thomas and Daniel McGlynn, Megan, Emily and Madeleine O'Shea, Stewart and Robert Paveley, and Tyrone Watkins

For lending the slide: The Early Learning Centre

For the following photographs taken especially for Conran Octopus: Cover, 2-3, 4-5 Ray Moller; 6 Nick Bucknall; 8-9, 80-81, 110-111, 178-179, 194-195 Ray Moller

For their kind permission to reproduce photographs: **10** Zefa Picture Library; **13** Pictor International; **16** Tim Woodcock; **18** Pictor International; **21** Jerrican (V. Clement); **22** Jerrican (Crampon); **24** Bubbles (Loisjoy Thurston); **28** Tony Stone Photo Library (David Sutherland); **29** Jennie Woodcock; **32** Sally & Richard Greenhill; **35** A. G. E. Fotostock; **40** Pictor International; **42** Bubbles (Loisjoy Thurston); **44** Sally & Richard Greenhill; **47** Jennie Woodcock; **49** Lupe Cunha; **52** Conran Octopus (Sandra Lousada); **54** Bubbles (Loisjoy Thurston); **57** Camilla Jessel; **58** Susan Griggs Agency (Sandra Lousada); **64-65** Camilla Jessel; **68** Susan Griggs Agency (Sandra Lousada); **72** Bubbles (Louisjoy Thurston); **73** CNRI/ Science Photo Library; **75** Camilla Jessel; **78** Sally & Richard Greenhill; **180** Bubbles (Ian West).